Henry Alford

The Queen's English

Stray notes on speaking and spelling

Henry Alford

The Queen's English
Stray notes on speaking and spelling

ISBN/EAN: 9783337282196

Printed in Europe, USA, Canada, Australia, Japan

Cover: Foto ©Andreas Hilbeck / pixelio.de

More available books at **www.hansebooks.com**

THE QUEEN'S ENGLISH

A MANUAL OF IDIOM AND USAGE

BY THE LATE

HENRY ALFORD, D.D.

DEAN OF CANTERBURY.

SEVENTH EDITION.

LONDON: GEORGE BELL AND SONS
YORK STREET, COVENT GARDEN
1888

CONTENTS.

	PAGE
PREFACE	vii
CHAP. I. INTRODUCTORY	1
II. SPELLING	6
III. PRONUNCIATION	30
IV. IDIOM AND CONSTRUCTION	54
CONCLUDING ADVICE	205
APPENDIX	209
INDEX	213

PREFACE

TO THE THIRD EDITION.

THE opening paragraphs of the present work will explain how far it differs from the previous editions. I may here say, that several portions have been re-written, and new matter has been added, to the extent of about seventy pages.

The motto at the back of the title-page has been borrowed from a little work by Signor Pagliardini, entitled "Essays on the Analogy of Languages." It expresses, in a jocular form, what every one who values our native tongue in its purity must feel: that most of the grammars, and rules, and applications of rules, now so commonly made for our language, are in reality not contributions towards its purity, but main instruments of its deterioration. These rules are often laid down by persons ignorant of the analogy of languages, of the laws of thought, and of the practice of those writers whose works are the great fountain-heads of our English usage. *Difficile est* . . . . *non scribere*, when we see men whose knowledge does not extend to the most ordinary facts of derivation, and requirements of speech, exalted into authorities whereby to judge of the correctness of Shakspeare, and Milton, and the English version of the Bible. We may not indeed say, *Malim cum Platone errare:* but we may say confidently, that the old writer had in his mind some reason for his mode of expression, which was far above the grasp of his modern critic.

I am happy to have been, in the course of my writing these "stray notes," made acquainted with some modern English Grammars which form exceptions to the description just given: Grammars based upon essential facts and principles which are utterly unknown to the "*pædagoguli*" of Count d'Arco's epigram.

I may mention among these, Dr. Latham's sensible English Grammar, and "An English Grammar specially intended for Classical Schools and Private Students," by Edward Higginson: Longmans, 1864.

It is my pleasing duty again to express my thanks to my many Correspondents, for their valuable contributions, inquiries, hints, and corrections; to my Censors, both gentle and ungentle, for their teaching by example and by precept: and to the Public in general, for the kind interest which they have shown in these stray notes on speaking and spelling.

CANTERBURY,
    March 12, 1870.

PUBLISHERS' NOTE TO THE SEVENTH EDITION.

In this reprint several small errors which still remained in the text have been corrected; and a full index, the want of which was felt in former editions, has been added.

February, 1888.

THE QUEEN'S ENGLISH:

A MANUAL OF IDIOM AND USAGE.

CHAPTER I.

INTRODUCTORY.

1. **Introductory.**—This work is a re-publication of the little treatise, which, under the former of these titles, has been for some years before the public. It was considered desirable to render more generally useful the matter contained in that treatise: and hence the adoption of the slightly varied form in which it now appears.

2. Besides the slight alteration of arrangement, considerable additions have been made, arising from correspondence, and observation, subsequent to the last edition of the former work.

3. It may be well to premise once for all, that it is my object not so much to enquire in each case what is according to strict rule and analogy, as to point out what is the usage of our spoken language.

4. In many, indeed in most cases, that usage will be found reasonable, and according to some assignable rule: and therefore we shall often find ourselves dealing with considerations pertaining to grammar, and referable to rule. But neither grammar nor rule governs the idiom of a people: and there will be a multitude of cases, where *Sic volo, sic jubeo* is the only measure of the tyranny of usage.

5. It was my intention to have arranged the contents of this new issue of "The Queen's English" under the *parts*

of speech. But the attempt at once shewed that such an arrangement would be undesirable. It would break the thread of continuity between matters naturally suggested the one by the other; and even if it had been rigidly adhered to, could hardly have been so managed as to be self-indexing.

6. Consequently the idea was abandoned, and the arrangement of the former work only so far modified as to clear, and bring out, and complete, the separate parts.

7. Queen's English, what?— I ought to begin by explaining what I mean by the term, "Queen's English." It is one rather familiar and conventional, than strictly accurate. The Sovereign is of course no more the proprietor of the English language than any one of us. Nor does she, nor do the Lords and Commons in Parliament assembled, possess one particle of right to make or unmake a word in the language. But we use the phrase, the Queen's English, in another sense; one not without example in some similar phrases. We speak of the *Queen's Highway,* not meaning that Her Majesty is *possessed* of that portion of road, but that it is a high road of the land, as distinguished from by-roads and private roads: open of common right to all, and the general property of our country. And so it is with the *Queen's English.* It is, so to speak, this land's great highway of thought and speech; and seeing that the Sovereign in this realm is the person round whom all our common interests gather, the centre of our civil duties and of our civil rights, the *Queen's English* is not an unmeaning phrase, but one which may serve to teach us some profitable lessons with regard to our language, and to its use and abuse.

8. And it may be, and is for us, a very useful phrase as conveying another meaning. That which we treat is not the grammarians' English, nor the Dictionary-writers' English, but *the Queen's English:* not that English which certain individuals, more or less acquainted with their subject, have chosen to tell us we ought to speak and write, but that which the nation, in the secular unfolding of its will and habits, has agreed to speak and write. We shall have to say more of this by-and-by.

9. I called our common English tongue the highway of

thought and speech; and it may not be amiss to carry on this similitude further. The Queen's Highway, now so broad and smooth, was once a mere track over an unenclosed country. It was levelled, hardened, widened, by very slow degrees. Of all this trouble, the passer-by sees no trace now. He bowls along it with ease in a vehicle, which a few centuries ago would have been broken to pieces in a deep rut, or would have come to grief in a bottomless swamp. There were no Croydon baskets, in the day when Henry II. and his train came to do penance from Southampton up that narrow, hollow, rough pilgrims' road, leading over Harbledown Hill to Canterbury.

10. Now just so is it with our English language—our Queen's English. There was a day when it was as rough as the primitive inhabitants. Centuries have laboured at levelling, hardening, widening it. For language wants all these processes, as well as roads do. In order to become a good highway for thought and speech, it must not have great prominent awkward points, over which the mind and the tongue may stumble; its words must not be too weak to carry the weight of our thoughts, nor its limiting rules too narrow to admit of their extension. And it is by processes of this kind in the course of centuries, that our English tongue has been ever adapted more and more to our continually increasing wants. If it ever was found too rough, too unsubstantial, too limited, for the requirements of English thought, it was smoothed, strengthened, enlarged,—till it has become for us, in our days, a level, firm, broad highway, over which all thought and all speech can travel evenly and safely. Along it the lawyer and the parliamentary agent propel their heavy waggons, clogged with a thousand pieces of cumbrous antiquated machinery, —and no wonder, when they charge freightage, not by the weight of the load, combined with the distance, but by the number of impediments which they can manage to offer to the progress of their vehicle. Along it the poet and novelist drive their airy tandems, dependent for their success on the dust which they raise, and through which their varnished equipages glitter. On the same road divines, licensed and unlicensed, ply once a week or more, with omnibus or carrier's cart, promising to carry their pas-

sengers into another land than that over which the road itself extends, just as the coaches out of London used to astonish our boyish eyes by the "*Havre de Grace*" and "*Paris*" inscribed on them. And along this same Queen's highway plods ever the great busy crowd of foot-passengers — the talkers of the market, of society, of the family. Words, words, words; good and bad, loud and soft, long and short; millions in the hour, innumerable in the day, unimaginable in the year: what then in the life? what in the history of a nation? what in that of the world? And not one of these is ever forgotten. There is a book where they are all set down. What a history, it has been well said, is this earth's atmosphere, seeing that all words spoken, from Adam's first till now, are still vibrating on its sensitive and unresting medium.

11. But it is not so much of the great highway itself of Queen's English that I would now speak, as of some of the laws and usages of the road; the by-rules, so to speak, which hang up framed at the various stations, that all may read them. The language of a people is no trifle. The national mind is reflected in the national speech. If the way in which men express their thoughts is slipshod and mean, it will be very difficult for their thoughts themselves to escape being the same. If it is high-flown and bombastic, a character for national simplicity and truthfulness, we may be sure, cannot be long maintained. That nation must be (and it has ever been so in history) not far from rapid decline, and from being degraded from its former glory. Every important feature in the language of a people has its origin in that people's character and history.

12. **Chatterton's imposture.**—Carefulness about minute accuracies of inflexion and grammar may appear to some very contemptible. But it would be easy to give examples in refutation of this idea. Two strike me, of widely different kinds. Some years ago a set of poems was published at Bristol, purporting to have been written in very early times by a poet named Rowley. Literary controversy ran high about them; many persons believed in their genuineness; some do even now. But the imposture, which was not easy to detect at the time, has been

now completely unmasked by the aid of a little word of three letters. The writer uses "*its*" as the possessive case of the pronoun "*it*" of the neuter gender. Now this possessive "*its*" was never used in the early periods of our language; nor, indeed, as late down as Elizabeth. It never occurs in the English version of the Bible, made in its present authorized form in the reign of James 1.:[1] "*his*" or "*her*" being always used instead. "They came unto the iron gate that leadeth unto the city; which opened to them of *his* own accord" (Acts xii. 10). "Of beaten work made he the candlestick; *his* shaft, and *his* branch, *his* bowls, *his* knops, and *his* flowers, were of the same" (Ex. xxxvii. 17). "The tree of life, which yielded *her* fruit every month" (Rev. xxii. 2). It is said also only to occur three times in Shakspeare, and once in "Paradise Lost." The reason, I suppose, being, that possession, indicated by the possessive case "*its*," seemed to imply a certain life or personality, which things neuter could hardly be thought of as having.

13. Detection of St. Peter by his speech.— The other example is one familiar to us, of a more solemn character. When St. Peter was stoutly denying all knowledge of his suffering Master, they that stood by said to him, "Surely thou art one of them; for thou art a Galilean, and thy speech agreeth thereto." So that the fact of a provincial pronunciation was made use of to bring about the repentance of an erring apostle.

[1] We have it in one place in our *present* copies, viz., Levit. xxv. 5: "That which groweth of *its* own accord." But this has been an alteration by the printers: King James's authorized copies have "of it own accord:" just as Shakspeare wrote "The innocent milk in it most innocent mouth:" and "go to it grandam, child, and it grandam will give it a plum." The usage of "*it*" for "*its*," is still found in the provincial talk of the Midland and Northern counties. (See on this subject Dr. Latham's "History of the English Language," pp. 527-9, 589.)

CHAPTER II.

SPELLING.

14. The character of this work will prevent, as has been already observed, anything like strictly classified arrangement of material. Those who use it must be content to trust entirely to the alphabetical index for finding the treatment of a word or a phrase of which they are in search.

Omitting the "u" in words in "-our."—My first remark shall be on the trick now so universal on the other side of the Atlantic, and becoming in some quarters common among us in England, of leaving out the *u* in the termination "-*our;*" writing *honor, favor, neighbor, Savior,* &c. Now the objection to this is, not that it makes ugly words, unlike anything in the English language (for we do thus spell some of the words thus derived, for example, *author, governor, emperor,* &c.), but that it is part of a movement to reduce our spelling to uniform rule, and to help forward the obliteration of all trace of the derivation and history of words. It is true that *honor* and *favor* are derived *originally* from Latin words spelt exactly the same; but it is also true that we did not get them direct from the Latin, but through the French forms, which ended in "-*our.*" Sometimes words come through as many as three steps before they reach us

> "'Twas Greek at first; that Greek was Latin made;
> That Latin, French; that French to English strait."

15. The late Archdeacon Hare, in an article on English Orthography in the "Philological Museum," some years ago, expressed a hope that "such abominations as *honor* and *favor* would henceforth be confined to the cards of the great vulgar." There we still see them, and in books

printed in America; and while we are quite contented to leave our fashionable friends in such company, I hope we may none of us be tempted to join it.

16. "**Neighbour.**"—We have spoken of these words in "*our*" as mostly having come to us from the Latin in "*or*," through the French in "*eur*." It has been observed, that this is not the case with some words involved in the "*or*" and "*our*" question. One of these is "*neighbour*." This has come from the German *nachbar*;[1] or perhaps

---

[1] I observe that the dictionaries derive it from the Anglo-Saxon "nehzebur:" in which case the *n* has more right in the word than the *o*. A very ingenious derivation, but I believe also wrong, has been sent me by a Scottish correspondent, dwelling under the shadow of Ben-Nevis. His letter is too interesting to be abridged, so I give it as it stands:—

"KILMALLIE MANSE, BY FORT WILLIAM, N.B.,
24*th June*, 1864.

"REV. SIR,—Seeing in your 'Queen's English' mention of the Danish word '*Nabo*' as possibly the original form of the English 'Neighbour,' I am induced to give you the following facts, and a conjecture regarding the further history of that word, hoping they may prove sufficiently interesting to plead my excuse for troubling you.

"In the northern counties of the Highlands the common Gaelic term for neighbour is still, as it has been for time immemorial, this Danish *Nabi* pronounced *Naabi*; whereas in the southern Highlands a totally different word, and one of pure Celtic lineage, is used.

"Now it is notorious that the Norsemen held the northern Highland counties, as well as the outer Hebrides, for ages, and still there are settlers in Caithness and in Lewis who boast of unmixed Danish blood. There are very few traces of Norse in the common language of the country, but the names of places generally are Scandinavian; and on the whole the wonder is, not that *Nabo* should retain his place in the Highlands, but that there are not many more of his kith and kin along with him.

"Having thus shown that *Nabo* is naturalised in the north Highlands, I proceed to tell how he travelled to the south Highlands. When the Caledonian Canal was being wrought (from about 1800 to 1822), many north-country Highlanders were, as a matter of course, employed on it, and after it was finished several of them went to the *Crinan* Canal—also a Government work—in the south of Argyleshire. There they naturally addressed one another as *Nabi*, just as an Englishman would say 'mate,' or 'comrade,' and the word, quite new to the Argyleshire-men, appeared so outlandish and odd that they fixed it as a nickname on the North-men, calling them all *Naabis*.

"This is a fact of which I have abundant proof, that about forty years ago a set of canal-workers in Argyleshire were called *Naabis*; and my conjecture about the further travels of the word may be easily antici-

from the Danish or rather Norse, *nabo*, compounded from the words *nœr*, near, and *boe*, to live or dwell; and it is therefore urged, that an exception should be made in its case to the ending with *our*, and it should be written "*neighbor*." I am afraid the answer must be, that English custom has ruled the practice another way, and has decided the matter for us. We do not follow rule in spelling the other words, but custom. We write *senator, orator, governor*, in spite of the French *senateur, orateur, gouverneur*. If we once begin reforming our spelling on rule, we ought to be consistent, and to carry our principles throughout. It is only the maintenance of our national custom and usage for which a reasonable man can plead. We have no Academy to settle such things for us; and as long as *neighbour* is universally spelt in England with a *u*, I fear we must be content to conform, even though it appear to have been

pated—that here we see whence came *Navvy*, about which there is so much disputing. *Navvy* is said to have been originally applied to canal-workers, and hence said to be a contraction of *Navigator*, which I do not consider at all likely. My own Dano-Celtic account appears much more probable; for though I cannot prove that any of the Highland workers went south from Crinan (though their having done so is most likely), I know that the contractors and superintendents were English and Scotch (it being a Government work), and they would easily convey the word with them, even though they knew not its original meaning."

So far my correspondent. Now first, his account does not quite stand upright by itself. For the North-men, who were " many " when working at the Caledonian Canal, which they left in 1822, became only " several " when they went to the Crinan Canal; and it was they only, not canal men in general, who were nicknamed *naabies*. So that the English contractors, who seem to be the only Link binding on the south to the story, would not be likely to adopt the term as a general name for all canal men when they returned to the south.

Besides, according to this account, the name did not come into England till after the completion of the Crinan Canal. Strangely enough, no history is given of this canal in Black's or in Anderson's Guide book; nor is the year of its completion to be found in Haydn's Dictionary of Dates, nor in the cyclopædias. It cannot have been finished till late in the *twenties* of this century. But I myself can remember, before the twenties came in, full fifty years ago, that when the canals were being made in the part of England where I was brought up, a common expression on people's lips was " the system of inland navigation;" and the men who worked at the canals were called at full length, " navigators;" the word had not yet been abridged. This my own remembrance, is to my mind decisive of the question.

first so spelt by those who forgot its derivation. It is when custom is various, and some rule is needed to decide which variety is right, that we must apply rules in order to that decision.

17. "**Control.**"—In the case of another word thus variously spelt, *control*, the rule is plain, and general usage conforms to it. Control never acquired any right to be spelt with a *u*. It comes from the French *contrôle, i.e.*, *contre-rôle:* and the original meaning is still found in the name *Controller*, when applied to finance: *i.e.*, an officer whose duty it is to keep a counter-roll, or check on the accounts of others. It seems also clear, from this account of the word, that it ought not to be spelt *compt*, as it frequently is, but *cont*.

18. "**Tenor**" and "**tenour.**"—With regard to one word of the class under consideration, *tenor*, some have thought that it bears different senses, according as we spell it with or without *u* in the last syllable: *tenour* signifying the character, or complexion, or drift of a course of action or speaking; and *tenor* signifying the part in music. But I can find no such distinction observed, either by writers, or by the compilers of our dictionaries. Some dictionaries give ten*or* for both, some ten*our;* and with regard to usage, the distinction attempted to be set up is certainly not observed. Sir Philip Sidney, Shakspeare, Dryden, Pope, Waterland, Locke, all use *tenor* in the sense of the *constant mode*, or *manner of continuity*, as may be seen in the dictionaries. The distinction is observed in French, but never appears to have been made a point of in English: and the word thus remains in the same predicament as the rest of those in this class—subject to be varied this way or that, according to prevailing usage.

19. **Phonetic spelling.**—The omission of the *u* is an approach to that wretched attempt to destroy all the historic interest of our language, which is known by the name of *phonetic* spelling; concerning which we became rather alarmed some years ago, when we used to see on our reading-room tables a journal published by the advocates of this change, called the "Phonetic News," but from its way of spelling looking like *Frantic Nuts*. Time has now happily confirmed the conviction expressed in the earlier

editions of this work, that the system will never prevail in England. It is a good thing to devise every means by which a short-hand writer,—whose object is to note down with all speed what he hears,—may be enabled to abridge his work. Let him by all means set at nought conventional spelling, and use what symbols he finds most convenient for the sounds expressed by combined letters. But *our* object is not expeditious writing only, nor is it easy spelling, nor uniformity in expressing the same sounds. We use, in writing, an instrument which has been adapted to our use by nearly sixty centuries; which bears on it the marks of many a conflict of thought and belief; whose very uncertainties and anomalies are records of our intercourse with other nations, and of the agglomeration of our mingled English people. You may gain, with no great trouble, uniformity of spelling, and of pronunciation according to spelling; but you will do it at the sacrifice of far more than the gain is worth. A smooth front of stucco may be a comely thing for those that like it; but very few sensible men will like it, if they know that, in laying it on, we are proposing to obliterate the roughnesses and mixtures of styles, and traces of architectural transition, from the venerable front of an ancient cathedral. I have heard that it is only the *short-hand department* of the phonetic movement which can at all be described as being in a flourishing state; and to that I wish all prosperity, provided always that it rises on the ruins of the other.

20. "-ent" and "-ant."—Here is another instance, in which our acknowledged English custom in spelling seems to defy all rule. How does it stand with the words ending in *-ent* and *-ant*, derived from the participles of Latin verbs? Some of these follow rule, others depart from it. The first conjugation of Latin verbs, forming its participle in *-ans*, genitive *-antis*, gives rise to a set of derivatives in our language which keep constant to the termination *-ant*. We have *abundant, reluctant, exuberant, remonstrant, recusant, recalcitrant*, and the rest. But in the case of the second, third, and fourth Latin conjugations, forming their participles in *-ens*, genitive *-entis*, we have not been able to keep the derivatives steady to the original type. In the greater number of cases, they follow it: in

some, usage varies; in a few, they have rejected the primitive form, and have adopted the -*ant*. We always write *different* and *difference*; indeed the derivative *differential* seems to fix these forms on us, as *transcendental* fixes *transcendent*. *Dependent* and *dependant* seem to be written indifferently. But *defendant* and *attendant* are universal. In some cases, the rules of pronunciation have kept the -*ent* unvaried. Take for instance the derivatives from Latin verbs ending in -*esco*,—*crescent, quiescent, acquiescence, arborescent* and such words as *detergent, emergency*. In all these, the substitution of *a* for *e* would change the soft sound of the preceding consonant into a hard one: we should be obliged to say *creschant, deterghant,* &c.

21. The question, *in-* or *en-*, in words beginning with the preposition variously thus represented in Latin and French, seems utterly to defy any answer according to rule. *Engrave, enrich, engross, enroll,* are universal; but so are *infant, intent, inflame:* while we have both *enquire* and *inquire,* both *enclose* and *inclose,* both *endorse* and *indorse,* used indifferently. We have also *insurance* and *assurance* indifferently used; and the liberty of choice in this case is owing to the fact that we may use both verbs, to *assure* and to *insure,* of that kind of making safe, which the substantive represents.

22. "Ecstasy" and "apostasy."—There seems to be considerable doubt in the public mind how to spell the two words *ecstasy* and *apostasy*. The former of these especially is a puzzle to our compositors and journalists. Is it to be *extasy, extacy, ecstacy* or *ecstasy?* In the absence of any preponderance of usage, the question is decided for us by the Greek root of the word. This is *ecstasis* (ἔκστασις), a standing, or position, out of, or beside, one's-self. The same is the case with apostasy. The root of this is *apostasis* (ἀπόστασις), a standing off or away from a man's former position. Consequently, *ecstasy* (or, if we prefer it, *extasy*) and *apostasy*, are right, not those forms which end in -*cy*.

23. "Lay" and "lie."—*Lay* and *lie* seem not yet to be settled. Few things are more absurd than the confusion of these two words. To "*lay*" is a verb active transitive: a hen *lays* eggs. To "*lie*" is a verb neuter; a

sluggard *lies* in bed. Whenever the verb *lay* occurs, something must be supplied after it; the proper rejoinder to "Sir, there it lays," would be "*lays what?*" The reason of the confusion has been, that the past tense of the neuter verb "*lie*" is "*lay*," looking very like part of the active verb:—"I lay in bed this morning." But this, again, is perverted into *laid*, which belongs to the other verb. I have observed that Eton men, for some reason or other, are especially liable to confuse these two verbs.

24. **The apostrophe of the genitive singular.**—There seems to be some doubt occasionally felt about the apostrophe which marks the genitive case singular. One not uncommonly sees outside an inn, that *fly's* and *gig's* are to be let. In a country town blessed with more than one railway, I have seen an omnibus with "RAILWAY STATION'S" painted in emblazonry on its side.

25. It is curious, that at one time this used to be, among literary men, the usual way of writing the plurals of certain nouns. In the "Spectator," Addison writes "*Purcell's opera's*" with an apostrophe before the *s*. And we find "*the making of grotto's*" mentioned as a favourite employment of ladies in that day.

26. Occasionally this apostrophe before the *s* in plurals is adopted to avoid an awkward incongruous appearance: as in another instance from the "Spectator," where Addison speaks of the way in which some people use "their *who's* and their *whiches*." Certainly "*whos*" would be an awkward-looking word, and so would "*whoes*." It would seem as if we were compelled to admit the intruder in these cases: for without him, how should we ever be able to express in writing that people drop their *h's*, or omit to dot their *i's* and cross their *t's?* But if we do, we must carefully bar the gate again, and refuse to tolerate his presence in any plurals where he is not absolutely required.

27. I have observed, on the part of our advertising posthorse-keepers, a strange reluctance to give the proper plural of *fly*, used to denote a vehicle. Where we do not see *fly's*, we commonly find "*flys*" instead, and very rarely indeed "*flies*," the obvious and only legitimate plural: the reason apparently being, that there is a fear of a ludicrous meaning being suggested by the word. But if we do not think

of the insect when we see "*fly*" in the singular, why should the plural form necessarily raise the thought in our minds?

28. It has been questioned, whether the name of the carriage be not really derived from the verb, seeing that certain night-coaches were once called "*fly-by-night*"? And if so, why should it be required to follow the rule of the substantive? But we may answer, was not that substantive itself also, in its time, derived from the verb? It is not merely the analogy of this particular substantive, but that of the language, to which we would bind the new noun.

29. A dispute was referred to me by the compositors of a certain journal, as to whether we ought to write *Messrs. Jacksons works* with the apostrophe before the final *s* in *Jacksons*, or after it: in other words—for it comes to the same—whether, in speaking of the firm, we ought to say Messrs. *Jackson*, or Messrs. *Jacksons*. It seems to me that, by using the plural appellative *Messieurs*, we have already adopted the former of these. Each member of the firm is Mr. Jackson: we may regard the whole firm, if we will, as made up of *Mr. Jacksons*. But in speaking of the firm as a whole, we use the other form, and say the *Messrs. Jackson*. It is plain that we have no right to mix both forms together, and to say the *Messrs. Jacksons*, with both names in the plural. So that, the practice of the commercial world having bound us to speak of the Messrs. Jackson,—when we speak of *Messrs. Jacksons works*, the apostrophe or sign of the genitive case ought to come before the final *s* (*Messrs. Jackson's works*), and not after it (*Messrs. Jacksons' works*). The example by which the other side in the dispute defended their view, was ingeniously chosen, but did not apply. They urged that in writing "*nine months imprisonment*," the apostrophe is put, not before, but after, the final *s* in months. Certainly: because we cannot say, and never do say, *nine month*: whereas we can and do always say, *Messrs. Jackson*.

30. **What is the apostrophe?**—We are led on by our last paragraph to say something about this same apostrophe itself.[1] First, what is it? what does it mean?

---

[1] See a learned and interesting Pamphlet by the late Mr. Sergeant Manning, "On the Character and Origin of the Possessive Augment in English, and its Cognate Dialects."

When I speak of "*the Senator*" in one sentence, and of "*the Senator's son*" in another, what has happened to the word *Senator* in becoming *Senator's*, with the apostrophe? The question was at one time answered by saying that "*the Senator's son*" was an abbreviation of "*the Senator, his son.*" And we may remember that the prayer for all conditions of men in our Common Prayer book ends with the words "*for Jesus Christ his sake.*" But more attention showed that this was an erroneous view of the matter. It failed to account for all feminine genitives: "*your wife's father*" cannot be "*your wife his father;*" and for all plural genitives: "*the children's bread*" cannot be "*the children his bread.*" More attention showed that the *s* preceded by the apostrophe is an abbreviation of the added syllable "*-is,*" marking the possessive or genitive case. Thus "*the Senator's son*" in English answers to *Senatoris filius* in Latin.

31. But if *the Senator's son*, with an apostrophe between the *r* and *s*, signifies *the son of the Senator*, how am I to express in a similar form *the sons of the Senators?* in other words, what becomes of the apostrophe when we want to make a possessive case in the plural? We have no inflexion, as in *Senatorum filii*, by which it can be expressed. Can we use the final -*is* to mark the possessive in the plural as we do in the singular? It would seem to a Latin scholar absurd so to do; yet we do it. We have already cited *the children's bread*. But most of our plural nouns already end in *s*; and to them we do not superadd another *s* with the apostrophe, but we indicate its omission by simply putting the apostrophe after the plural noun. We say "*the senators' sons;*" "*the senators' sons' wives;*" the *senators' sons' wives' jewels.*" I mention this, not to inform any one of so well-known a practice, but because it gives rise to a few cases in which there is some difficulty. The reason of the usage may be, a desire to avoid the occurrence of the two sibilant letters together. This seems likely, because we extend it to other words ending in *s*, or in a sound like *s*, though they may not be plural. Thus we say, "*for thy goodness' sake,*" meaning, for the sake of thy goodness: in which case the word "*goodness*" ought plainly to be written with the apostrophe after it. Thus,

too, we should say "*for patience' sake*," meaning, for the sake of patience; and again, we ought to put the apostrophe after "*patience.*"

32. But we are not consistent in this. If we were speaking of a *person* named Patience, we should say, *Patience's* father is here": and we form the possessive cases of James, and Thomas, and Charles, not by the mere apostrophe, but by the apostrophe with the *s*. "Thomas is Charles's son: James is Thomas's son: therefore Charles is James's grandfather." Again, we say and write "Bass's Ale," not "Bass' Ale": "Chambers's Journal," not "Chambers' Journal."

33. **Plurals of compound names.**—Very nearly related to the last question is the following. Which of these two is right,—the *Misses Brown*, or the *Miss Browns?* For the former it may be said, that *Brown* is the name of the whole species, and that the young ladies, being individuals of that species, are *Misses;* for the latter, that each of the young ladies being *Miss-Brown*, the whole taken together, or any two or more, are *Miss-Browns*. So that either way is justifiable. Usage is all but universal in favour of the latter in conversation. We may say we met *the Miss Browns*, not *the Misses Brown*. But we can hardly justify this our colloquial practice, if we bring in *Mrs. Brown*, and say we met *Mrs. and the Miss Browns*. For, by enumerating thus first the individual, and then the species, we bind ourselves to the *former* way of spelling. The sentence, as I have last given it, is inaccurate; because it really says that we met *Mrs.*, *and the Miss*, *Browns;* i.e., one *Mrs.* and one *celebrated Miss*, rejoicing in the name of, not *Brown*, but *Browns*. If we had wished to keep to the ordinary colloquial usage in this case also, we ought to have said that we met *Mrs. Brown and the Miss Browns*.

34. A correspondent writes: "*Calf-skin* is spoken of in the singular. Does the plural admit of the word *calf* being transformed into *calves*, with the letter *s* added to the word *skin?*" The answer, I conceive, must be, that in the compound term *calf-skin*, we use the first word as a generic adjective, *calf-skin*, not *calf's skin*: as we do when we say, "*bound in calf:*" and that we have no more right to change *calf* into *calves* when we change *skin* into *skins*,

than we have to say "One book is bound in calf," "two books are bound in calves."

35. A similarly doubtful case presents itself in *calves'-head* or *calf's-head*. The former of these, as describing a dish made of a single calf's-head, is hardly defensible on any rules of propriety; but it is universally used in preference to the other. The reason possibly may be that ease of pronunciation favours the *v* rather than the *f*. We should naturally write, not *pigs'-face*, but *pig's-face*.

36. It may be asked, whether of these two is right, "*spoonfuls*" or "*spoonsfull*." The answer seems very obvious. If spoonful is to be regarded as one word, as I suppose it is, then spoonfuls is its plural. "The earth brought forth by handfuls" (Gen. xli. 47). But if we keep the compounding syllables separate, *a spoon full*, then we ought of course to say *two spoons full*, and so on. The composite word "*spoonful*" has an existence of its own, and must follow the laws of that commonwealth of words to which it belongs. To make its plural "*spoonsfull*," is to blot out its separate existence as a word. Besides, this form of plural does not convey the meaning intended. "*Three spoons full*" is a different thing from "*three spoonfuls*." The former implies that three separate spoons were used: the latter expresses three measures of the size indicated.

37. "Attorneys" and "moneys." — There seems to be a liability to error in the formation of some plurals themselves. The words "*attorney*" and "*money*" are often made into "*attornies*" and "*monies*" in the plural. This is of course wrong: we might as well turn the singular "*key*" into a plural "*kies*." I am not aware that any one ever wrote "*monkies*" or "*donkies*" for "*monkeys*" or "*donkeys*." And this is not a case of rule against usage: for all our better and more careful writers use the right plurals, viz., "*attorneys*," and "*moneys*."

38. A correspondent is about to dedicate a book to a royal patroness. He wishes to express gratitude for "many kindnesses;" but feeling uncomfortable as to the correctness of the expression, is afraid he shall have to write "*much kindness*," which does not so well express his meaning, "*kindness shown on many occasions*."

It is a very easy matter to calm his apprehension, and allow him the full expression of his gratitude. Nothing is commoner than the making of abstract nouns into concrete in this manner. I trust we all remember the verse in the Lamentations of Jeremiah, ch. iii. 22, " It is of the Lord's *mercies* that we are not consumed, because His *compassions* fail not." In the same chapter we read of "all their *imaginations* against me." And in Ps. lxxxix. 49, we have the very word in question : " Lord, where are thy former *loving-kindnesses*, which Thou swarest unto David in thy truth ? "

In all these examples, the word which originally signified an attribute, is taken to indicate an instance of the exercise of that attribute. " *Loving kindnesses* " are, instances of loving kindness.

A curious case of this licence in speech may be seen at present on the walls of our railway stations, where an agent announces that he has upwards of 500 "*businesses*" to dispose of.

39. " **Means.**"—A question arises as to the proper construction of certain nouns bearing the plural form. The first which I shall notice is " *means*." " Those pieces of hypocrisy were, with him, means to an end." " That piece of hypocrisy was with him, a "—what ?—a *mean* to an end ? No,— this is not English, though it may be correct in grammatical construction. " That piece of hypocrisy was, with him, a *means* to an end." This is how we speak. And we say, " the best *means* of accomplishing your end *is*," if we are going to speak of one mode of action only ; not " the best *mean* is," nor " the best *means are*," unless we mean to enumerate more than one.

40. The plural "*acquaintances*" is found fault with because acquaintance itself is a plural noun—"they sought Him amongst their kinsfolk and acquaintance." But here is another instance of that which we have been just treating. " *A loving kindness*," is an example of the abstract quality loving-kindness, and so we have the plural " *loving-kindnesses*." So " *an acquaintance* " is an example of acquaintance, concretely present in an individual with whom we are acquainted : and if this substitution is to be allowed, we cannot object to its taking a plural form, and becoming " *acquaintances*." It is precisely analogous to "*relations*" used in the same concrete sense.

c

41. "**News.**"—Very similar is our way of dealing with "*news.*" If we are about to mention one fact, only, we say the latest news "*is,*" not "*are.*" In this case indeed the use of the plural verb at all is unusual, even if several things are to be mentioned. If we pick one out of several, we sometimes say, "The latest *piece of news* is." "*Here lies the remains of,*" has been justified, on the ground that "*remains*" is equivalent to "*remainder,*" there being no such singular noun as "*a remain.*" But the defence is unquestionably wrong. The word "*remains*" is, and is intended to be, plural, in signification, as well as in form. The human body is broken up by death, and is no longer regarded as a whole, but as a heap of decomposing parts. And the same idea is present in speaking of any thing which has passed into decay or dismemberment: we speak commonly of *the ruins* of a church or castle, though in this case we may say that it has become "*a ruin;*" we have "*les restes,*" "*trümmer,*" "*rudera,*" "*ίψίπια,*" all plurals.

42. "**Mewses.**"—There is another word which, by conspicuous notices on the London walls, appears to have become one of this class. I mean "*mews.*" I should have been inclined to say, "South Portman Mews are on the left as you go up Orchard Street." But clearly this is not the way of speaking which is most intelligible to the coachmen and grooms of London. For at the entrance of every one of the Marylebone mews (I am using my own plural), I see a notice posted for the regulation of the "*mewses*" of the metropolis.¹ Besides the incongruity of its poetic

¹ In my article printed in "Good Words" for November, 1863, I had supposed this form of the notice to be current throughout London, and had ascribed it to the late Sir Richard Mayne. I received the following letter from Dr. Thomson, the medical officer of health for Marylebone, which enables me to correct my former statement:—

"DEPARTMENT OF MEDICAL OFFICER OF HEALTH.
"Court House, St. Marylebone, W.
"November 5, 1863.

"Sir, I observe that in your last interesting paper on the English language in 'Good Words,' you ascribe the use of the term Mewses to Sir Richard Mayne. In justice to him, allow me to state that the regulations to which you refer are only attached, so far as I am aware, to the Mews in the parish of St. Marylebone. They were drawn up by

associations, this word "*mewses*" is a very queer monster. Fancy ordering "*two Daily Newses*," by way of two copies of the "Daily News." Still, we must allow the Marylebone parish authorities this much indulgence, as to confess that their word is not altogether without precedent.

43. "Summons."—With regard to *summons*, which appears to be another of these plural words become singular, and in the usage of which we have long ago become accustomed to read that "*summonses* were served on all the offenders," a barrister has suggested to me that it is in fact derived from the French *semonce*. Probability is given to this idea, from the fact that the verb representing the serving of the legal process, is in English most commonly pronounced, not to "*summon*," but to "*summons*," as it naturally would be, if from the French verb "*semoncer*." In Landais' large French dictionary, the meanings are thus given:—

"Semonce, subst. fem. (du latin *submonitio*, fait de *submonere*, avertir secrètement, à demi-mot), invitation faite dans les formes pour quelque cérémonie.—Avertissement fait par quelqu'un qui a autorité.—Reprimande.

"Semoncer, v. act., faire une *semonce*; donner un avertissement."

So that, at all events, the proposed derivation is not far-fetched; for the signification exactly corresponds. The only missing link is, the historical proof, from the old French of our courts, that "*semonce*" and "*semoncer*" were actually used in them, and from French passed into English. This, which I am not able to give, some of my legal correspondents may perhaps supply. I observe that Todd, in his edition of Johnson, derives summons from the formal Latin name of the writ, "*summoneas*." But this does not seem so probable.

44. Is "*chickens*" a legitimate plural? If we go by

myself, and in my original copy of the draught they are styled Mews. In correcting the proofs, however, the legal authorities of the parish substituted the term you object to, in defiance of the Queen's English, but in direct obedience to the inexorable 35 Geo. 3, cap. 73, passed in 1795, where the term Mewses occurs throughout.

"Very faithfully yours,
"R. Dundas Thomson, M.D., F.R.S.
"Medical Officer of Health."

authority, yes: for the English Version of the Bible has it, Matt. xxiii. 37, and Shakspeare, "Macbeth" (act iv. sc. 3), "What, all my pretty chickens at a swoop?"; and three times more. If "*chickens*" is an allowable plural, it can of course be only because "*chicken*" is an allowable singular. And apparently it is so used by Shakspeare, "2 Henry VI." (act iii. sc. 1); for "the chicken" there represents the king only. At all events, usage has long ago sanctioned both the singular and the plural. No one would now say, "We had a chick for dinner"; and we have all our lives been used to the sign of the "Hen and Chickens." But we use the other and more strictly correct plural also: making, I think, a slight distinction between the two forms. We say, "Do you keep chicken?" But we read, "Gathereth her chickens beneath her wings." Does not this indicate a leaning to "*chicken*" for the generic plural, "*chickens*" for the individualised? For the chicken are kept *en masse*: the chickens run in, one by one.

45. "**Diocess**" or "**diocese**."—Ought the district over which a bishop has ecclesiastical jurisdiction to be spelt *diocese*, or *diocess?* The latter form is found in a few of our older writers, and is by some persons retained in our own days. The "Times" newspaper once pertinaciously adhered to it. In letters inserted and extracts given, the spelling was even altered to this form. Of late it appears to have been abandoned. There is really no justification for it. The word seems to have come from the Norman-French *diocisse;* but its derivation, as well as the usage of the great majority of English writers, fixes the spelling the other way. The word is derived from the Greek "*dioikesis*," with the "*eta*" or long *e* in the last syllable but one; and ought no more to be spelt diocess, than *cheese* ought to be spelt *chess*.

46. "**Need**" and "**needs**." A correspondent asks, whether the suppression of the *s* in the third person singular of "*to need*" may be regarded as sanctioned by use?

Certainly, no one in these days would think of saying, "Tell the housemaid she needs not light the dining-room fire to-day." Our practice in this case is to abridge "needs not" into "needn't." But it is to be observed that the *s* is dropped only when another verb follows: we say "He need have the strength of Hercules to lift that stone:" but if we leave out "have," we must say, "He needs the strength."

47. Division of a word between lines.—The division of a word, when the former portion has to be written in one line and the latter in another, may seem but a trifling matter; but it is one worth a few moments' attention. The ordinary rule is, that the break should be so made, as to let the new line begin with a consonant. And notice that this is not the same matter as division of the word into its component parts. This latter process must follow the order of derivation and inflexion of the word: but in division between line and line, we are obliged to transgress this order. For instance, in dividing the word *attainted* into its component parts, we say that *at-* is the first, *taint-* the second, and *-ed* the third: *taint* being the root of the word, and *-ed* the added sign of the past tense. But in dividing this word between two lines, we should put *attain-* in the former line, and *-ted* in the latter. If any one is disposed to object to this way of dividing, and to require that we should in all cases follow the composition and inflexion of the word, and begin the new line with the *-ed*, he may at once be shown the impossibility of doing so, by trying it in the case of any verb ending with *e* preceded by a mute and a liquid, as *humble*, or any which turns a final *y* into *ie*, as *multiply*, in making its past tense. The word *humbled* is confessedly of two syllables: but if we are to divide on the *rational* plan, where is the break to occur? It is true that, in this particular case, on no plan is the account to be given quite satisfactory. The pronunciation of the word in reading, making the *e* of *ed* mute, may be represented by "*humbld*." But this is not expressed by *hum-bled*, nor by *humb-led*, nor indeed by any mode of division that can be devised. The inference is, that we should, if possible, avoid dividing such a word at all. But in such words as *multiplied*, though the rational division according to inflexion fails, the ordinary rule is easily followed: *-plied*, when the *e* is mute, becomes the last syllable, and the division is made accordingly.

48. "**To**" and "**too**."—I have observed that Mr.

Charles Dickens speaks in one of his works of "shutting *too*." Now it is true that "*to*" and "*too*" are originally the same word; in German, *zu* expresses them both; but it is also true that usage with us has appropriated "*too*" for the adverb of addition or excess, and "*to*" for the preposition; and that in the expression "shutting *to*," it is the preposition, and not the adverb that is used; that *to which* the door is shut being omitted, and the preposition thus getting the adverbial sense of *close* or *home*.

49. **Doubling the final letter.**—There seems to be a habit of expressing any less usual sense of a monosyllabic word by doubling the final letter. Thus I have sometimes seen "This house to *lett*." And in one of the numerous mining circulars which are constantly swelling one's daily parcel of letters, I observe it stated, that the "*sett*" is very rich and promising. Thus, likewise, *clear* profit is sometimes described as "*nett*," instead of "*net*."

50. **Benefitted.**—This reminds us of another doubling of a final letter, respecting which there is considerable doubt. Does the verb to *benefit*, in forming its past participle, double its final letter? Is it true, as stated in the first edition of this work, that this doubling only takes places in a syllable on which the accent is laid, and that the purpose of it is to ensure the right pronunciation? At first sight it would seem so. If the participle of quit were spelt *quited*, it would be pronounced as in *requited*, and would lose the sound of its verb: whereas by spelling it *quitted*, that sound is retained. And so of *fit*, *cabal*, *abhor*, and other words of the same kind. When the syllable has no accent on it, the reduplication seems not to be needed, for there can be but one way of pronouncing it; we might as well make the participle of *remember*, *remembered*, as that of *benefit*, *benefitted*. But the intelligent Irish correspondent, whom I quote at length in paragraph 331, observes justly that this view does not seem borne out in the case of *cavilling, travelling, grovelling,* and the like words. So that, after all, it seems as if usage were our only safe guide in the matter.

51. **"Caviller."** A correspondent asks why we double the *l* in *caviller*, when the accent is undoubtedly on the first syllable? The answer, I suppose, is that we wish to keep

some difference evident between such words as "*reviler*" and "*caviler*." That no rule requires us to lay the accent on the second syllable on account of the doubling, is evident from such words as "*cruelly*," "*royally*," "*jovially*," &c.

52. "**Dare**."—The same correspondent asks whether good writers make "*dare*" do duty for the past tense of "to dare"?

I do not quite understand this question. I never saw that done which is described. Does my correspondent mean that he doubts whether good writers would say, "They urged him to take the leap, but he dare not"? I imagine that every one would write "he dared not:" I am sure that every one would *say*, "he didn't dare to."

Let me put in a word to rescue "*dare*" from being treated as we just now saw "*need*" must be treated. It is not according to the best usage to say, "*he dare not do it*." The *s* of the third person present must not be suppressed: but we must say "*he dares not do it*."

53. **Double letters in compound words.**—When do we, and when do we not, express double letters coming together in certain compound words? No one writes *camelleopard*: but *withhold* is universal in the Authorised Version of the Bible, and in Shakspeare, and in all careful modern writers. I have observed a tendency gaining ground to drop one *h* and spell "*withold*," but we do not write *washouse*, *watchouse*; which shows that the double *h* need not be avoided as intolerable.

54. Sometimes, when a double letter occurs at the end of a monosyllable used in compounding a word, we drop one letter. Thus from *well*, we have *wel-fare*, *wel-come*: from *full*, *ful-some*: from *all*, *al-ways*, *al-mighty*, *al-so*. But these seem to be adverbs, or adjectives adverbially used. The same does not happen to substantives. From *bell* we have not *bel-pull*, but *bell-pull*, and *bell-tower*: from *wall*, *wall-flower*: from *gall*, *gall-bladder*, *gall-nut*: from *hell*, *hell-fire*: from *mill*, *mill-stream*, *mill-dam*, *mill-stone*: from *pill*, *pill-box*, &c. The only verb that occurs to me, "*pass*," is compounded both ways: from it we have *pas-time*, but we have also *pass-book* and *pass-word*.

55. "**Lose**" and "**loose**."—I have several times

noticed the verb to *lose* spelt *loose*. A more curious instance of the arbitrary character of English usage as to spelling and pronunciation, could hardly be given, than these two words furnish: but usage must be obeyed. In this case it is not consistent with itself in either of the two practices: the syllable "-*oose*" keeps the sound of *s* in *loose*, *noose*, *goose*, but changes it for that of *z* in *choose*: the syllable "-*ose*" keeps the sound of *s* in *close*, *dose*, but changes it for *z* in *chose*, *hose*, *nose*, *pose*, *rose*. But when usage besides this requires us to give the *o* in *lose* the sound of *u* in *luminary*, we feel indeed that reasoning about spelling and pronunciation is almost at an end.

56. "**Sanitary**" and "**sanatory**."—*Sanitary* and *sanatory* are but just beginning to be rightly understood. *Sanitary*, from *sanitas*, Latin for soundness or health, means, appertaining to *health*; *sanatory*, from *sano*, to cure, means appertaining to *healing* or *curing*. "The town is in such a bad sanitary condition, that some sanatory measures must be undertaken." I was surprised to see, in the "Illustrated News" of October 31, 1863, a print and description of Murree, one of the "*Sanitariums*" for our troops in India.

57. "**Pharaoh.**"— I have noticed that the title of the ancient Egyptian kings hardly ever escapes mis-spelling. That title is Phar*ao*h not Phar*oa*h. Yet a leading article in the "Times," not long since, was full of PHAROAH, printed, as proper names in leading articles are, in conspicuous capitals. Nay, even worse than this: on my first visit to the South Kensington Museum, an institution admirably calculated to teach the people, I found a conspicuous notice with the same mis-spelling in it. I gave a memorandum of it to the attendant; but whether it has been corrected or not I cannot say.

58. **Mis-spelling in newspapers.** It is in newspapers, and especially in provincial newspapers, that most frequent faults in spelling are found. No doubt there is much to be said which may account for this. Sometimes their editors are men of education, aided by a very inefficient staff, and are at the mercy of their compositors and readers; sometimes they are half-educated men, aspiring to the use of words which they do not understand.

Examples might be gathered of the most absurd misspelling and misuse of words, from almost any copy of any provincial journal in the kingdom. In a country newspaper, not long since, I read that a jury might be "*immersed*" in a heavy fine; the meaning being, of course, that they might be "*amerced*." We were informed once, in the "Evening Star," a London penny paper now extinct, that the Pope went to the "*basilisk*" of St. Peter's; meaning "*basilica*," the name given by the Romans to several of their largest churches.

59. "**-ize**" or "**-ise.**"—How are we to decide between *s* and *z* in such words as anathematize, cauterize, criticize, deodorize, dogmatize, fraternize, utilize, and the rest? Many of these are derived from Greek verbs ending in *-izo*; but more from French verbs ending in *-iser*. It does not seem easy to come to a decision. Usage varies, but has not pronounced positively in any case. It seems more natural to write *anathematize* and *cauterize* with the *z*, but *criticise* is commonly written with the *s*. I remember hearing the late Dr. Donaldson give his opinion that they ought all to be written with *s*. But in the present state of our English usage the question seems an open one.

60. "**Show**" and "**shew.**"—It is not easy to say how the verb corresponding to the substantive *show* comes to be spelt *shew*. Here again we seem bound to follow usage, and not rashly to endeavour to reform it. Still, perhaps, something may be said tending to illustrate the present usage.

It has seemed to me from observation as if the tendency were to write the verb *show*, as the substantive is unquestionably written, when an outward demonstration is intended, and *shew*, when we speak of a demonstration to the mind: "He showed me his house, and shewed me that it was worth the rent he asked." If there be anything in what has been said, it would seem to follow that the substantive, "a show," should always be spelt with an *o*: its meaning being restricted to an outward display made to the senses. But perhaps this is mere fancy. In the English Version of the Scriptures, *shew* seems without exception, both for verb and substantive. The same use is found also in the Common Prayer Book. The tendency of the modern printer has been to abandon this spelling altogether, and to use the *o* in every case.

61. "**Scottish**" and "**Scotch**." A correspondent enquires about "*Scottish*," and "*Scotch*," asserting that the latter form is a mere corruption, and that "no intelligent Scots-, or educated English man, makes use of this corruption." With reference to the question itself, I can only say, "Non nostrum .... tantas componere lites." But as regards my correspondent's assertion, I can only say, that I read in Shakspeare, "Much Ado about Nothing" (act ii. sc. 1), "Wooing, wedding, and repenting, is as a Scotch jig, a measure, and a cinquepace: the first suit is hot and hasty, like a Scotch jig, and full as fantastical." I conclude that Shakspeare will satisfy the requirements as to intelligence and education. In three other places, he has "Scottish."

62. "**Overflown**" for "**overflowed**."—We not unfrequently read that the whole valley was "*overflown*," instead of "*overflowed*." "No one," writes Dr. Latham ("History of the English Language," p. 556), "has (I hope) brought himself to say "the water *overflew* the field.""

63. **Words terminating in "-ery" or "-ry."**— Usage does not seem to be uniform in regard to such nouns as *deanery, fishery,* &c. Dr. Latham (p. 478) tells us that *fishery* is a double derivative, *fish, fisher, fishery*: and so of *brewery, cutlery,* &c. But the same cannot be said of *deanery, shrubbery, piggery*: and it may be a question how they got their *e* in the termination. There is much to be said on the attraction exercised by common sounds in a language over those which nearly resemble them. In our old books at Canterbury we find usually *deanry,* and this form still subsists in *heronry* (although we pronounce it *hernery*), *foundery, laundry.* Such words as *pinery, vinery,* might be quoted on both sides. For if the termination were -*ery,* the mute *e* preceding would be suppressed: and if -*ry,* the word stands as it ought—*pine-ry, vine-ry.*

64. There are some curious instances of this termination: witness *buttery,* which may have been *butt-e-ry*; and the above-quoted *shrub-be-ry, pig-ge-ry.*

65. "**Cemetery.**"—There is a word with a similar ending, but not to be placed in the same category, or dealt with by the same analogy. I mean *cemetery*, which owes its *-ery*, not to any habit of the English language, but to the ending of the Greek κοιμητήριον, cœmetērium, a sleeping-place.

66. **Meanings of such words.**—It may be observed that words with this termination are of two meanings: one local, as in all the instances hitherto quoted: the other abstract, describing the pursuit, or the general quality, pertaining to the simple root. In this, as well as in the former case, the uncertainty of usage as to the spelling prevails. We write *chemistry, palmistry, devilry;* but *witchery, lechery, venery, treachery.*

67. "**Stationery,**" "**confectionery.**"—Is the generally assumed difference between *stationary* and *stationery* worth keeping up? I venture to think it is. The adjective comes to us direct from a lower Latin form, *stationarius*, and signifies, abiding at rest. The substantive comes from the same, but through another derivative, *stationer*, the man who keeps a station or shop for books (as distinguished from an itinerant vendor). This being so, it had far better retain the trace of its derivation by ending in *-ery*, than be referred back, by ending in *-ary*, to a meaning which is wholly passed from it. There is an analogy in *confectionery;* in which case there is no adjective *confectionary* requiring the distinction to be made.

68. **Diphthongs.**—One word which occurred above reminds us to say something respecting the transference of Greek and Latin diphthongs into our own language. First we have the cases where the diphthongal form is by usage retained. In these, it is desirable to keep the distinction between *ae* and *oe* clear. An author has always to look keenly at his proofs with this view: and very few books are without some examples of mistake. The matter is complicated by the awkward circumstance that in *italics* the difference is so slight as to be almost imperceptible: that while in roman type we can print correctly Cæsar, homœopathy,—the former from "Kaisar," the latter from "homoiopatheia,"—in italics we print *Cæsar, homœopathy,* with hardly any appreciable distinction.

69. **Shall we drop diphthongs?**—Then comes the question, Is it desirable to drop altogether these awkward, un-English-looking diphthongs, and substitute *e* for them everywhere, as usage has already done in *equal* and *economy?* Possibly, so that it be not done rashly. But we should lose by it in some cases: *e.g.*, home-opathy would lie in danger of losing its right pronunciation though it would, perhaps, acquire a meaning not altogether inappropriate. In this, as in other cases, we must wait upon usage.

70. **"Cherubim," "seraphim."**—The varying plurals of *cherub* and *seraph*, as found in our Bible and Common Prayer Book, occasion some perplexity. Being anxious to give an account of them, I obtained the following from a friend whose scholarship I can trust:—

"The forms, '*cherubs*,' '*cherubim*,' '*cherubin*,' '*cherubims*,' and '*seraphs*,' '*seraphim*,' '*seraphin*,' '*seraphims*,' are, or profess to be, plurals of the words '*cherub*' and '*seraph*' respectively. The words themselves are taken directly from the Hebrew, and in that language the plurals are '*cherubim*' and '*seraphim*.' In the English Version the plurals appear as *cherubims* and *seraphims*, the translators finding *cherubim* (or '*in*') and *seraphim* (or '*in*') in the Latin and Greek Versions, and, it may be, thinking that these terminations would not carry to the majority of their readers the plural sense without the addition of *s*.¹ Cherub*in* and seraph*in* are properly Chaldaic or Rabbinic forms, and are those generally used in the oldest MSS. of the Septuagint Version (*or*), that version having probably been made by persons to whom the Rabbinic form was most familiar. (The form has, however, in later MSS. and in the editions of the Septuagint, been altered to *im*.) From the Septuagint this form was introduced to the Latin Versions, and so found its way into the Te Deum, where it has remained untranslated in the English Prayer Book."

71. **"Clue" or "clew"?**—Ought we to write *clue*, or *clew?* Beyond doubt, the latter is the original and the right orthography. We are, however, reminded that no

---

¹ The earlier English Bibles have generally *cherubins*, &c.

less an authority than Shakspeare has *clue* ("All's Well that Ends Well," act i. sc. 2). So that it seems the spelling now becoming universal has something to be said for it. Still we think the lovers of accuracy may, without imputation of pedantry, make a point of the original form.

CHAPTER III.

PRONUNCIATION.

72. Pronunciation.—I pass from spelling to pronunciation. And here a few introductory words may be desirable. In pronouncing, as in most things that we do, two extremes are to be avoided; precision and slovenliness. Few outward indications mark a man more plainly than his habit of pronouncing his own tongue. To be accurate without being precise, distinct without being artificial, to be everywhere heard, and always understood, without noticeable effort,—these are the excellences of good pronunciation; and while they come by a happy instinctive tact to some men, others seem never able to attain them, and seldom, if they lack them, to feel their deficiency.

73. In this matter, the accidents of birth and early training go for much; but they are not insuperable. I have known cases of men who have risen from the ranks, —whose provincial or vulgar utterances I could myself remember, who yet before middle age have entirely cast off every trace of these adverse circumstances, and speak as accurately as their high-born and carefully trained compeers.

74. Misuse of the aspirate.—These remarks lead me first to notice that worst of all faults, the leaving out of the aspirate where it ought to be, and putting it in where it ought not to be. This is a vulgarism not confined to this or that province of England, nor especially prevalent in one county or another, but incident throughout England to persons of low breeding and inferior education, principally to those among the inhabitants of towns. Nothing so surely stamps a man as below the mark in intelligence, self-respect, and energy, as this unfortunate habit: in intelligence, because, if he were but moderately keen in perception, he would see how it marks him; in self-respect and energy, because if he had these, he would long ago have set to work and cured it. Hundreds of stories are current about the absurd consequences of this vulgarism. We remember the barber in "Punch" who, while operating on a gentleman expresses his opinion, that, after all, the cholera was in the *hair*. "Then," observes the customer, "you ought to be very careful what brushes you use." "Oh, sir," replies the barber, laughing, "I didn't mean the *air* of the *ed*, but the *hair* of the *hatmosphere*."

75. As I write these lines, which I do while waiting in a refreshment-room at Reading, between the arrival of a Great-Western and the departure of a South-Eastern train, I hear one of two commercial gentlemen, from a neighbouring table, telling his friend that "his *ed* used to *hake* ready to burst."

76. The following incident happened at the house of friends of my own. They had asked to dinner some acquaintances who were not perfect in their aspirates. When they made their appearance somewhat late, imagine the consternation of my relative, on receiving from the lady an apology, that she was very sorry they were after their time, but they had some *ale* by the way. The well-known infirmity suggested the charitable explanation, that it was a *storm*, and not a *tipple*, which had detained them.

77. I had once a very curious communication on the subject of the pronunciation of the aspirate. My correspondent objected, that the portion of my Essay which treated of this matter conveyed no meaning to him, for that from a child he had never been able to tell the difference in pronunciation between a word beginning with an *h*, and one beginning without: and he insisted that I ought to have adopted some method of making this plainer. He adds, "In all cases where the *h* is used, *to me* it appears superfluous." I adduce this to shew that there are some cases in which the neglect of the aspirate is simply incurable. Still, I have known instances where it has been thoroughly eradicated, at the cost, it is true, of considerable pains and diligence.

78. "**Umble**," &c. But there are certain words with regard to which the bad habit lingers in persons not other-

wise liable to it. We still sometimes, even in good society, hear "*ospital,*" "*erb,*" and "*umble,*"—all of them, in my opinion, very offensive, but the last of them by far the worst, especially when heard from an officiating clergyman. The English Prayer-book has at once settled the pronunciation of this word for us, by causing us to give to God our "*humble* and *hearty* thanks" in the general thanksgiving. "*Umble* and *hearty*" few can pronounce without a pain in the throat; and "*umblanarty*" we certainly never were meant to say; "*humble* and *hearty*" is the only pronunciation which will suit the alliterative style of the prayer, which has in it "not only with our *lips*, but in our *lives*." If it be urged that we have "*an humble* and contrite heart," I answer, so have we the "strength of *an horse;*" but no one supposes that we were meant to say "*a norse.*" The following are even more decisive: "holy and humble men of heart:" "*thy* humble servants," not "*thine.*" It is difficult to believe that this pronunciation can long survive the satire of Dickens in "David Copperfield": "I am well aware that I am the umblest person going," said Uriah Heep, modestly, "let the other be who he may. My mother is likewise a very umble person. We live in a numble abode, Master Copperfield, but have much to be thankful for. My father's former calling was umble; he was a sexton."

79. The unaspirated pronunciation of *humble* has been defended, partly on the ground of being borrowed from the Italian, partly by the allegation that I have failed to prove from the Prayer-book the intention of the compilers of our Liturgy that the aspirate should be pronounced. It has been asserted that the alliteration in the words, "humble and hearty," is as perfect without the aspirate on the former word, as with it; and I am told that the fact of the occurrence of "*thy humble servants,*" and "*thine unworthy servants,*" decides nothing, because we have "*thy honour and glory.*" But be it observed, that in order to answer my argument, an instance ought to have been produced, not of a *different* unaspirated vowel with "*thy*" before it, but of the *same* unaspirated vowel, (the short *u*); because some vowels have in themselves sounds more or less nearly approaching to the power of a consonant, and therefore

enduring "*thy*" and "*a*" before them. The long *u* has this power; we may say "*a unit*," "*a university*," because the first syllable sounds as if it began with "*you*," and *y* has here the power of a consonant. But the short *u*, as in "*humble*," is not one of those vowels which require a consonant to enunciate them : one could not say "*a unlearned man :*" and I must therefore still maintain that the occurrence of "*thy humble*," and "*thine unworthy*," shews that the *h* was meant to be aspirated in the former case, as we know it was not in the latter.

80. An apparently more formidable objection has been brought against my conclusion from "*thy humble*" and "*thine unworthy*." "Were I," it is said, "to find the words '*my umbrella*' in some standard work, should I at once exclaim, 'Oh, this writer calls it '*humbrella*'? Here is an example of the short *u*." My answer is very simple. *Mine* is now almost universally disused: and *my* has taken its place before vowels. The translators of the Bible wrote "*mine eyes :*" but if I found "*my eyes*," or "*my own*," in a modern book, I certainly should not charge the writer with meaning me to read "*my heyes*," "*my hown*." I must still maintain that, when the same persons, in the same book, wrote "*thy humble*," and "*thine unworthy*," they meant to indicate a difference, in respect of the aspirate, between the pronunciation of the two words thus differently preceded.

81. A correspondent, writing from Ireland, charges me with being in error for finding fault with those who drop the aspirate in the word "*hospital*," "for," says he, "no one in *Ireland*, so far as I am aware, ever thinks of aspirating the *h* in that word." This is certainly a curious reason why we should not aspirate it in England. It reminds me of an American friend of ours, who, after spending two or three days with us, ventured to tell us candidly, that we all "*spoke with a strong English accent.*"

82. "**Which.**"—The same correspondent states that he never met an Englishman who could pronounce the relative pronoun "*which*." He charges us all with pronouncing it as if it were "*witch*." I may venture to inform him that it was his ear which was in fault. The ordinary English pronunciation "*which*" is as distinguishable

D

from "*witch*," as it is from the coarse Irish and Scotch "*wh-ich*."

83. **"A" or "an" before a vowel.**—What is our rule—or have we any—respecting the use of *a* or *an* before words beginning with an aspirated *h*? The rule commonly given is this: that when the accent on the word thus beginning is on the first syllable, we must use *a*; when it is on the second or any following syllable, we may use *an*. This is reasonable enough, because the first syllable, by losing its accent, also loses some portion of the strength of its aspiration. We cannot aspirate with the same strength the first syllables in the words *history* and *historian*, and in consequence, we commonly say *a history;* but *an historian*.

84. Still, though this may define our modern practice, it is rather a reasonable description of it, than a rule recognised by our best writers. They do not scruple to use *an* before aspirated words, even when the accent falls on the first syllable. In the course of an examination through the letter *h* in the Concordance, verified by the text in all passages which seemed doubtful, I have found in the English Version of the Bible very few instances of the article *a* used before a word beginning with *h*. We have *an half, an hammer, an hand, an high hand, an handmaid, an harp, an haven, an head, an heap, an heart, an hedge an helmet, an help, an herdsman, an heretic, an heritage, an hill, an high hill, an hissing, an holy day, an holy man, an holy angel, an horn, an horrible thing* (I may mention that Cruden has cited *a horrible* in every instance, but that in every instance, it stands *an*, both in the edition of 1611 and in our present Bibles), *an horse, an host, an house, an hundred, an husband, an hymn, an hypocrite*. The only exceptions which I have found are, *a hill*, Josh. xxiv. 33: *a holy solemnity*, Isa. xxx. 29. So that the surprise of a correspondent at Archbishop Trench's having written *an hero* was hardly justified. I do not, of course, mean to say that the usage of the translators of the Bible should be our rule now; but in the absence of any general fixed rule, we can hardly find fault with writers who choose to follow a practice once so widely prevalent, and still kept before the public in the Book most read of all books. I must just

remark, that the fact, that we are more particular about this matter than our ancestors were, seems to shew that, notwithstanding the very common vulgarism of dropping the aspirated *h*, the tendency of modern times has been rather to aspirate more, than less.

85. "**Such an one.**"—A correspondent questions the propriety of the common use of "*an*" before "*one*," in the phrase "*such an one.*" I bring this forward not with any idea of deciding it, but because in my examination of the usage of our translators of the Bible, a curious circumstance has come to light. They uniformly used "*such a one*," the expression occurring about thirteen times. In the New Testament, the printers have altered it throughout to "*such an one:*" in the Old Testament, they have as uniformly left it as it was. It seems to me that we may now, in writing, use either. In common talk, I should always naturally say "*such a one*," not "*such an one*," which would sound formal and stilted.

86. **An "ear," "a year."**—A correspondent enquires how the indefinite article should be expressed before the words *ear, year*. Here is just one of the instances in which the distinction between "*a*" and "*an*" is valuable. By always saying "*an ear*," "*a year*," we ensure at all events that something like the right pronunciation of both words should be heard.

87. **Only one hen in Venice.**—A student at one of our military academies had copied a drawing of a scene in Venice, and in writing the title, had spelt the name of the city *Vennice*. The drawing master put his pen through the superfluous letter, observing, "Don't you know, sir, there is but one *hen* in Venice?" On which the youth burst out laughing. Being asked what he was laughing about, he replied he was thinking *how uncommonly scarce eggs must be there.* The master, in wrath, reported him to the colonel in command, a Scotchman. He, on hearing the disrespectful reply, without in the least perceiving the point of the joke, observed, "An a varra naatural observaation too."

88. "**Idear,**" &c.—A worse fault even than dropping the aspirate, is the sounding words ending with *a* or *aw*, as if they ended with *ar*. A correspondent, accustomed

apparently to attend the Houses of Parliament, sends me a strong remonstrance against this practice. He says, "Woe betide any unfortunate member if he strews the floor with '*aitches*': the laughter is open and merciless: but honourable members may talk of the '*lawrr*' of the land, or '*seaien the idear*,' with perfect impunity. One of the greatest offenders in this matter is a well-known opposition speaker whom I shall not name. The startling way in which he brings out *idear* is enough to make the hair of any one but a well-seasoned Cockney stand on end." My correspondent goes on to say, "*Amelia Ann* is a great stumbling-block to people with this failing, becoming of course in their mouths *Amelia ran*. I remember once seeing a little elementary tract on French pronunciation, in which, opposite the French *a*, was placed *ar*, by way of indicating to British youth the pronunciation thereof. I showed the curiosity to several Londoners, but they could not be made to see the point of the joke."

89. **Calling** "u" "oo."—There is a very offensive vulgarism, most common in the midland counties, but found more or less almost everywhere: giving what should be the sound of the *u* in certain words, as if it were *oo*: calling "*duty*," *dooty*; "*Tuesday*," *Toosday*; reading to us that "the clouds drop down the *doo*;" exhorting us "*dooty* to do the *dooties* that are *doo* from us;" asking to be allowed to see the "*noospaper*." And this is not from incapacity to utter the sound; for though many of these people call "*new*," *noo*, no one ever yet called "*few*," *foo*; but it arises from defective education, or from gross carelessness.

90. "**Heritor**"—"**curātor**."—A Scottish correspondent, speaking of some usages prevalent in the north, says: "'Heritor,' proprietor of landed property, is most commonly pronounced '*eritor*,' which is manifestly inconsistent with '*heritage*,' '*hereditary*,' &c., in which the aspiration is always given. In our Scottish courts of law, we hear of entries being made on the '*recórd*,' never *récord*: but in other than law uses the word is always accented on the first syllable. This reminds me of another term in Scottish law—'*Curátor*,' pronounced *curátor*, in violation, certainly, of the Latin analogy. It is told of a witty

Scottish counsel, that when pleading before the House of Lords, being corrected by one of their lordships for his false quantity in the pronunciation of this word, he replied, with a profound bow, that he must submit to the authority of so learned a *senātor*, and so eloquent an *orātor*."

91. "**Decanal**," &c.—In one letter sent to me, fault is found with the pronunciations "*decānal*," "*ruri-decānal*," "*optātive*," on the ground that it is the genius of our language always to throw back the accent to the first syllable of a tri-syllabic word, as in "*senātor*," "*orātor*," "*minister*." In such a case, custom is our only guide. It is not to be thought that, because we say "*senātor*," "*orātor*," "*minister*," we have any objection to tri-syllabic words with the accent on the penultima; we have hundreds of them: witness "*objector*," "*protector*," "*reflector*," "*assertor*," &c. So that no rule can be laid down, except the "*norma loquendi*." Think of "*disputer*," and "*disputant!*"

92. **Manifold.**—A correspondent asks for a comment on the pronunciation of the word "*manifold*." He thinks that we lose the idea of its original composition by calling it, as we generally do, "*mannifold*," and that it ought to be called "*many-fold*," as if it were two words. My reply would be, that the end proposed is a praiseworthy one, but I am afraid it will not justify the means used in attaining it—viz., the violation of common usage, which has stamped "*mannifold*" with its approval. It may be that the mispronunciation first originated in the apparent analogy with "*manifest*." I would remind him, that this is not the only word which suffers change of pronunciation when compounded. We call a "*vine-yard*," "*vinyard:*" the man would be deservedly set down as a pedant who should do otherwise. We call a "*cup-board*" a "*cubbard*," a "*half-penny*" a "*haepny*," and we similarly contract many other compound words. The great rule, I take it, in all such cases of conventional departure from the pronunciation of words as spelt, is to do nothing which can attract attention. We naturally think somewhat less favourably than we otherwise should of a person who says "*vic-tu-al*," when the rest of the world say "*vittal;*"

"*med-i-cine*," when others say "*med'cine*;" "*ve-ni-son*," where we thought we should hear "*ven'son*." We commonly expect that such a man will be strong-willed, and hard to deal with in ordinary life: and I think we are not often wrong.

"**Prophecy.**"—A correspondent complains of the stress laid on the final syllable of the substantive *prophecȳ*: and says, "What should we think of *ecstasy, fallacy, phantasy*, especially if put in the plural?" But in this case, usage is right, and apparent analogy wrong. *Ecstasy*, as we have already seen, is from the Greek *ecstasis*; *phantasy*, from the Greek *phantasia*; *fallacy*, from the Latin *fallacia*. But *prophecy* is from the Greek *propheteia*: and it is therefore not without reason that we lay the stress on the last syllable. The verb, *to prophesy*, we pronounce in the same way; I suppose, by a double analogy: partly guided by the sound of the substantive, partly by that of the last syllable in other verbs ending in *y*, to qualify, to amplify, to mystify, &c.

93. I have an enquiry whether the long name for a giraffe, cited above, in paragraph 53, should be pronounced according to its correct spelling, "*camelopard*," or according to the conventional spelling, "*camcleopard*." There can be little doubt that the latter is a corruption of the former; but it has gained universal acceptance, and it now would be pedantic to depart from it.

94. A word may be said here on a pronunciation, confined, as far as I have observed, to my own countrymen of the west of England. The general tendency of the Somersetshire dialect is to sound the voice where ordinary English speakers suppress it. For example: the letters *s*, soft *c*, *f*, and *th*, are properly pronounced by the mouth, without the aid of the voice. But the Somersetshire man never intermits the sound of his voice; and consequently he sounds *s* and soft *c* as *z*, *f* as *v*, and *th* as *dth*: he calls *Sunday, Zunday; fire, vire;* and *thick, dthick*.

95. This habit has been in the main overcome by people of education; but it lingers in certain words. And among them the two just treated of, "*prophecy*" and "*prophesy*" may be numbered. The Somersetshire man very commonly says for both, "*provezy*."

96. **Vocal and oral sounds.**—This continual use and disuse of the vocal organs in speaking is a curious thing to think of. A hundred times in a minute the stop is pushed in and pulled out by every speaker, and without any conscious effort. For it is this which makes the difference between *p* and *b*, between *t* and *d*, between *f* and *v*, between *s* (and soft *c*) and *z*, between *th* and *dth*. In such a sentence as, "*A big pig fell down into a very thick thorn bush, but was saved*," we have the alternatives coming pretty fast. But not faster than in much of our ordinary talk. The words take two and a half seconds to pronounce, and we push in our vocal stop seven times.

97. "**Alms**," &c.—Complaint has been made of the pronunciation of the words *alms*, *psalms*, *calm*, after the fashion of *elm* and *film*. No doubt the marked utterance of the *l* in these words would savour of affectation; at the same time, there is a subdued sound of it which should be heard in "*alms:*" even less audibly in "*psalm*," and hardly at all in "*calm:*" usage, as learnt in society, being in this, as in other uncertain pronunciations, the only safe guide.

98. A correspondent mentions an amusing result of provincial pronunciation in the mind of an ignorant man:—

"Many years ago, in the Isle of Skye, I was reasoning with a man who thought himself very religious, who, in common with the class to which he belonged, fancied that he possessed the power of 'discerning spirits,' especially those of preachers, and reckoned it a sacred duty to refuse to listen to any one of whose conversion he felt not fully assured (the test, I am sorry to say, being the use of certain formal phrases, and specially the tone of voice). I said what I could about the truth being God's truth—to be received as such in a meek, humble, and self-searching spirit; and referred to the well-known passage—'Take heed *how* ye hear,' &c. &c. 'No, no,' says my friend; 'it is take heed *who* (*hoo*) ye hear, and proves I am right.' He had been taught to pronounce *how*, *hoo*. He saw no necessity for *whom*—the objective—before the verb. He was convinced thoroughly that he had floored me with my own weapons, and was more and more confirmed in his spiritual pride."

99. "**Cowper.**"—There are two words, the pronunciation of the former of which can easily be settled, whereas that of the latter seems to defy all settlement. How are we to call the Christian poet who spells his name C-o-w-p-e-r? He himself has decided this for us. He makes his name rhyme with *trooper*. We must therefore call him *Coo-per*, not *Cow-per*; seeing that a man's own usage is undeniably the rule for the pronunciation of his own name. I have had a letter from a correspondent, urging that this rhyme may have been only a poetical pronunciation of the name, not the usual one; as Coleridge in one place makes his name rhyme to "polar ridge." But I have received an interesting testimony from Dr. Goddard Rogers, confirming the settlement of the pronunciation as given above. "Cowper," he says, "not only decided the matter by 'making his name rhyme to trooper;' but in conversation always begged his friends to call him Cooper. I have this from a very old gentleman whom I attended in his last illness. He was Thomas Palmer Bull, son of Cowper's friend, 'smoke-inhaling Bull,' and had himself heard the poet make the remark."

100. "**Cucumber.**"—Another word also brings into question the "*coo*" and "*cow*," but without any such chance of a settlement. It is the agreeable but somewhat indigestible gourd spelt c-u-c-u-m-b-e-r. Is it to be *coo*cumber? *cow*-cumber? or *kew* cumber? The point is one warmly debated: so warmly in certain circles, that when I had a house full of pupils, we were driven to legislation on it, merely to keep the peace of the household. Whenever the unfortunate word occurred at table, which was almost every day during the summer months, a fierce fray invariably set in. At last we abated the nuisance by enacting that in future the first syllable should be dropped, and the article be called for under the undebateable name of "*cumber*." Perhaps, of the three, the strongest claim might be set up for *kew*, or *Q-cumber*; seeing that the Latin name, *cucumis*, can hardly by English lips be otherwise pronounced.

101. "**Revenue**" and "**Trafalgar.**" – It will, we suppose, never be settled whether we are to say révenue or revénue. The latter is hardly possible in certain combina-

tions; *e.g.*, in that of " revenue cutter." Trafálgar and Trafalgár again, will, we suppose, both hold their ground. But, inasmuch as it is not easy to pronounce Trafalgár Square, the other pronunciation has a fair chance of becoming universal.

102. " -ough."—It were hardly to be expected that a writer on pronunciation could escape questioning on that *crux Anglorum* the *-ough*. " Should the word '*hough*' be pronounced huff, hoff, hoe, hoo, or how?" This puts one in mind of the amusing " squabble of the vowels " over the title of Lord Houghton, inserted a few years ago in " Notes and Queries." It will at once be seen by enumerating the various sounds attaching to this combination of letters, how utterly hopeless it must be to lay down any rule, and how necessary to ascertain the prescriptions of usage.

In cough } we have the sound of off.
trough }
rough ⎫
enough ⎪
chough ⎬   "   "   uff.
sough ⎭
dough }   "   "   oe.
though }
plough   "   "   ow.
through   "   "   oo.

The general practice, I believe, is to pronounce " hough " as if it were *huff*. I have heard a clergyman read " He hoffed their horses," but " He huffed " is more usual.

103. **Mis-pronunciation of Scripture names.**—I cannot abstain from saying a few words on the mispronunciation of Scripture proper names by our clergy. This, let me remind them, is quite inexcusable. It shows a disregard and absence of pains in a matter, about the least part of which no pains ought to be spared. To take it on no other ground, is it justifiable in them to allow themselves to offend by their ignorance or carelessness the ears of the most intelligent of their hearers? This was not the spirit of one who said he would not eat meat while the world lasted, if it scandalised his neighbour. But this is not all. When I hear a man flounder about among St.

Paul's salutations, calling half of them wrongly, I am sure that that man does not know his Bible. The same carelessness is sure to show itself in misappropriation of texts, wrong understanding of obsolete phrases, and the like. The man who talks of Aristobulus in the Lesson, is as likely as not to preach from St. Paul's " I know nothing by myself," to show us that the Apostle *wanted divine teaching*, and not to be aware that he meant, *he was not conscious of any fault.*[1]

104. Examples.—Three Sundays before this was written, Jan. 18, 1863, we had the crucial chapter, Rom. xvi., for the evening lesson. A friend writes to me from a distant city in Italy:—" In the afternoon a stranger officiated; but as he saluted *Assyncritus* and *Patrŏbas*, I knew what to expect in the sermon, and so it was." Another writes from London, that he was on that day at a fashionable London church, and heard Epenētus and Patrŏbas introduced to the congregation. A clergyman in the West of England found on his breakfast-table one Monday morning a note from his congregation to this effect :—

> " To-day you said, ' ye know Stephănas ; '
> This misconception, sir, doth pain us :
> For it is Stephănas we know,
> And beg that you will call him so." [2]

A friend of mine heard the following in a London church, and, strange to say, from a schoolmaster :—" Trophimus have I left at Milētum sick." But it perhaps may be said to me, with the beautiful inconsequence of the logic of the present day, Is a man a perfect Christian minister, because he knows how to pronounce these names? To which I fearlessly answer, " No, by no means ; but he is, at all events, as near to it as if he did not know how to pronounce them."

---

[1] See the text explained, in paragraph 477 below.

[2] I have had a very amusing letter, written anonymously, from the clergyman in the West of England to whom these verses were sent. He comes to a rather curious conclusion from the fact of my having told the story. He infers that I was present, and that I made the verses. As this may be my only means of communicating with him, let me assure him that this was not the case. I merely tell the tale as 'twas told to me.

105. "**Johnny Stittle.**"—I am put in mind, by this question, of "Johnny Stittle," a redoubtable preacher who used to hold forth at Cambridge, in a chapel in Green Street. The tradition of him and his sayings was yet a living thing, when I went up as an under-graduate in 1828. His wont was to rail at the studies of the University; and in doing so on one occasion, after having wound himself up to the requisite pitch of fervour, he exclaimed, in a voice of thunder, "D'ye think *Powl* knew Greek?"[1]

106. A writer in a now extinct newspaper adds the following to many instances of mispronunciation of Scripture proper names. "Too well do I remember the city of *Colossé* pronounced *Coloss*, as if it were a word of only two syllables; *the epistle to Philêmon*, '*the gainsaying of Core*' (one syllable), betraying that the speaker had no conception he was talking of the person who in the 16th chapter of Numbers is designated 'Korah.' An informant, whom I well know, heard the name of the returned slave in St.

[1] I have had two interesting communications from Cambridge, giving accurate details respecting "Johnny Stittle."

He is mentioned in the Rev. Abner Brown's "Recollections of Rev. Chas. Simeon," Introduction, p. xiii., where he is described as a "day labourer," and it is said that Mr. Simeon thought well enough of him to encourage him by pecuniary assistance.

In a memoir of Rowland Hill, by Mr. Jones, are the following notices of Stittle:—

"During Mr. Hill's residence at Cambridge he was much attached to 'Johnny Stittle,' one of Mr. Berridge's converts. He was naturally a gifted man, though, like his patron, he moved in his own orbit. He preached for many years in Green Street, Cambridge, and died in 1813, in his 87th year.

"As Mr. Hill was on his way to Duxford to preach for the Missionary Society, he suddenly exclaimed, 'I must go to Cambridge, and see the widow of an old clergyman who is living there, for I have a message to leave with her.' On being asked if the message was important, he replied, 'Yes, sir, I want the old lady—who will soon be in heaven—to give my love to Johnny Stittle, and to tell him I shall soon see him again.'"

Another correspondent says, "I am old enough to remember, and to have actually heard, Johnny Stittle at Cambridge. He compared eternity, in one of his sermons, to a great clock, which said 'tick' in one century, and 'tack' in the next. Then suddenly turning to some gownsmen, he said, 'Now go home, and calculate the length of the pendulum.'"

One must acknowledge that if there was eccentricity here, there was something very like genius also.

Paul's Epistle to Philemon, read, 'One (monosyllable) Simus,' instead of Onésimus." I have also a complaint sent me of a clergyman who insists on always saying "*Achaicus*;" and an anecdote of a remark being made, how well the *Venite exultemus* was chanted.

107. Samaria and Philadelphia.—A correspondent requests me to endeavour to correct the very common mispronunciation Timothéūs, into the proper sound, Timothé-ŭs. On the other hand, one of my Censors expresses a hope that as I so strongly advocate our following the Greeks in the pronunciation of their proper names, I shall be consistent, and never again, in reading the lessons, call those ancient cities, Samaria and Philadelphia, otherwise than *Samaria* and *Philadelphia*. The answer to this is very simple—viz., that I do not advocate the following of the Greeks in the pronunciation of their proper names, in any case where English usage has departed from their pronunciation. It is in cases where there is no such usage, and where the reader is thrown back on what ought to be his own knowledge of the form and composition of the name, that we are pained at discovering that one who ought to be able rightly to divide the Word of Truth, is not in the habit of consulting his New Testament in the original Greek.

108. But there is more to be said about the two rather unfortunate instances given by my critic. The tendency of our language has been universally to shorten the last syllable but one, in those names of cities which in Greek ended in *ia*. *Alexandria* is now called *Alexandria*; *Seleucia*, *Seleucia*; and *Samaria* and *Philadelphia*, *Samaria* and *Philadelphia*. But no such usage infringes the proper Greek pronunciation of *Epænetus*, *Asyncritus*, *Patrobas*, *Aristobulus*, and the like. Of course, usage is not immutable. We now say *Zabulon*, but the day may come when the stricter scholars may have overborne common usage, and we may say *Zabulon*, which is right according to the Hebrew and the Greek. We now say *Sennacherib*; and so universal is this usage, that a correspondent writes in strong terms, stigmatising the strictly accurate pronunciation, *Sennacherib*, as a blunder. When I was at school, the common practice was to pronounce the names of two of the

Greek letters, as "*Epsilon*" and "*Omicron:*" now, such sounds are unknown in schools, and the right pronunciation, "*Epsilon*" and "*Omicron*," is universal.

109. "**Inimical.**"—One word, in which the proper classical pronunciation has gradually overborne the conventional, is *inímical*. Our forefathers called this *inímĭcal*; but no one would venture on such a pronunciation now; all the world says inimícal.

110. **Urbane.**—Three correspondents have written about another Scripture name. It is that of a person saluted in Rom. xvi. 9, and in our present Bibles spelt *U-r-b-a-n-e*. The common idea respecting this name is that it belongs to a woman, and most readers pronounce it as three syllables, *Urbānè*. But it is simply the English for the Latin name *Urbanus*, in English *Urbane*, or, as we now call it, *Urban*. We have not forgotten "Sylvanus Urban," the Editor of "The Gentleman's Magazine" in its good old times. The royal printers, who have made so many unauthorised alterations in the text of our Bibles, might with advantage drop out the final "*e*" from this word, and thus prevent the possibility of confusion.

111. **Junias.**—I may mention that in verse 7 of the same chapter, *Junia* (so in our Authorised Version), who is mentioned with Andronicus, is not a woman, but a man, *Junias*.

112. **Covetous.**—While treating of the pronunciation of those who minister in public, three other words occur to me which are very commonly mangled by our clergy. One of these is "*covetous*," and its substantive "*covetousness*." I hope that some of my clerical readers will be induced to leave off pronouncing them "*covetious*," and "*covetiousness*." I can assure them, that when they do thus call the words, one at least of their hearers has his appreciation of their teaching disturbed.

113. A second injured word is the adverb "*wholly*." It is not uncommon to hear in the Communion Service, "submitting ourselves *holy* to His holy will and pleasure." "*Wholly*" admits of very distinct pronunciation, short of all affected precision.

114. **The Revelation.**—The third hint I would venture to give is, that the mysterious concluding book of

Scripture is the *Revelation*[1] of St. John, not the *Revelations*. I imagine this very common mistake must have arisen from our being accustomed to speak of the Lamentations of Jeremiah, in which case the word *is plural*. [I am sorry to find this blunder becoming more and more common: so much so, as to be fast superseding the right name.]

115. "Able" for "Abel," &c.—A complaint respecting slovenly pronunciation has been sent me, which seems to bring before us a matter of some delicacy and uncertainty. A correspondent blames rightly the slovenly habit of pronouncing "Abel," "Mabel," "Ethel," as if they were "*Able*," "*Mable*," "*Ethle*;" and speaks with proper severity of Walker, who, in his "Pronouncing Dictionary," has set down "*evle*," as the pronunciation of "evil." So far seems clear. But, when we come to the question, whether all words in -*el* or -*il* are to be rigidly pronounced in full, we are, I think, compelled to yield somewhat to custom. Nay, custom has, as matter of fact, prevailed in some cases, even to the alteration of our conventional *spelling*. What was once "*battail*," then "*battel*," has now become "*battle*;" "*chattail*," or "*chattel*," has become "*cattle*;" "*subtile*," or "*subtil*," has become "*subtle*;" "*castell*," or "*castel*," has become "*castle*." The word "*devil*" is far more frequently pronounced "*devle*," than "*de-vill*;" indeed, this latter pronunciation, in the mouth of an affected precisian, is offensive. Good taste, and the observance of usage, must in such matters be our guides.

116. A correspondent enquired about the pronunciation of *oasis*. Is it to be *óasis* or *oásis*? A search among classic authorities resulted in favour of *óasis*; but custom in our own language has, I think, sanctioned *oásis*. So the reader may take his choice.

117. Criticism in a newspaper.—A very curious and choice bit of newspaper criticism on these remarks was sent me. A writer says: "There is, to our mind, something small, not to say ludicrous and absurd, about

---

[1] I had a strong letter of remonstrance for having called this book the "*Revelation of St. John*," whereas it is, by ch. i. 1, "the Revelation of Jesus Christ." Here we have a misapprehension of the meaning of the preposition; so puerile, as not to be worth recording, were it not to illustrate a point hereafter to be treated of.

the notion of a dignitary of the Church of England constituting himself the censor and reporter of small slips of pronunciation, such as *Sophœnētus* for *Sophœnĕtus*, and the like. We should think none the worse of a man for tripping once, or even twice, in those long Pauline lists of salutations. Not to trip at all would, except in the case of practised and familiar scholars, suggest to us the notion that rather more pains and time had been bestowed upon the matter than it deserved."

118. Where this critic found the name *Sophænetus* among the Pauline salutations, I am at a loss to say : at all events it shows that he practised his own advice, and had not bestowed more time or pains on the matter than it deserved.[1]

119. But it is his doctrine, that in knowledge of the proprieties of these minute points in Scripture, inaccuracy is better than accuracy, that I would especially hold up for reprobation. Very little time or pains is really required in the matter. Every clergyman is, or ought to be, familiar with his Greek Testament ; two minutes' reference to that will show him how every one of these names ought to be pronounced. If he is in the practice of regular reading in the original, he will not want even this two minutes' reference. And those who cannot refer to the original will be kept right without any pains at all, if the clergy are right ; for they will simply follow their leaders. Surely this doctrine of the writer in the newspaper cannot represent the general opinion among those bodies who have of late years been making such remarkable advance in the accurate study of the original text of the Scriptures, and have by the results of the training in some of their admirable colleges done so much for the credit of biblical scholarship in England.

120. For my own part, I was disposed to put together

[1] The blunder was rather amusingly defended thus : " We accidentally substituted for the less known Epænetus what is to the classical scholar the more familiar and analogously formed name Sophænetus." Now as regards the *classical scholar*,—Epænetus, the writer on cookery, is about as often mentioned in Athenæus, as Sophænetus in Xenophon : and the matter in question being *St. Paul's lists of salutations*, I do not see why the critic should have gone to Xenophon for his example, unless he had believed that the name occurred in St. Paul also.

this critique and a letter which I received from a friend, saying that he had heard a person, not a clergyman, read *Arcturus* and *Orion* and the *Pleiades*. I could not help imagining that I had tracked my critic *tripping twice or even more* in what I daresay he believes to be some more of these Pauline salutations.

121. Serious accompaniments of ignorance in this matter.—The really serious aspect of the matter comes before us when we hear what my friend adds, that the man thus reading proceeded to *expound the chapter*. An error in pronunciation may be, in an ordinary person, a trifle; but when a *teacher* makes it, it is no longer a trifle: and for this reason, that a teacher is bound to be acquainted with the real meaning of that which he expounds and enforces; with the context of the passages, and with the spirit and force of the sacred word as the Spirit has given it to us. And when we find a teacher ignorant of even outward matters of common information respecting the text, we are not led to hope much for his power of rightly divining the word of truth. That it may please Him who is the fountain of wisdom, to make exceptions, and to endow even ignorant men with insight into the meaning of His word, no one would deny; still, it is not our business to take such exceptions for granted, but rather to take for granted His ordinary course of proceeding on our part, and to provide for its success as we best may. He who feels this, will not think correctness even in the lists of Pauline salutations a trifling matter.

122. Pronunciation of "-éd."—A word about a practice very common with our clergy:—the pronouncing of the full *éd* at the end of the " weak " past tenses of verbs. Is it not full time to leave off this pedantry? The excuse made for it, of course, is that it puts a difference between solemn utterance in church or anywhere of divine things, and our ordinary talk. But it is for this very reason that I desire to challenge it. There are just ten times too many differences between these two things; and by their means it is, that we are enabled to wrap up in napkins and to bury so many of the matters that dearly concern us.

123. Archbishop Longley.—I remember, when Archbishop Longley, after his enthronement on a Friday, spent the Sunday with us at Canterbury, feeling a sense of relief and pleasure at hearing him give out the "comfortable words" of our Lord, "*God so lov'd the world....,*" instead of the ordinary starched form, *lovéd*. When a man reads of the great fact thus, the thought rushes unbidden all over my heart, " What a love that was ! " But I am afraid that when I hear the other, there only goes up from the outer court of my thoughts the poor compliment, " How carefully you are reading ! "

124. **Difference in Singing.**—Mind, I do not grudge the full starched utterance in singing, or in any strictly rhythmical pronouncing. Those are of necessity artificial things, and do, it can hardly be denied, gain much of their force from the art which accompanies them. Many vowels are differently uttered in singing and in reading.

125. **" Knowledge " and " knolledge."**—Surely all affectations in public reading of solemn things ought to be at once and finally laid aside. I know clergymen who, when talking of *knowledge*, pronounce it as all the world does,—*knolledge:* but in church always say *know-ledge.* An American friend who was staying with me had heard this in our cathedral, and remarked that he should as soon have thought of a clergyman in a buff jerkin and boots, as of his uttering such a portent. I do not set up our cousins as standards of English pronunciation, but I cannot help thinking that in this case the Yankee was right.

126. Another word which gets disguised, when men are reading on stilts, is *sacrament*. English usage has ruled the pronunciation to be *sácrament*, and so almost every one calls it. Yet in church we not unfrequently hear *sācrament*. Sometimes the stiff plan is too absurd to be carried out. I once heard *vic-tu-al* read out, each syllable with a *vis* in it, as if the reader were discharging a solemn duty. But I do not suppose one in a thousand has courage for this.

127. **" Blesséd," &c.**—Of course it will be understood that there are certain words which general usage pronounces full : such as *bless'd, curséd* (in their participial form, unless they are simply past tenses, they follow the ordinary rule and drop their *e*). It would be mere pedantry,

in reading Gen. xiv. 19, because we say, in the former part of the verse, "*And he bless'd him,*" to insist on continuing, "and said, *Bless'd be Abram.*" As we drop the *e* according to usage in the former case, so we enounce it according to usage in the latter.

128. "**Heron.**"—A correspondent in Scotland writes that an English friend questions the correctness of pronouncing *heron* as a word of two syllables, and affirms that the usage in the south is to pronounce the word as though spelt *hern*. And he enquires,—1, whether, under both forms of spelling, the word is pronounced as of one syllable; 2, whether when spelt and pronounced *héron*, it departs from English usage.

129. My answer was that the spelling *hern* is at present unknown, except in cases presently to be noticed; but the pronunciation *hern* is universal, except rarely in poetry. That this has very long been so is testified by such proper names as Herne Hill (a name not peculiar to the railway junction at Camberwell, but also found in Somersetshire, near Ilminster, and I dare say elsewhere) and Herne Bay. Another and a very curious testimony to this is found in the corruption of a proverb in which the bird is mentioned. We now say of a stupid fellow that "he doesn't know a hawk from a hand-saw." But thus the proverb over-does its work: for, out of idiotcy itself, such stupidity could not occur, as should confound things so entirely and essentially different. As the proverb originally stood, it described a degree of unversedness in common things which doubtless was, and certainly now is, very common. In the days when hawking was to be seen in almost any neighbourhood, not to know a hawk from a *herneshew* (for so the bird at which the hawk was flown was then called) would be well understood. And *herneshew* having become *handsaw*, is another witness to the antiquity of the monosyllabic pronunciation of *heron*.

130. The contraction of "herneshew" into "heron," puts us in mind of the little gentleman in black velvet, toasted of old by the Jacobites, whose name "mole," is the only surviving syllable of a much longer word, "*mouldywarp*," or "mould-warp," a creature that turns the mould.

131. A sportsman friend who has long lived (and long

may he live) in the most beautiful part of Charnwood Forest, in Leicestershire, told me, years ago, that the people round Bradgate Park, when they want to summon a passer-by, call out, not "Hallo" or "Halloo," but "*Halloop!*" and he thought that the exclamation, by this form, betrayed its having come down from the days when one cried to another, "A loup!" or as we say, "wolf, wolf!" This may or may not be the fact; it is at all events interesting.

132. **Ingenious derivation : Teddington.**—Considering how commonly ingenious derivations are wrong, it is surprising that any grave writer in these days should allow himself to be taken in by one. Yet no less a person than the present Emperor of the French has fallen into this trap. We all know that there is a place on the Thames, above London, called Teddington. It so happens that its situation nearly corresponds with the limit to which the tide ascends in the stream. So some ingenious person made what was little better than a pun upon the name, and called Teddington Tide-end-town. In process of years, the public, who are always ready to accept a likely-sounding derivation, reported Tide-end-town as the origin of the name. And the Emperor Napoleon, in the 2nd vol. of his Life of Julius Cæsar, has gravely stated the fact, and worked it into his argument. His words are these :—

"The only thing which appears to us evident is, that the Romans did not cross anywhere below Teddington. It is known that this village, of which the name is derived from Tide-end-town, marks, in point of fact, the last point of the Thames at which the tide is felt. It would be impossible to believe that Cæsar exposed himself to the risk of being surprised, during his passage, by the swelling of the water." (Vol. ii. p. 191, Eng. transl.)

The Edinburgh Reviewer well remarks on the singular simplicity, often observable in the Emperor's book, with which "a Cockney myth, such we conceive the popular derivation of Teddington to be, is transformed into a serious piece of archæology."

133. **Ingenious correction, "rack."**—If ingenious derivations are often wrong, so also are ingenious correc-

tions of common readings. I may give as an instance, a correction, often made with some confidence, of a word in the famous passage in Shakspeare's "Tempest," beginning, "The cloud-capt towers." We commonly read in the modern editions, "And, like the baseless fabric of a vision, leave not a *wreck* behind." No, says the corrector, not *wreck*, but *rack*: rack being thin floating vapour, such as is seen on the blue sky before a change of weather. Now the original word, it is true, is *wrack*, but there is every probability that by this Shakspeare meant *wreck*, not *floating vapour*. Two reasons may be given for this opinion: 1. In this very play, he calls the wreck of a ship by the name *wrack*:—"The direful spectacle of the wrack, which touched the very virtue of compassion in thee;" and in "Measure for Measure" (act iii. sc. i.), "her brother Frederick was wracked at sea." 2. The word *rack*, in the sense of the thin cloud spread over the blue sky, is never found except with the definite article, "*the rack*." Thus in "Hamlet," "We often see against some storm, a silence in the heavens, the rack stand still." And Bacon, in his "Natural History," says, "the clouds above, which we call 'the rack.'" In all other examples given in the dictionaries, the same is the case; and it would appear as contrary to usage to say "*a rack*," as it would be to say "*a north*," or "*a zenith*." This being so, we have no resource but to face the corrector boldly, and to maintain that "leave not a wrack behind," means, leave not behind so much as a ship when she has broken up,—not even a spar to be remembered by.

134. **Emphatic reading: "princess."**—A question has been asked, naturally enough, at the present time, about the pronunciation of *princess*. It appears that many of our best speakers and readers say *princéss*; but my correspondent thinks that the tendency of modern education is to call it *prίncess*. I think, and hope it will be felt, that modern education, as against the speakers and readers, ought to prevail. The other pronunciation has, it seems to me, arisen mainly from that foe to good reading, emphatic antithesis. I hold the rule for all good reading to be, when two terms specifically distinguished occur together, let what emphasis is laid, in the absence of any special re-

quirements of the context, be on that which they have in common, not on that in which they differ. Thus, "the prínce and prínccss," not "the prínce and princéss."

135. Thus we heard one speak of "the French *Emprér and his Empréss;*" and thus might it be said that an Indian officer had a *tigér eaten by a tigréss*.

136. And the same emphatic reading gives rise to offence in regard to matters of a more solemn import. We not unfrequently hear in church such emphases as "*Give* us this day our daily bread; and *fórgive* us our trespasses:" "Maker of all *things*, Judge of all *men*." This last is a sad descent from the sublime address to Him who is "all in all."

137. The very pronunciation which we are blaming probably took its rise in church:—"Albert Edward, Prince of Wales, the Princéss of Wales," &c.

138. While these sheets are in the press, a correspondent has written to ask whether the *o* in *among* and *amongst* should be sounded as *o* in *belong*, or as *u* in *sung*. He is aware that the latter is the general pronunciation, but ventures to think it is not the correct one. The case seems to be one in which usage must rule. The sounds of the English vowels are not so fixed that we can found upon them any law applicable to a particular case, as against common practice. Even if *among* and *amongst* required justification by precedent, the pronunciation of the *o* in *tongue, one,* and *done* might be cited to bear it out.

CHAPTER IV.

IDIOM AND CONSTRUCTION.

139. **Usage and construction.**—I now come to that which must form a principal part of my work,—consideration of the usage of words and construction of sentences. And let me repeat, in order to prevent mistakes, that my object in these notes is not to lay down nor to exemplify mere rules of grammar,—though of course the consideration of such rules must often come before us,—but to illustrate the usages and tendencies of our common language, as matter of fact, by the discussion of questions arising out of doubtful words and phrases. One of the most interesting subjects connected with a language is its tendencies: the currents, so to speak, which set in for or against certain modes of speech or thought. These are to be discovered in all languages, and in none more notably than our own. We are a mixed race, and our tongue everywhere bears traces of the fact. We have gone through more crises of religious and political strife than most nations, and thought and speech have ever been freer in England than in other countries. From these, and from other circumstances, the English language has become more idiomatic than most others; and the tendency is still going on among us, to set aside accurate grammatical construction, and to speak rather according to idiom than according to rule.

140. **Idiom.**—The word "*idiom*" is derived from the Greek, and properly signifies a thing or habit peculiar to one person or set of persons, and forming an exception to general rules. Our usage of the term has confined this its meaning in English to matters of *language*. When we speak of an idiom, we mean some saying, or some way of speaking, peculiar to some one language or family of languages, which can only be accounted for by the peculiar

tendency, or habit of thought, of those who use it. When we say that a phrase is *idiomatic*, we mean that it bears this character.

141. Now let us see to what this amounts. Such expressions, if judged by strict rules, will commonly fail to satisfy them. In so far as they are idiomatic, they are departures from the beaten track of that grammatical construction, and that characteristic analogy, which are common to all languages. For the rules of grammar and of logic, being dependent not on local usage, but on the constitution of the human mind, are common to all nations. And when any nation sets up, so to speak, for itself, and indulges in the peculiarities which we call idioms, it takes a course which these general rules do not justify.

142. **Idiomatic mode of address.**—Let us show this by some examples. It is the habit of modern European nations to avoid the second person singular in addressing individuals. Some languages use the second person plural instead: some the third person. The English, the French, and others, say "*you*" for "*thou:*" the Germans, and those cognate to them, say "*they*" for "*thou:*" the Italians, still more strangely, say "*she*," meaning "your excellency." These are the *idioms* or *idiomatic usages* of these languages respectively. Every one speaking any of those languages must use the idiomatic expression, or he will render himself ridiculous.[1]

[1] Nay, the consequences may sometimes be much more serious. A correspondent sends me the following story: "My friend, a student in the University of Heidelberg, acquired his first knowledge of German chiefly by colloquial exercise with his fellow-students, who habitually addressed each other in the second person singular. '*du*.' Having thus acquired enough of the language to blunder through a conversation, he was present at a party, where he danced with the sister of one of his fellow-students, and entertained her with the choicest German at his command, but unfortunately always addressed her as '*du*.' This (to a German ear) impertinent familiarity was either overheard by, or reported to, the young lady's brother, who deemed it impossible to wipe out the scandal by any other means than a duel. In vain my friend explained his ignorance of the German conventional mode of address. The offence had been committed in public, and if the culprit wished to remain at Heidelberg in peace in future, he must fight there. They fought accordingly, and the skilful German cleverly inflicted a slight wound which drew blood; honour was satisfied, and the affair ended in pipes, friendship, and beer."

143. But, if we judge such expressions by strict rules, they cannot be defended. It cannot be correct to address one person as if he were many: it cannot be correct to look at and address one person as if he were not present, and, being absent, were more than one. We all know this: notwithstanding we do not criticise and carp at every such usage, but simply acquiesce in it as being the common custom.

144. **Elliptic usages.**—Let us take another instance. Some languages are more *elliptic* than others: that is, the habits of thought of some nations will bear the omission of certain members of a sentence, better than the habits of thought of other nations. In English we should say, "*At the Equinox the sun rises at six and sets at six.*" But if we were speaking in French, we should say, "At the Equinox, the sun rises at six hours of the morning, and sets at six hours of the evening." Now here there is no doubt that the Frenchman has the advantage in fulness and propriety of expression. Any one disposed to cavil at our English sentence, and to treat it as some of my sentences have been treated, might say, "Rises at six and sets at six! Six what! Six miles, or six minutes, or six occasions?" But we do not in practice thus cavil, because we are in the enjoyment of common sense, and we are prepared, in the daily use of our language, to omit that which the thought will naturally supply.

145. **Caprice of idiom.**—One more example. In English, our common mode of salutation to one another is, "*How d'ye do?*" Now of course we all understand, that in this phrase we use the verb "*do*" in a neuter sense: in the same sense which it bears in the reply of the disciples concerning Lazarus: "Lord, if he sleep, he shall do well." But suppose a person were to insist on this usage being carried throughout our converse, and to make it an objection to the question "*How d'ye do?*" that one cannot say in the same sense, "I went to see A or B, and he *did well.*" We should at once reply, if we thought on the matter, that while the verb admits of being thus used in certain tenses, and in certain connexions, it does not admit of being thus used in certain other tenses, and in certain other connexions; and that the account to be given of this

is, that the English people will have it so: it is an idiom, or arbitrary usage, of their language.

146. The capricious character of idiomatic usage is admirably illustrated by this very example. For though it is admissible to say, "I went to see A or B, and he was doing very well," the words would not carry the sense, that I was able to say to him "How d'ye do?" and he to reply, "Very well, thank you;" but would convey the impression that he had lately met with an accident or had been lately ill, and was going on favourably.

147. **Example from the Greek.**—I want yet one more example for the purpose I have in view, and I will take it from a dead language. In the Greek,—which is perhaps the finest and most subtle vehicle ever formed for human thought,—it is the practice to join a plural noun of the neuter gender to a verb in the singular number. Now, of course, according to the rules of universal grammar, this is wrong. A plural noun should be joined to a plural verb. But the Greek had his reason, and a very good one it was. He felt, that things without life, when spoken of in the plural, formed but one mass, and might be treated as one thing. And so the tendency of the national thought, which was to define and to express the subtle distinctions of thought, prevailed over the rule of grammar, and the usage became idiomatic.

148. **Spoken and written English.**—Let another thing also be remembered. We must distinguish between the English which we speak, and that which we write. Many expressions are not only tolerated but required in conversation, which are not usually put on paper. Thus, for instance, everyone says "can't" for *cannot*, "won't" for *will not*, "isn't" for *is not*, in conversation; but we seldom see these contractions in books, except where a conversation is related. This is a difference which the foreigner is generally slow in apprehending. He says, "I will not," "I cannot," "I must not," "I shall not:" "I am," for "I'm," "they are," for "they're:" and he often may be detected by his precision in these matters, even after he has mastered the pronunciation and construction of our language. This difference between our spoken and our written language should always be borne in mind, when we

are treating of expressions commonly found in colloquial English. Many persons, in judging of them, bring them to the test of the stricter rule of written composition, to which they are not fairly amenable.

149. "**Those kind of things.**"—Let me further illustrate this tendency of nations by another usage now almost become idiomatic, and commonly found in the talk of us all. I mean the expression "*these*" or "*those kind of things*." At first sight, this seems incorrect and indefensible. It would appear as if we ought to say "*this kind of things*," "*that kind of things*." It becomes then an interesting inquiry, as it was in the other case, why this should be so. And here again my readers must excuse me if I go to a dead language for my illustration—not for my *reason*: the *reason* will be found in the laws of thought: but it will be best illustrated by citing the usage of that language in which, more than in any other, the laws of thought have found their expression.

150. "**Attraction.**"—In the Greek language, there is an idiomatic usage called *attraction*. It may be thus described. If an important noun in a sentence is in a certain case, say the genitive or dative, a relative pronoun referring to it is put in the same case, though by the construction of the sentence it ought to be in another. Thus, if I wanted to put into Greek the sentence, "*I gave it to the man whom I saw*," the relative pronoun "*whom*" would not be in the accusative case, as it ought to be, governed by the verb "*saw*," but in the same case as "*man*," viz., dative, and the sentence would be roughly represented, as far as the mere form of it is concerned, by the English "*I gave it to the man, to whom I saw*."

151. Now in the way of speaking of which I treat, it is evident that this same tendency, to draw the less important word into similarity to the more important one, is suffered to prevail over strict grammatical exactness. We are speaking of "*things*" in the plural. Our pronoun "*this*" really has reference to "*kind*," not to "*things*;" but the fact of "*things*" being plural, gives a plural complexion to the whole, and we are tempted to put "*this*" into the plural. That this is the account to be given, appears still more plainly from the fact that not unfre-

quently we find a rival attraction prevails, and the clause takes a *singular* complexion from the other substantive, "*kind.*" We often hear people say, "*this kind of thing,*" "*that sort of thing.*" It must be confessed that the phrases, "*this kind of things,*" "*that sort of things,*" have a very awkward sound; and we find that our best writers have the popular expression, These kind, those sort. Thus we have in Shakspeare, "King Lear," (act ii. sc. 2):

"These kind of knaves I know."

"Twelfth Night," (act i. sc. 5):

"That crow so at these kind of fools."

"Othello," (act iii. sc. 3):

"There are a kind of men so loose in soul."

In Pope:

"The next objection is, that these sort of authors are poor."

Examples are also stated to occur in Lord Bacon, Swift, and Addison.

152. "This" and "that."—One word on "*this*" and "*that,*" as we pass onward. "*This*" and "*these*" refer to persons and things *present*, or under immediate consideration; "*that*" and "*those*" to persons and things *not present*, or not under immediate consideration; or if either of these, one degree further removed than the others of which are used "*this*" and "*these.*" We find this rule sometimes curiously violated in conversation and in writing. A barrister tells me that the confusion is common in the Irish law courts: "Those arguments I now use," &c. Another Irish correspondent is often greeted with, "That's a could day, yer riv'rence." I have a Scottish friend, who always designates the book which he has in his hand as "*that book;*" the portfolio of drawings which he is turning over as "*those drawings.*"

153. We have this usage in England, but it carries another meaning. If I have a book in my hand, and say, "*that book will make a great sensation,*" I mean to remove my own and my hearer's attention from the particular

volume, or even the present consideration of its contents, and to describe it in its general, and as it were historical, effect on the world.

154. The oddest departure from the common usage of "*this*" and "*that*," which I remember to have observed, was in a notice which I repeatedly saw, in the summer of 1863, posted on houses in Devonshire, " *Those houses to let*," " *That house for sale*."

155. "**To-day**," "**to-night**."—In "*this day*," "*this night*," the somewhat stiff and formal demonstrative pronoun is curiously abbreviated. "*To-day*," "*to-night*," are universally used. In the dialect of the western counties, "*this year*," is commonly expressed by "*to-year*." In Scotland and Ireland, "*the day*," "*the night*," "*the year*," are the ordinary expressions: "it'll no rain the day," &c.

156. **Triple meaning of "that."**—Confusion sometimes arises in our language from the triple meaning of "*that*," which, with us, is a demonstrative pronoun, a relative pronoun, and a conjunction. It is possible to use six "*thats*," consecutively in the same sentence. Take the sentence, " He said, that the meaning which the report which that man told him had been thought to bear was more than had been intended." Here I have already "*that*," conjunction; and I may express "*the meaning*," by "*that*," demonstrative pronoun; "*which*," by "*that*," relative pronoun; "*the report*," by "*that*," demonstrative pronoun; "*which*" again, by "*that*," relative pronoun; and then I end with "*that man*." "*that*" being in this last case again a demonstrative pronoun. So that I get the following sentence, with, as I said, six "*thats*," occurring consecutively : " He said *that that that that that that* man told him had been thought to mean, was more than had been intended." Nay, *seven* "*thats*" may be used together, if one of them is a mere *citation*. " I assert *that that* 'that,' *that that that that* person told me contained, was improperly emphasized." And this use may be carried even further yet: " I assert, *that that, that that* 'that,' *that that that that* person told me contained, implied, has been misunderstood."

157. From this threefold import of the word it sometimes is not apprehended which of its meanings it bears

in a given sentence. Ps. xc. 4, in the Prayer-book version, runs thus—" A thousand years in Thy sight are but as yesterday, *seeing that is past as a watch in the night.*" Here, of course, *that* is the demonstrative pronoun, and refers to "*yesterday,*" which has just been spoken of;[1] and it ought, in reading, to have a certain emphasis laid on it. But not unfrequently we hear it read in the responses of the congregation, as if it were the conjunction: "Seeing thăt is past as a watch in the night." I remember having some trouble in curing our choristers at Canterbury of singing it thus.

158. "This much," "that much."—What are we to think of the very common expressions, "*this much,*" "*that much?*" We continually hear and read, "*This much I know,*" "*Of that much I am certain,*" and the like. It might be supposed at first sight that this way of speaking was indefensible. "*Much*" is an adjective of quantity, and requires, in order to define it, not a pronoun, but an adverb. We may say *very much, pretty much* (where "*pretty*" is used in its colloquial adverbial sense of *tolerably, moderately*), *as much, so much,* or *thus much;* but from such a view it would appear that we must not say "*this much,*" or "*that much.*" Still, may not another view be taken? High, deep, long, broad, are adjectives of measure; but we may say *a foot high, a yard long, an ell broad.* And if we choose to designate with the hand, or otherwise, the measure of a foot, yard, or ell, we may substitute the demonstrative pronoun for the substantive, and say with precisely the same construction of the sentence, "*this high,*" "*this long,*" "*that broad.*" Now, how is this with "*much*"? If I may use *this* and *that* to point out the extent of length, height, and breadth which I want to indicate, why not also to point out the extent of *quantity* which I want to indicate? When I say "*Of this much I am certain,*" I indicate, by the pronoun *this,* something which I am about to state, and which is the extent of my certainty. When I say, "*That much I knew before,*" I

---

[1] Not, as one correspondent insists, to "a thousand years." The rendering is not exact; literally, the words stand as in our Bible version, "as yesterday when it is past, and [as] a watch in the night." But in both cases, the reference is to "*yesterday.*"

indicate, by the pronoun "*that*," the piece of intelligence which my friend supposed to be new to me. But it may be replied, I might have said, "*Of this I am certain*," "*That I knew before.*" True: but then I should express nothing as to *the extent* of my certainty or previous knowledge. I believe both expressions to be correct; not so elegant perhaps as "*Thus much*," but at the same time more fitted for colloquial use.

159. "**That ill.**"—There is one use of *that*, which is quite indefensible, and indeed is not found except as a provincialism. I mention it, because some might suppose that what I have said might be cited in defence of it likewise. I mean, when it is used as a qualifying word with adjectives not denoting extent, and when itself must be explained by "*to that extent.*" I have heard in the midland and eastern counties, "I was *that ill*, that I could not go to work:" "He was *that drunk*, that he didn't know what he was about."

160. "**Ever so**," or "**never so?**"—Are we to say "*ever so*," or "*never so*," in expressions like "be he *ever* (*never*) so old," and the like? Usage seems divided. In familiar speech we mostly say "*ever so:*" in writing, and especially in the solemn and elevated style, we mostly find "*never so.*" We say to a troublesome petitioner, "If you ask me *ever* so much, I won't give it you:" but we read, "Which refuseth to hear the voice of the charmer, charm he *never* so wisely." Can we give any account of this? What is the difference between the expressions? Because one would think there must be some difference, when two such words are concerned, which are the very opposites one of another. Sentences similarly constructed with these two words are as different in meaning as possible. "Had he *ever* loved at all," and "Had he *never* loved at all," are opposite in meaning to one another. And so, actually and literally, are the two which we are now considering: but in the general sense they both convey the one meaning which is intended. This may be made plain as follows: "Be it *ever* so large," means, "though it attain every imaginable degree of size:" "be it *never* so large," means, "though there be no imaginable degree of size which it does not attain." The former is inclusively affirmative;

the latter is exclusively negative; and these two amount to the same.

161. "**What was,**" "**what was not.**"—There are some curious phenomena coming under the same head as this last. I may say, "What was my astonishment," and I may say, "What was not my astonishment," and I may convey the same meaning. By the former I mean, "how great was my astonishment;" by the latter, that no astonishment could be greater than mine was.

162. "**No**" **and** "**yes**" **the same.**—Another correspondent mentions a curious fact about negatives and affirmatives. If we were to ask the question, "Had you only the children with you?" a person south of the Tweed would answer "*no*," and a person north of the Tweed, "*yes*," both meaning the same thing—viz., that only the children were there. I think I should myself, though a Southron, answer *yes*. But there is no doubt that such questions are answered in the two ways when the same meaning is intended to be conveyed. The account to be given of this seems to be, that "only" is "none but." "Had you none but the children with you?" and the answer is "*None*," affirming the question. So that the negative form naturally occurs to the mind in framing its answer, and "*none*" becomes "*no*." Whereas in the other case this form does not occur to the mind, but simply to affirm the matter inquired of, viz., the having only the children: and the answer is "*Even so*," or "*Yes*."

163. "**Excuse,**" "**excuse . . not. . .**"—"How is it," asks a correspondent, "that, 'excuse my writing more,' and 'excuse my not writing more,' mean the same thing?" We may answer that the verb "excuse" has two different senses: one being *dispense with*, and the other, *pardon*. When a school is called over, the master may excuse (dispense with) a certain boy's attendance: or he may excuse (pardon) his non-attendance. This will be at once seen, if we put, as we properly ought, the *person* as the object to the verb "excuse," as in, "I pray thee have me excused:" the sentence will then stand in the one case, "Excuse me *from* attendance;" but in the other, "Excuse me *for* non-attendance."

164. "**Oldest inmate.**"—In some sentences unobjec-

tionably expressed, it is impossible to be sure of the meaning. An establishment has been founded fifty years. A person tells me that he is "one of its oldest inmates." Am I to understand that he is one of the few survivors of those who came to it at or near its first foundation, in which case he may be any age above fifty; or am I to understand that he is at the present moment one of the oldest in age of the inmates there, which might bring his age up to between eighty and ninety? In other words, does the term "*oldest*" qualify him absolutely, or only as an inmate of that establishment?

165. "Lesser."—The mention of degrees of comparison leads me to another point, which I have been requested to notice by more than one correspondent. It is the use of *lesser* in certain combinations, instead of *less*. Are we to stigmatise this as an impropriety, or to regard it as an idiomatic irregularity which we must be content to tolerate? It seems to me that the latter must be our course. The usage is sanctioned by our best writers, and that not here and there, but uniformly. "God made two great lights: the greater light to rule the day, and the *lesser* light to rule the night."

166. The account to be given of it seems to be somewhat like that which we gave of a former irregularity: that it has arisen originally by the force of attraction to another word, *greater*, which in such sentences precedes it. For example, when we have spoken of "*the greater light*," "*the less light*" sounds halting and imperfect; and the termination *er* is added to balance the sentence. Sometimes the usage occurs where the other word is not expressed: as when we say "the *lesser* of two evils:" but still the comparison is in the mind, though not on the tongue. It may be too, that it is not only the sound of the one word "*greater*," which is usually the companion of "*lesser*," but that of almost every other comparative in the language, which has produced the effect; for they are almost without exception dissyllables. It is a confirmation of the account which we have been giving of this usage, that no one thinks of attaching the additional syllable to "*less*" when it is combined with '*more;*" *more and less* being already well balanced.

167. "**More than probable.**"—"More than probable" is found fault with. "If a thing be more than probable," says a correspondent, "it must be certain; but this expression does not denote certainty, only a great probability,—a meaning which the words do not naturally convey." But does not the expression do good service? Does it not supply a link between "very" or "highly" probable, and "certain." To say that a thing is probable, invests it with a character of uncertainty, of which "more than probable" almost divests it. In spite of purism, I think we can ill spare the phrase.

168. "**Methinks.**"—Some idiomatic expressions seem to defy any attempt to give a satisfactory account of them. Take the phrase "*methinks.*" It is believed to have arisen from a strange impersonal use of the verb, and the transposition of the pronoun, which should come after it. We have the similar phrase, "*meseems,*" which can more easily be resolved: viz., into "it seems to me." That this is the account to be given of both, appears plain, seeing that in both cases we find in use the other and more formal third person, "*me-thinketh*" and "*me-seemeth.*" But what an expression to come under the ferule of the strict grammarian!

169. A further account may be given of these phrases, by observing that the latter syllable is found sometimes in the form think'st, or seem'st. In "Hamlet," (act v. sc. 2,) we have, "Does it not, *think'st thee....?*" On which Dyce's note says, "The quartos, 1604, have 'Does it not, thinke thee?'.... The folio has, 'Does it not, think'st thee?'.... Walker observes, that, 'thinks it thee?' occurs in the Elizabethan poets in the sense of the Greek πῶν δοκεῖ σοί (does it seem to thee?): and after citing and correcting the present passage, he adduces from Cartwright's Ordinary, 'Little think'st thee, how diligent thou art to little purpose.' In 'All's well that Ends well,' (act ii. sc. 3,) we have 'Methink'st thou art a general offence.'"

170. This note seems to give a clear account of the origin of the phrase. And we may add, that the dropping out of the final *t* was done not only for the sake of the sound, but as being needed in the elliptical construction. The Somer-

F

setshire people have an ellipsis of the same kind in their phrase "*do zim t' I*", meaning, *it seems* to me.

171. "Replace."—We may notice the growing practice of using the word "*replace*," to signify something quite alien from its real meaning. "Lord Derby went out of office, and *was replaced* by Lord Palmerston." This, as now used, conveys the meaning, "*was succeeded by* Lord Palmerston." But put the sentence before our grandfathers, and they would have understood it to mean that Lord Derby went out of office, and Lord Palmerston *put him in again*; he was *replaced* by Lord Palmerston.

172. I hardly need say that the usage is borrowed from that of the French "*remplacer*." But there is this difference, that the French verb does not mean to *replace*, in its true English sense, nor has it in its derivation anything to do with "*replace*," but is "*remplir la place*," "*to fill the place*," and thus has for its proper meaning that which it is now attempted to give the English word *replace*. Lord Derby went out of office, and was "*remplacé*," i.e., *his place was filled*, by Lord Palmerston; but he was not *replaced*, i.e., *put back again*, by his rival.

173. "Enclosure."—The "*enclosure*" of a letter, what is it? Is it that which *encloses* the letter, viz., the envelope? or is it something *enclosed in* the letter, as a dried flower, or a lock of hair? or is it something *enclosed with* the letter, as another letter of the same size, or a map or plan of a larger size?

174. Strictly speaking, I suppose the noun is an abstract one, signifying *the act of enclosing*, as *exposure* means *the act of exposing*. In this sense we might say "the *enclosure* of letters in envelopes, before the penny postage was established, incurred the payment of double postage." Then, when we pass from the abstract to the concrete use of the word, *i.e.*, use it to signify not the act of enclosing, but something which is the instrument, or object, or result of that act, the question arises, ought it to signify the thing *enclosing*, or the thing *enclosed?* There are examples both ways. *Cincture* is properly the act of girding. *A cincture* is the thing which girds, not the thing which is girded. But, on the other hand, *a fissure* is the rift produced by cleaving, not the thing which cleaves it. And *Clausura*, in

Italian, is inscribed over that part of a cloister which is strictly shut. There seems no reason why *enclosure* may not be used in both senses, that which encloses, and that which is enclosed. We may say of sheep in a fold, "the flock was all within the enclosure," meaning, within the hurdles surrounding the square; or we may say that "the flock occupied the whole of the enclosure," meaning the whole of the square enclosed. In the case in question, usage seems to have fixed the meaning in the latter of these two senses, viz., the thing enclosed. An envelope is not said to be the enclosure of the letter, but the letter is said to be the enclosure of the envelope. If I write to the Committee of Council on Education, I receive printed directions as to our correspondence, the first of which is, "Every letter *containing enclosures* should enumerate them specifically."

175. Clearly however, in strict propriety, the word ought to apply to matter enclosed *in*, and not merely *with*, the letter. But when this is departed from, when we write on a sheet of note-paper, and speak of a drawing three times its size as *the enclosed*, or the *enclosure of this letter*, we may say that we are using the word *letter* in its wider sense, as meaning the envelope as it is received unopened from the post.

176. A curious extension of this licence is sometimes found. I remember some years ago receiving a letter from my tailor to the following effect:—" Rev. Sir, *the enclosed* to your kind order, which hope will give satisfaction, and am, respectfully and obliged." Now "*the enclosed*" in this case was a suit of clothes, sent by coach, and arriving some two days after the latter.

177. "Emergency."—A clerical correspondent finds fault with the word "*emergency*" used as a *straight* (sic) or difficulty, instead of *immergency*, which signifies falling into, or being immersed overhead, while "emergency signifies just its opposite, or scrambling out." But he is certainly wrong. An *emergency* is any special occasion, which *emerges from* ordinary occasions. That this has come to be understood in the bad sense exclusively is one of the very frequent instances of words taking a partial meaning as time goes on. That Johnson, who gives this sense, should

have characterised the now universal meaning of the word as "a sense not proper," can only be classed among the many blemishes of his great work. "Immergency" is a monster, unknown to the language. It is difficult to say, judging by analogy, what meaning it could bear.

178. "Who" and "which."—It will be well to attempt some explanation of the usages of "*who*" and "*which*," especially in our older writers. It may perhaps serve to clear up a matter which may have perplexed some, and to show that there is reason and meaning, where all has appeared confusion and caprice. The common modern distinction between these two forms of the relative pronoun is, that "*who*" is used of persons, "*which*" of things. And this, if borne in mind, will guide us safely throughout. It may be well to notice that what I am about to say does not apply to colloquial English; indeed, hardly to modern English at all: for this reason, that now we do not commonly use either the one or the other of these pronouns, but make the more convenient one, "*that*," do duty for both. We do not say, "the man who met me," nor "the cattle which I saw grazing," but "the man that met me," "the cattle that I saw." We must take care, however, to remember that *which* was not always accounted the neuter of *who*, nor is it so in grammar. Dr. Latham says: "To follow the ordinary grammarians, and to call *which* the neuter of *who*, is a blunder. It is no neuter at all, but a compound word." It is made up of *who* and *like*: and this he shows by tracing it through the various Gothic and German forms, till we come to the Scottish *whilk* and the English *which*.'

179. Both *who* and *which* are in our older writers used of persons. When this is so, is there any distinction in meaning, and if so, what is it? I think we shall find that the composition of the word *which*, out of *who* and *like*, will in some measure guide us to the answer; and I think, without presuming to say that every case may be thus explained, that the general account of the two ways is this: "*who*" merely identifies, whereas "*which*" classifies. Let us quote in illustration one of the most important and well-known

' An Irish correspondent informs me that "*which!*" is used in Ireland as equivalent to our "*what!*" or "*what did you say!*"

instances. If, in the solemn address, "Our Father *which* art in heaven," "*who*" had been used instead, then we should have been taught to express only the fact that HE, whom we address as our Father, dwelleth in heaven. But as the sentence now stands, if I understand it rightly, we are taught to express the fact that the relation of Father in which He stands to us is not an earthly but a heavenly one; that whereas there is a fatherhood which is on earth, His is a Fatherhood which is in heaven. And herein I believe that our translators have best followed the mind of Him who gave us the prayer. The bare construction of the clause in the original does not determine for us whether the relative pronoun applies to the person only of Him whom we address, or to His title of Father. But from our Lord's own use so frequently of the term "your heavenly Father," I think they were right in fixing the reference to the relationship, rather than to the Person only.

180. **Use of "but."**—There is a use of the word "*but*," principally to be found in our provincial newspapers, but now and then "leaking upwards" into our more permanent literature. It is when that conjunction is made the connecting link between two adjectives which do not require any such disjoining. We may say that a man is *old, but vigorous*, because vigour united with age is something unexpected; but we have no right to say *old but respectable*, because respectability with old age is not something unexpected. Even while I write, my train stops at a station on the Great Western Railway, where passengers are invited to take a trip to Glasgow, "to witness the *wild but grand* scenery of Scotland." Now, because scenery is wild, there is no reason why it should not be also grand; nay, wildness in scenery is most usually an accompaniment of grandeur. *Wild but not grand* would be far more reasonable, because wildness raises an expectation of grandeur, which the "*but*" contradicts.

181. The expression "allow me *respectfully, but earnestly* to represent to you," is objected to. Yet here we seem to require the disjunctive particle. A *respectful* representation carries with it the idea of a certain distance and formality, with which the zeal implied in *earnestness* is at first sight inconsistent: and the disjunctive particle seems

to show that though the latter is present, the former is not forgotten.

182. "As" and "so."—A correspondent writes: "Many, especially I think ladies, say, 'He is not *as* tall as his brother.' Am I not right in saying that after a negative '*so*' should be used—'He is not *so* tall as his brother'?" Such certainly appears to be the usage of our language, however difficult it may be to account for it. We say, "one way of speaking is as good as the other;" but when we deny this proposition, we are obliged to say, "one way of speaking is not so good as the other." *So* cannot be used in the affirmative proposition, nor *as* in the negative. Change the form of the sentence into one less usual and still allowable, "the one way of speaking is equally good with the other," and the same adverb will serve for both affirmative and negative: "the one is equally good with the other;" "the one is not equally good with the other."

183. The accuracy of this rule has been called in question by one of my censors, and he gives as his example "There are few artists who draw horses as well as Mr. Leech": in which sentence he rightly observes that "so well" ought to have been used. But why? Simply because the sentence is *not affirmative*, as he designates it, but *negative*. *There are few* (= not many), *denies* the existence of many; *there are a few*, *affirms* the existence of some. It never could be said "There are a few artists, who draw horses so well as Mr. Leech." His example confirms the rule, instead of impugning it. Carry the negative a little further, and we have "There are *no* artists who draw horses so well as Mr. Leech."

184. A correspondent asks respecting "the use which is now becoming pretty general of the conjunctions 'so' and 'as,' in such expressions as these— 'He has been well conducted for so long as I have known him': 'So far as I know, he is alive:' 'So soon as he comes, I will leave.'" In all three cases it seems to me that "as" might with advantage be substituted for "so," and in the first, "for" might be omitted. But if "so" is to be used, the account to be given is very simple. "So far as I know," "So soon as he comes,"—"To that extent to which my knowledge reaches," "At that limit of time which marks his arrival."

"So" carries the mind on by anticipation over an extent to which the subsequent clause places a limit. The same may be said of "Be so kind as to . . ." and indeed of every sentence so constructed. "So" opens an indefinite extent, which "as" closes by a particular example.

185. "**Had rather.**"—A question has been asked about the expressions "*I had rather,*" "*I had as soon,*" or "*as lief.*" What is the "*had*" in these sentences? Is it really part of the verb "*have*" at all? If it is, how do we explain it? We cannot use "*to have rather*" in any other tense: it is no recognised phrase in our language. And therefore it has been suggested, that the expression "*I had rather*" has originated with erroneous filling up of the abbreviated *I'd rather*, which is short not for *I had rather*, but *I would rather*. "*I would rather be*" is good English, because "*I would be*" is good English; but "*I had rather be*" is not good English, because "*I had be*" is not good English. Yet "*I had rather be,*" "*I had as soon be,*" are completely sanctioned by usage.

186. **Colloquial contractions.**—One word with regard to the colloquial contractions which I just now mentioned. We occasionally hear some made use of, which cannot be defended. For instance, "*I ain't certain,*" "*I ain't going.*" This latter, in the past tenses, degenerates still further into the mere vulgarism, "*I warn't going.*" The last is heard only as a vulgarism; but the other two are very frequently used, even by highly educated persons. The main objection to them is that they are proscribed by usage; but exception may also be taken to them on their own account. A contraction must surely retain some trace of the resolved form from which it is abbreviated. What, then, is "*ain't?*" It cannot be a contraction of "*am not.*" What "*arn't*" is contracted from is very plain; it once was "*are not,*" which, of course, cannot be constructed with the first person singular. The only legitimate colloquial contraction of "*I am not,*" is "*I'm not:*" "*I'm not going;*" "*I'm not quite sure.*" The same way of contracting is used in the case of "*are not.*" It is usually contracted by attaching the verb to the personal pronoun, not by combining it with the negative particle. We say "*You're not in time,*" not "*you arn't;*" "*they're not coming,*" not "*they arn't,*" or "*ain't.*"

187. A few remarks may be made on the use in English of feminine substantives. Certain names of occupations and offices seem to require them, and others to forbid them. We say "*emperor*" and "*empress;*" but we do not in the same sense say "*governor*" and "*governess.*" In this latter case the feminine form has acquired a meaning of its own, and refuses to part with it. I remember, during the first weeks of our present Queen's reign, hearing a clergyman pray for " *Alexandrina*, our most gracious Queen and *governess.*" Very many, indeed most names of occupations and offices, are common to both sexes, and it savours of pedantry to attempt by adding the feminine termination, to make a difference. The description "*pilgrim,*" for instance, may include both men and women; yet I remember once seeing advertised, " The Wanderings of a *pilgrimess,*" &c. "*Porter*" is another of these words. When we are told to apply to the porter, we are not surprised to see " her that keeps the gate" answer to our knock. But in many public establishments we see the " *portress*" announced as the person to whom we are to apply. It is true, the *word* "portress" is legitimate enough. We have in Milton " the portress of hell gate." But it does not follow, because it is used in poetry, that we may use it in our common discourse. I expect we shall soon see "*groceress*" and *tea-dealeress*, and licensed *venderess* of stamps."

188. A rule regarding the classification of both sexes together is sometimes forgotten. When both are spoken of under one head, the masculine appellation is used. Thus, though some of the European rulers may be females, they may be correctly classified, when spoken of altogether, under the denomination " *kings.*" It has been pointed out that Lord Bacon does this even in the case of two, " Ferdinand and Isabella, kings of Spain." This would hardly be said now; and in ordinary language, we should perhaps rather choose to call the European rulers "sovereigns." But this is no reason why the rule should be forgotten, nor why sentences, when it is observed, should be charged with incorrectness, or altered to suit modern ears. I am informed that a clergyman, in the following sentence in the prayer for the Queen, in the Communion Service, " We are taught

that the hearts of kings are in Thy rule and governance," alters the word *kings* into *sovereigns*.

189. Punctuation : commas.—From speaking of the forms of words, we will come to punctuation, or stopping. I remember when I was young in printing, once correcting the punctuation of a proof-sheet, and complaining of the liberties which had been taken with my manuscript. The publisher quietly answered me, that *punctuation was always left to the compositors*. And a precious mess they make of it. The great enemies to understanding anything printed in our language are the *commas*. And these are inserted by the compositors, without the slightest compunction, on every possible occasion. Many words are by rule always hitched off with two commas ; one before and one behind ; *nursed*, as the Omnibus Company would call it. "*Too*" is one of these words ; "*however*," another ; "*also*," another ; the sense in almost every such case being disturbed, if not destroyed by the process. I remember beginning a sentence with—" However true this may be." When it came in proof, the inevitable comma was after the "*however*," thus of course making nonsense of my unfortunate sentence.

190. In a book generally so accurate as Dr. Latham's "English Language," (p. 57,) the following occurs : " This difference is, by no means, unimportant." Now by this punctuation the words "by no means" are parenthesized ; that is, are pronounced non-essential to the sentence, and may, as the words included between commas in the sentence of " He is, on this very day, twenty years old," be omitted. Let us omit them. The sense is at once reversed. What the author meant to say, and doubtless did say before the compositor misrepresented him, was, "This difference is by no means unimportant:" without the offensive commas.

191. In a note (p. 95) to the Bishop of St. David's remarkable Charge to his Clergy in 1869, we read, " It may be asked, Why revive these painful memories? It is because they are only, to a very small extent, things of the past." Here again the commas misrepresent the sense. Take out the clause parenthesized by them, and we shall have left, "because they are only things of the past," a sense the very opposite of that which the sentence was

meant to convey; which was, of course, this, "because they are only to a very small extent things of the past."

192. **Comma after "now."**—Another word which constantly suffers from this *commatose* treatment is the unfortunate adverb *now*. It has, as we all know, two usages: one, temporal, the other, resumptive or connexional. "Then, every one believed him guilty; now, the world is of a different opinion." This is an example of the temporal *now*; which, though it does not require a comma after it, admits of one, and is sometimes made clearer by having one. But when *now* is used in the other sense, as a resumptive or connecting particle, the comma is absurd. This sense is constantly found in the English Version of the gospel of St. John. "Now Philip was of Bethsaida . . ." (i. 44): "now when he was in Jerusalem at the passover . . ." (ii. 23): "Now Jacob's well was there . . ." (iv. 6): &c. In every one of these cases, the modern compositors would insert a comma after *now*, reducing the unhappy sentences to utter nonsense. I have some satisfaction in reflecting, that, in the course of editing the Greek text of the New Testament, I believe I have destroyed more than a thousand commas, which prevented the text being properly understood.

193. **Comma between two adjectives.**—One very provoking case is that where two adjectives come together, belonging to the same noun-substantive. Thus, in printing *a nice young man*, a comma is placed after nice, giving, we may observe, a very different sense from that intended: bringing before us the fact that a man is both nice and young, whereas the original sentence introduced to us a young man that was nice. Thus too in the expression "*a great black dog*," printed without commas, everybody knows what we mean; but this would be printed "a great, black dog." Take again the case where meaning is intensified by adjectives being repeated—as in "*the wide wide world*," "*the deep deep sea*." Such expressions you almost invariably find printed "*the wide, wide world*," "*the deep, deep sea*," thereby making them, if judged by any rule at all, into nonsense.

194. "The French, and not the German, system." Is this rightly punctuated? There seems to be some defence

for the omission, as there is also for the insertion, of the comma. On the one hand it may be said that the words "and not the German" are parenthetical, and therefore want the two commas: on the other, that "German" is just as much an epithet of "system" as if it stood alone, and that we do not insert a comma between an epithet and the noun which it precedes. And to my mind this argument rather preponderates, affecting as it does the look of the sentence. It seems better to regard the construction as elliptical in the former member, and to omit the comma in the latter: " The French (system), and not the German system."

195. **Too few commas.**—Still, though too many commas are bad, too few are not without inconvenience also. I remember a notice of " the Society for Promoting the Observance of the Lord's-day which was founded in 1831," giving the notion that the *day, not the society*, was founded in that year. Had the date been 1631, instead of 1831, an awkward interpretation might have been possible.

196. I take the following, verbatim and *punctuatim*, from a religious newspaper: " EDUCATION.—In a Ladies' School conducted on Evangelical principles about nine in number, good instruction is given, &c."

197. **Stops not unimportant.**—Some people, especially such as somewhat plume themselves on knowing the world and the ways of business, will tell us that stops are never to be regarded,—make no imaginable difference. But in this, as in many of their off-hand assertions, this class of layers-down of the law are in the wrong. There are sentences which cannot possibly be understood without the intervention of commas. Notably among such are constructions where the relative may either describe or limit, according as it is or is not preceded by a comma. Thus when we write, *All voted for him except the Jews, who live in Houndsditch,*—we assert that the Jews as a class did not vote for him, and that the Jews as a class live in Houndsditch. This is the descriptive force of the relative. But if we write *All voted for him except the Jews who live in Houndsditch*, we say nothing about the Jews in general, but assert that those Jews who live in Houndsditch did

not vote for him. This is its limiting force. And sentences of this form are constantly occurring, in legal documents, as well as in ordinary writing.

198. A curious example of sense vitiated by the insertion of a comma occurred the other day in a circular received by me from the south of France: "M. Nègre above all things is most careful in the primitive matters used in his laboratory, being perfectly healthy and free from all injurious matters."

199. **Notes of admiration.**—While I am treating of stops, a word is necessary concerning notes of admiration. These *shrieks*, as they have been called, are scattered up and down the page by the compositors without mercy. If one has written the words "*O sir*," as they ought to be written, and are written in Genesis xliii. 20, viz., with the plain capital "O" and no stop, and then a comma after "*sir*," our friend the compositor is sure to write "*Oh*" with a shriek (!) and to put another shriek after "*sir*." We should use, in writing, as few as possible of these nuisances. They always make the sense weaker, where we can possibly do without them. The only case where they are really necessary, is when the language is pure exclamation, as in "How beautiful is night!" or, "O that I might find him!"

200. **Semi-colon and colon.**—Is there any difference between the *semi-colon* and the *colon*? And, as a question consequent on this, do we want both? I venture to think that there is a difference, and that we do want both. The *semi-colon* serves to separate clauses between which the sense is not immediately carried on, as after a comma, nor disjunctively broken off, as after a colon. It is useful, after perhaps a series of commas, to indicate a somewhat greater break in the sense, or at all events one differing in kind. A colon, on the other hand, marks a considerable break; and is useful before a disjunctive particle, or where, for the sake of the style, a connecting particle is omitted.

201. We will give some examples. Take the sentence, "He saved others—himself he cannot save." (I use the dash, as not having yet determined the punctuation.) Now here a comma is hardly enough, considering that we have

two distinct propositions. A colon is too much, because the two propositions are closely connected, and regard the same act of *saving*. It is precisely the case for a semicolon: and accordingly we find it so punctuated. Take, on the other hand, the examples so often recurring in the Book of Proverbs, where two propositions, contrary the one to the other, are asserted of persons contrary in character: "A righteous man regardeth the life of his beast—but the tender mercies of the wicked are cruel." Here is a clear case for the colon. The two propositions are related only by their antithetical character: there is no term common to the two: if there be, the colon at once passes into the semi-colon, or even into the comma. For example: "Wisdom is before him that hath understanding; but the eyes of a fool are in the ends of the earth." Here the idea of the look-out, so different in the case of the wise man and the fool, binds the antithetical propositions together. And in the following, the connexion is even more close: "There is a way that seemeth right unto a man, but the end thereof are the ways of death."

202. **Standards of punctuation.**—Much might be said about the different standards of punctuation to be adopted according to differing matter and style. Very short sentences require hardly any stops except the comma and the period. Moderately short ones can do without more than the comma, period, and colon. But sentences of ordinary length require combinations of all four. The *dash* should never be admitted if it can be helped. Sometimes it is indispensable. A clause, or a set of clauses, requires marking off as a departure from the main line of thought, and then a dash before and after can hardly be spared. But in the majority of cases where the dash is so freely used, either the colon may with advantage be substituted, or the style wants reforming, and the abruptness toning down.

203. "**Centre.**"—We return to the idiomatic usage of words and constructions. The very simple and intelligible word "*centre*" comes in for a good deal of mal-treatment in our days. *Centre* is from the Greek word "*Kentron*," meaning merely *a point:* the point of a needle, or of a sting, or of anything else: and hence is used in geometry

to denote that point round which a circle or any other symmetrical curve is drawn. And in accordance with this its original meaning ought its use always to be: a centre should always designate a point, never a line, nor, except as presently defined, a middle space. But we see this often departed from. "A gangway will be left down the centre of the room," is a clear case of such departure. I do not of course mean to advocate absolute strictness in this or in any other usage. Accuracy is one thing, punctiliousness is another. The one should be always observed, the other always avoided. While I should take care not to say that I *walked up and down the centre* of the lawn, I should not object to say that there is a large bed of geraniums *in the centre*, although strictly speaking the centre of the lawn is in the bed, not the bed in the centre.[1]

204. And in the figurative use of this word, and of all words, intelligent common sense, rather than punctiliousness, ought to be our guide. *Centre*, and its adjective *central*, are often used in speaking of objects of thought, as well as of sight. Let it be borne in mind, when this is done, that these words apply only to a principal object round which others group themselves, and not to one which happens to be pre-eminent amongst others. To say that some conspicuous person in an assembly was *the centre of attraction* is perfectly correct; but to say that some subject of conversation, merely because it happened to occupy more of the time than other subjects, was the *central topic* of the evening, is incorrect and unmeaning.

205. "**By and by.**"—The following question may be regarded as pertaining rather to orthography, but it has its bearing on construction also. Ought we to write *by and by*, or *by and bye? by the by*, or *by the bye?* There is a tendency to add a vowel, by way of giving emphasis in pronunciation, when a preposition is used as an adverb. Thus "*too*" is only the preposition "*to*," emphasized; a "*bye*"

---

[1] A correspondent informs me, that a parliamentary notice to landowners, which has been in use for many years, and is issued to the number of hundreds of thousands at once, contains the words "within eleven yards, or thereabouts, of the *centre-line* of the proposed work." This is not absolutely wrong; for the *centre-line* is the line which *passes through the centre*, as the *Chatham-line* is the line which passes through Chatham.

ball, at cricket, is only a ball that runs *by*. In this latter case the added "*e*" is universal: but not so in *by-play*, *by-end*, which are sometimes spelt with it and sometimes without it. And we never add it when "*by*" is used as an adverb in construction in a sentence, as in *passing by*. This being so, it is better, perhaps, to confine this way of spelling to the only case where it seems needed, the *bye ball*, and to write "*by and by*," "*by the by*."

206. "**Endeavour ourselves.**"—A mistake is very generally made by our clergy in reading the collect for the second Sunday after Easter. We there pray, with reference to Our Lord's death for us, and His holy example, "that we may thankfully receive that his inestimable benefit, and also daily endeavour ourselves to follow the blessed steps of his most holy life." This is often read with an emphasis on the word "*ourselves*," as if it were in the nominative case, and to be distinguished from some other person. But no other persons have been mentioned; and the sense thus becomes confused for the hearer. The fact is, that "*ourselves*" is not in the nominative case at all, but in the accusative after the verb "*endeavour*," which at the time of the compiling of our Prayer-book was used as a reflective verb. To *endeavour myself*, is to consider myself in duty bound. That this is so, appears clearly from the answer given in the Ordination service, where the Bishop asks, "Will you be diligent in prayers and in reading of the Holy Scriptures, and in such studies as help to the knowledge of the same . . . ?" And the candidate replies, " I will *endeavour myself* so to do, the Lord being my helper."

207. "**To be mistaken.**"—The usage of the verb to *mistake* is somewhat anomalous. Its etymology seems simple enough—*to take amiss*. And by the analogy of "misunderstand," "misinterpret," "mislead," "misinform," "miscalculate," it ought to be simply an active verb, as in the phrases, "you mistook my meaning," "he had mistaken the way." This would give as its passive use, "my meaning was mistaken by you." But our English usage is different; we have these phrases, it is true, but we far more commonly use the verb in the passive, to carry what should be its active meaning. To *be mistaken* is not,

with us, to be misapprehended by another, but to commit a mistake oneself. This is a curious translation of meaning, but it is now rooted in the language and become idiomatic. "I thought so, but I was mistaken," is universally said, not "I mistook." We expect to hear "you are mistaken," and should be surprised at hearing asserted "you are mistaking," or "you mistake," unless followed by an accusative, "the meaning," or "me." When we hear the former of these, we begin to consider whether we were right or wrong; when the latter, we at once take the measure of our friend, as one who has not long escaped from the study of the rules of the lesser grammarians, by which, and not by the usages of society, circumstances have compelled him to learn his language.

208. "Good looking" or "well looking."—A correspondent asks me, *good looking* or *well looking?* Here is another instance of idiom versus accuracy. And idiom decidedly has it. To speak of a *well-looking* man would be to make oneself ridiculous: all usage is against the word. But, at the same time, to be *good looking* is not to *look good*. It is, in one sense, to *look well*; or, if we will, to have good looks. So that the whole matter seems to be left to usage, which in this case is decisive.

209. "Very pleased."—Is the expression "*very pleased*" admissible? The ordinary usage before a participle is "very much:" "I was very much pleased." No one would think of saying, "I was very cheated in the transaction." But on the other hand, we all say "very tired," "very ailing," "very contented," "very discontented." Where then is the distinction? The account seems to be this. If the participle describe only the action or the suffering implied in its verb, in other words, if it continue a verb, "very" alone will not serve to qualify it. "Very" simply intensifies: and it must have some quality to intensify. You cannot intensify a mere event. In other words, if "very" alone be used, it must be followed by an adjective, or by something equivalent to an adjective. "Tired" is equivalent to "weary:" it is a participle used as an adjective: therefore we may say, "very tired;" "ailing" is equivalent to "poorly;" "contented" and "discontented" are qualities and tempers, not records of an event which has

happened. Judging "very pleased" by this rule, it is inadmissible. " Pleased " is a state of mind, carried on beyond the mere occasion which gave rise to it. Introduce a marked *reference to the occasion*, and "very" becomes at once inappropriate. We cannot say "very flattered," but must say "very much flattered." I own I prefer "very much pleased," as more conformable to usage.

210. **" Latter," of more than two ; "last," of only two.**—One point made very much of by the precisians is, the avoiding of the use of "*latter*" when we have spoken of more than two things, and of "*last*" when we have spoken of only two. Is this founded in any necessity or propriety of the laws of thought; or is it a mere arbitrary regulation laid down by persons who know little and care little about those laws?

211. Let us inquire into the matter. The notion is, that in speaking of two things, we can have only positive and comparative ; that for a superlative we require three or more ; and when we have three or more, we must use the superlative. Thus if I speak of two invasions of Great Britain, I must call the earlier the *former*, not the *first*, and the second the *latter*, not the *last*. But if I speak of three invasions, I must call the third, in referring to it, the *last* not the *latter*. Is there reason in this ? Let us look at it in this light. Of two invasions, the earlier is undoubtedly the *first*, the latter the *second*. Now "*first*" is a superlative ; and if of two, one is designated by a superlative, why not the other ?

212. Still, this is not digging to the root of the matter ; it is only arguing from the acknowledged use of a form in one case, to its legitimate use in an analogous one. Let us take it in another point of view. "*First*" is unavoidably used of that one in a series with which we begin, whatever be the number which follow ; whether many or few. Why should not "*last*" be used of that one in a series with which we end, whatever be the number which preceded, whether many or few ? The second invasion, when we spoke of only two, was undoubtedly the *last* mentioned ; and surely therefore may be spoken of in referring back to it, as the last, without any violation of the laws of thought.

213. Nor does the comparative of necessity suggest that only two are concerned, though it may be more *natural* to speak of the *greatest* of more than two, not of the *greater*. For that which is *greatest* of any number, is *greater* than the rest.

214. "Superior," "inferior."—There is an expression creeping into general use which cannot be justified in grammar, "a *superior* man;" "a very *inferior* person." We all know what is meant: and a certain sort of defence may be set up for it by calling it elliptical: by saying that the comparatives are to be filled up by inserting "to most men," or the like. But with all its convenience, and all the defence which can be set up for it, this way of speaking is not desirable; and if followed out as a precedent, cannot but vulgarize and deteriorate our language.

215. It may be hard to assign exactly the difference between "*oldest*" and "*eldest*." Whatever it may be, it is clearly matter of idiomatic usage, and not derivable from any distinction in the words themselves. But that there is a difference, may in a moment be shown. We cannot say, "Methuselah was the *eldest* man that ever lived;" we must say, "the *oldest* man that ever lived." Again, it would hardly be natural to say, "his father's *oldest* born," if we were speaking of the first-born. If we were to say of a father, "He was succeeded by his *oldest* son," we should convey the impression that that son was not the *eldest*, but the oldest surviving after the loss of the eldest. And these examples seem to bring us to a kind of insight into the idiomatic difference. "*Eldest*" implies not only more years, but also priority of right; nay, it might sometimes even be independent of actual duration of life. A first-born who died an infant was yet the *eldest* son. If all mankind were assembled, Methuselah would be the oldest: but Adam would be the eldest, of men. Whether any other account is to be given of this than the caprice of usage, I cannot say, but must leave the question to those who are better versed in the comparison of languages. My object is to describe the current coin, rather than to inquire into the archæology of the coinage.

216. Connected with this inquiry about "oldest" and

"eldest" is the subject of a letter which I will give entire:—

"SIR,
"When I came on deck the other morning in the Red Sea (very near the place at which Moses and the Israelites are supposed to have crossed), I was seized by three fellow-passengers—a Russian, a Frenchman, and a Swiss—who, *nolentem volentem*, constituted me umpire in a dispute which they were carrying on upon a point of English grammar. The Russian, it seems, was his father's eldest son, and he had four brothers, all, *ex necessitate*, younger than himself. In speaking of the oldest of these four, he called him 'my elder brother'; on which the Frenchman said, 'I thought you were your father's eldest son.' 'So I am,' he replied; 'but I spoke of the elder *of my brothers*. I am not one of my own brothers, and therefore when I speak of my elder brother, I don't include myself. He I spoke of is the oldest of *my* brothers, not the oldest of my father's sons.' To this I replied by quoting Milton—'Adam the goodliest of his sons since born, the fairest of her daughters, Eve.' That, however, we agreed was only justified by poets' licence. Finally, I ruled that though my Russian friend was strictly and grammatically correct, yet, according to common usage, the expression employed by him was calculated to mislead. He seemed to think it rather hard that the English people, having constructed a grammar, should not conform to its rules; and hinted that in Russia no such liberty of the subject would be permitted—that when laws were made, people were expected to obey them; and that a man who talked bad grammar would be in danger of the knout.

"Will you be so good as tell us in your next edition whether the Russian or the Frenchman was right, and whether you approve of my ruling?   "Your obedient servant,
"W. F."

217. It was somewhat curious that the Russian should have blamed us for inconsistency: for surely "*my elder brother*" must mean "the elder brother of me," just as "*my better half*" means, "the better half of me." We may also hereby illustrate what was just now said about "oldest" and "eldest:" "my eldest brother" could never be said by the first-born of a family, seeing that the title belongs to him alone: whereas when "my oldest brother" is said, he excludes himself, and indicates the brother next to him in age.

218. "**Talented.**"—We seem rather unfortunate in our designations for our men of ability. For another term by which we describe them, "*talented*," is about as bad as possible. What is it? It looks like a participle. From what verb? Fancy such a verb as "*to talent!*" Cole-

ridge somewhere cries out against this newspaper word, and says, Imagine other participles formed by this analogy, and men being said to be pennied, shillinged, or pounded. He perhaps forgot that, by an equal abuse, men are said to be "*moneyed*" men, or as we sometimes see it spelt (as if the word itself were not bad enough without making it worse by false orthography), "*monied*." [1]

219. "**Gifted.**"—Another formation of this kind, "*gifted*," is at present very much in vogue. Every man whose parts are to be praised, is a *gifted* author, or speaker, or preacher. Nay, sometimes a very odd transfer is made, and the pen with which the author writes is said to be "*gifted*," instead of himself.

220. "**To leave,**" absolute.—Exception has been taken to what has been called the *neuter* use of the verb to leave: "I shall not *leave* before December 1." But it is not correct to describe this as a *neuter* use; it is rather the *absolute* use. The verb is still active, but the object is suppressed. Thus, if there are three persons in a room, one reading the Bible, another the newspaper, and the third a review, I say that they are all *reading*, without depriving the verb of its active force; using it as an absolute predicate applicable to them all. Thus too, if of three persons one is leaving his own home to-morrow, another a friend's house, and the third an hotel, I may say that they are all *leaving* to-morrow. And this absolute usage is perfectly legitimate where one person only is concerned. "I shall not read this morning, but I shall write." "It is my intention to leave when my lease is up." How far it may be more or less elegant under given circumstances to speak thus, is another question, which can only be decided when those circumstances are known; but of the correctness of the usage I imagine there can be no doubt.

221. "**I beg to . . .**"—A correspondent is highly offended with the very common expression, "I beg to inform you," "I beg to state," &c., requiring that the word "leave" should be inserted after the verb, otherwise, he says, the words are nonsense.

[1] A friend has directed my attention to the fact that in "The New Whig Guide," printed in 1824, the word "*talented*" is noticed as an Irish expression, equivalent to the English "*clever*."

In this case, I think custom has decided for us, that the ellipsis, "I beg," for "I beg leave," is allowable.

222. "**Could not get.**"—Connected with the last are, or may seem to be, certain elliptical usages which cannot be similarly defended. Thus when the object has been to visit a friend, or to attain a certain point, we sometimes hear the excuse for failure thus expressed, "I meant to come to you,"—or, "I fully intended to be there;" "but *I couldn't get.*" The full expression would in this case be, "I couldn't get to you;" or, "I couldn't get there." But the verb "*to get*" is used in so many meanings, that it is hardly fit for this elliptical position. Besides that the sentence ends inelegantly and inharmoniously, an ambiguity is suggested: "couldn't get what?" a horse? or time? or money to pay the fare? or some one to show the way?

223. "**Does not belong.**"—Another word objectionably thus used is the verb "*to belong.*" "Is Miss A. coming to the Amateur Concert to-night?" "No: she does not *belong;*" meaning, does not belong to the Society. And then perhaps we are told that "though she does not *belong* this year, she means to *belong* next." Here again we may say that *belong* is a verb of so wide a signification, that it will hardly admit of being thus detached from its accidents, and used absolutely and generally.

224. To "**belong Leeds,**" &c.—I am reminded by a valued correspondent, of another use of the verb "*to belong,*" already familiar to me, as having been long resident in the north-midland counties. "We have," he says, in these parts a provincial usage of the word "*belong:*" as, "belong to Halifax," "belong to Leeds:" or, more commonly, "belong Halifax," "belong Leeds:" meaning, live there. The late Mr. F. W., one of the largest proprietors of land in Yorkshire, and M.P. for the yet undivided county—and, let me add, a wise and munificent friend to the Church,—was withal so little lavish on his person, that he might easily pass for a very humble farmer. He was one day accosted on the roadside by two strangers in a gig on their way to Wighill, near York. "My man, do you belong Wighill?" He answered, "No, Sirs, Wighill belongs me."

225. "**To progress.**"—The verb to "*progress,*" is challenged by one of my friends as a modern Ameri-

canism. This is not strictly accurate. Shakspeare uses it in King John (act. v. sc. 2):

"Let me wipe off this honourable dew,
That silverly doth *progress* on thy cheeks." [1]

But you will observe that the line requires the verb to be pronounced *prógress*, not *progréss*, so that this is perhaps hardly a case in point, except as to the word, a verb formed on the noun *progress*.

226. **Passage from Milton.**—Milton also uses such a verb, in the magnificent peroration of his "Treatise of Reformation in England." I cannot forbear citing the whole passage, as it may be a relief to my readers and to myself in the midst of these verbal enquiries:

"Then amidst the Hymns and Hallelujahs of saints, some one may perhaps be heard offering at high strains in new and lofty measures, to sing and celebrate thy divine mercies, and marvellous judgments in this land throughout all ages; whereby this great and warlike nation, instructed and inured to the fervent and continual practice of Truth and Righteousness, and casting far from her the rags of her old vices, may press on hard to that high and happy Emulation, to be found the soberest, wisest, and most Christian people at that day, when Thou the Eternal and shortly expected King, shalt open the clouds to judge the several kingdoms of the world, and distributing national honours and rewards to religious and just commonwealths, shalt put an end to all earthly Tyrannies, proclaiming thy universal and mild Monarchy through heaven and earth. Where they undoubtedly, that by their labours, counsels and prayers, have been earnest for the common good of Religion and their country, shall receive above the inferior orders of the Blessed, the regal addition of Principalities, Legions, and Thrones into their glorious Titles, and, in supereminence of beatifick vision, *progressing* the dateless

---

[1] I mention, as in courtesy bound, an account of this construction which has been sent me by a correspondent anxious to vindicate Shakspeare from having used a modern vulgarism. He would understand "doth progress" as "doeth progress," the latter word being a substantive. Surely, he can hardly be in earnest. I am surprised to see this advocated in the very sensible little English Grammar of Mr. Higginson.

and irrevoluble circle of Eternity, shall clasp inseparable Hands with Joy and Bliss, in over measure for ever."

227. It may be noticed again that Milton's use of the verb is not exactly that which is become common now. He seems to make it equivalent to "*moving along,*" or "*moving throughout,*" in an active sense. These favoured ones are to *progress* the circle of Eternity, i.e., I suppose, to revolve for ever round and round it. The present usage makes the verb neuter; to *progress* meaning to advance, to make progress. I can hardly say I feel much indignation against the word, thus used. We seem to want it; and if we do, and it does not violate any known law of formation, by all means let us have it. True, it is the first of its own family; we have not yet formed *aggress, regress, egress,* or *retrogress,* into verbs; but we have done in substance the same thing, by having admitted long ago the verbs *suggest, digest, project, object, reject, eject;* for all these are formed from the same part of the original Latin verbs, as this "*progress*" on which we have been speaking.

228. Some of these words are set down as English verbs in the folio edition of Bailey's Universal Dictionary, published in 1755. But there is as wide a difference between *dictionary words* and English words, as between vocabulary French and spoken French. We might in a few minutes find a list of dictionary words which would introduce us to some strange acquaintances. What do we think of "abarcy," "aberuncate," "abolishable," "abstringe," "abstrude," "acervate," "acetosity," "adjugate," "admetiate," "adminicle," "advolation," "adustible," &c., &c.? Thousands of words in the Dictionaries are simply Latin, made English in form, without any authority for their use.

229. **Nouns made into verbs.**—In treating of this verb to "*progress,*" a correspondent notices that there prevails a tendency to turn nouns into verbs: "The ship remained to *coal:*" "the church is being *pewed:*" "he was prevailed on to *head* the movement." I do not see that we can object to this tendency in general, seeing that it has grown with the growth of our language, and under due regulation is one of the most obvious means of enriching it. Verbs thus formed will carry themselves into

use, in spite of the protests of the purists.[1] Some years ago, precise scholars used to exclaim against the verb "*to experience;*" and a very ugly candidate for admission into the language it was. Milton introduced its participle when he wrote, "He through the arméd files Darts his *experienced* eye." Still, as we know in the case of "*talented*" and "*moneyed*," the participle may be tolerated long before the verb is invented; and no instance of the verb "*to experience*" occurs till quite recently. But all attempts to exclude it *now* would be quite ineffectual.

230. **Does an organ "blow"?**—A correspondent referred to me the question whether in Milton's line,

"Then let the pealing organ blow,"

the verb "*blow*" is rightly used. The organ, it was urged, is *blown*: and it might as well be said that the fire "*blows*," when it is blown.

But I believe Milton to be quite correct. The whole action of the organ is, to produce sound by *blowing* into the pipes: and this it is, rather than the filling the bellows with wind, that is meant. The action of fire is, not to blow, but to burn: when it *is blown*, it *burns*; but when the organ *is blown*, it, by aid of its valves, opened by the pressure on the keys, *blows*, and produces music.

231. **"To treat of," or "to treat"?**—To *treat of,* or *to treat?* Plainly, which we please. To *treat* is to *handle,* to *have under treatment*, to *discuss*. The verb may be used with an object following it, to "*treat a subject;*" or it may be used absolutely, to "*treat concerning,*" or "*of,*" a subject. It is one of those very many cases so little understood by the layers down of precise rules, where writers and speakers are left to choose, as the humour takes them, between different ways of expression.

232. **Fallacy:—of two ways of expression, one must be wrong.**—And I may once for all notice a fallacious way of arguing, into which the sciolists who would legislate for our language are continually betrayed. It consists in assuming that, of two modes of expression, if one be shown to be right, the other must necessarily be

---

[1] I have before me "The Joiner's Instructor in *staircasing* and *handrailing*."

wrong. Whereas very often the varying expressions are equally legitimate, and each of them full of interest, as bearing traces of the different sources from which our language has sprung.

233. "**The book Genesis**," "**the city London**."— There is a piece of affectation becoming sadly common among our younger clergy, which I had already marked for notice, when I received a letter, from which the following is an extract:—"I wish to call your attention to the ignorance which is sometimes exhibited by clergy and others of the true meaning of the preposition in such expressions as 'the city of Canterbury,' 'the play of "Hamlet."' We sometimes hear it proclaimed from the desk, 'Here beginneth the first chapter of the book Genesis:' and we read in parochial documents of 'the parish of St. George,' 'the parish of St. Mary,' instead 'of St. George's,' 'of St. Mary's,' &c."

234. I believe the excuse, if it can be called one, set up for this violation of usage is, that "the book of Genesis" and "the book of Daniel" cannot both be right, because the former was not written by Genesis, as the latter was by Daniel. But, as my correspondent says, this simply betrays ignorance of the meanings of the preposition "*of.*" It is used, in designations of this kind, in three different senses: 1. To denote authorship, as "*the book of Daniel:*" 2. To denote subject-matter, as "*the first book of Kings:*" 3. As a note of apposition, signifying, "which is," or "which is called," as "*the book of Genesis*," "*of Exodus*," &c. This last usage meets us at every turn; and the pedant who ignores it in the reading desk, must, in consistency, drop it everywhere else. Imagine his letter describing his summer holiday: "I left the city London, and passed through the county Kent, leaving the realm England at the town Dover, and entering the empire France at the town Calais, on my way to the Republic Switzerland."

235. It has been suggested that the "*of*" in "*the city of Canterbury*," may be *territorial*: that as it is rendered in Latin by "*de*," this "*de*" may be the same that we find in "*Henricus de Estria*." But I cannot quite agree with this view: because though it might seem to be justified in the case of a town, it clearly would not be in that of a book,

or in any other in which the territorial connexion is out of the question.

236. I may remark in passing, that here again usage comes in with its prescriptive laws, and prevents the universal application of rules. While we always say "the city of Cairo," not "the city Cairo," we never say "the river of Nile," but always "the river Nile." So too "the city of London," but "the river Thames." In Ireland, "the county Wicklow," &c., is according to usage.

237. "**Reverend**" and "**reverent**."—It seems astonishing that many of our writers should not yet be clear in their distinctive use of "reverend" and "reverent." I saw lately a description of a certain person as being "unintentionally irreverend." The writer (or printer) of this forgot that "*reverent*" (*reverens,-entis*) is the *subjective* word, describing the feeling within a man as its subject, whereas "*reverend*" (*reverendus*) is the *objective* word, describing the feeling with which a man is regarded,—of which he is the object from without. Dean Swift might be "very reverend," by common courtesy; but he was certainly not "very reverent" in his conduct or in his writings.

238. **Subjective and objective words.**—A few words more about these *subjective* and *objective* words. It has been the fashion to laugh at and decry these terms, *subjective* and *objective*. I have generally found that those who do so are wanting in appreciation of the distinction which these words are intended to convey, and which can hardly be conveyed but by their use. Take the case where one and the same word is used in both senses. We say "a fearful heart," and we say "a fearful height." In the former phrase we use *fearful* in its *subjective* sense, as describing a quality inherent in the subject of the sentence; in the latter phrase, we use *fearful* in its *objective* sense, as describing an effect produced by being an object contemplated. The heart is *subject to fear*, the height is *an object of fear*. How otherwise than by the use of these terms are we clearly and shortly to indicate this difference? Other instances of this double use of one and the same word may be found in "a hopeful spirit," "a hopeful youth,"— "a joyful multitude," "a joyful occasion;" and an example of the distinction in the use of two words, in the

adjectives "*tall*" (subjective,—high with reference to himself as compared with others) and "*high*" (objective, contemplated as an object from without).

239. "**Obnoxious.**"—One correspondent asks, whether of these two is right, "Death is obnoxious to men," or "Men are obnoxious to death!" Here the adjective "obnoxious" is used in two different senses. In Latin, "*obnoxius*" means "subject to:" "Omnes homines morti obnoxii sunt,"—All men are obnoxious, subject, to Death. But this meaning has almost vanished out of our English usage, and that of noxious, hurtful, has taken its place. I need not tell scholars that this meaning crept into later Latin probably from the similarity of sound in "noxius" and "obnoxius," and was altogether unknown in the better days of the language.

240. To "**attain one's —th year.**"—A newspaper stated in 1864, that Lord Palmerston had *attained* his eightieth year. On this a household at Beckenham fell out. The ladies maintained that the expression was equivalent to—had *completed* his eightieth year. And matter of fact was with them: for Lord Palmerston, having been born in 1784, was full eighty in 1864. But the gentlemen held that, however the fact might seem to bear out the ladies' interpretation, and however the writer may have intended to express the meaning, *attained* and *completed* cannot be the same: but the expression "attained his eightieth year" must properly mean "entered his eightieth year."

It seems to me that the gentlemen were right. A youth has attained his majority the very day he enters upon it, not the day he dies and quits it, his life being complete. A man attains a position in life the moment he is appointed to it, before he has begun any of his duties. And so a man attains his eightieth year the first day that it can be said of him that he is in his eightieth year: not the last day that this can be said: for he has then attained his eighty-first year.

241. "**Or**" and "**nor**" **in a negative sentence.**—A good deal of confusion is prevalent in the usages of "*or*" and "*nor*" in a negative sentence. When I wrote, in the last paragraph but three, "he was certainly not very reverent in his conduct or in his writings," was I

right or wrong? Ought I to have said, "he was not very reverent in his conduct *nor* in his writings?" We may regard this sentence in two ways, which may be represented by the two following modes of punctuation: 1. "He was not very reverent in his conduct, or in his writings." 2. "He was not very reverent, in his conduct or in his writings." According to the former punctuation, "*or*" is wrong; it should be "*nor*." But observe that thus we get a somewhat awkward elliptical sentence: "He was not very reverent in his conduct, nor (was he very reverent) in his writings." In the second form of the sentence, "*or*" is right, and "*nor*" would be wrong. This will be evident in a moment by filling up the sentence with the other alternative particle, "He was not very reverent, *either* in his conduct *or* in his writings;" not, "He was not very reverent, *neither* in his conduct, *nor* in his writings."

242. We may, if we will, strike out the negative altogether from the part of the sentence containing the verb, and attach it entirely to the alternative clauses. But in this case it is usual to place those clauses before the predicative portion of the sentence: "neither in his conduct, nor in his writings was he very reverent."

243. The commonly received rules respecting "*or*" and "*nor*" do not seem to have been observed by our best writers. Cowley has,

> "For 'tis not buildings make a court,
> Or pomp: but 'tis the king's resort."

The truth is, that these same rules are, in almost every case, of doubtful application. In these lines, we may resolve the former proposition in two ways: "'tis not buildings or pomp that make a court," "'tis not buildings that make a court, nor [is it pomp that makes a court]." And the same may be said of almost every similar sentence.[1] Only we must take care to be precise, where the use of one or the other really alters the sense. "Whosoever shall not honour father or mother . . ." has a very different meaning from "Whosoever shall not honour father nor mother . . ." In the former case, dishonour done to *either*

---

[1] e.g., "not grudgingly, or of necessity," 2 Cor. ix. 7.

parent incurs the penalty which follows: in the latter case, only dishonour done to *both*.

244. Elliptical sentences.—As I have been speaking of an elliptical sentence, I may remark that it is astonishing what an amount of ellipsis the English ear will tolerate: in other words, how great an effort the mind of a hearer will make in supplying that which is suppressed. This extends sometimes even to changing the construction, and turning affirmative into negative, tacitly and unconsciously, as the sentence falls upon the eye or ear. A remarkable example of this occurs in one of the most solemn prayers in our English Communion Service: " We do not presume to come to this Thy Table, most merciful Lord, trusting in our own righteousness; but (*we do presume to come, trusting*) in thy manifold and great mercies." Put this admirable sentence into the hands of our ordinary rhetoricians, and it would be utterly marred. The apparently awkward ellipsis would be removed thus: " We presume to come to this Thy Table, trusting not in our own righteousness, but in thy manifold and great mercies." But at the same time, the whole character of the sentence and of the prayer would be altered. Who does not see, that by the opening words, " We do not presume," the *key-note* of the whole prayer is struck—the disclaiming of presumption founded on our own righteousness? It was worth any subsequent halting of the sentence in mere accuracy of construction, to secure this plain declaration of the spirit in which the prayer was about to be made.

245. General rule in such cases.—And this leads us to a rule which we should do well to follow in such cases. To secure the right sense being given, and the right emphasis laid, is the first thing: not to satisfy the rules of the rhetoricians. Many a sentence, which the mere rhetorician would pronounce faulty in arrangement, does its work admirably, and has done it for centuries: let him correct it and re-arrange it, and it will do that work no more. Its strong emphasis will have disappeared: its nervous homeliness will have departed, and it will sink down into vapid commonplace.

246. Arrangement of words in sentences.—Let us now enter on this matter somewhat more in detail.

The one rule which is supposed by the ordinary rhetoricians to regulate the arrangement of words in sentences, is this: that "*those parts of a sentence which are most closely connected in their meaning, should be as closely as possible connected in position;*" or, as it is propounded by Dr. Blair, "*A capital rule in the arrangement of sentences is that the words or members most nearly related should be placed in the sentence as near to each other as possible, so as to make their mutual relation clearly appear.*"

247. Ordinary rule.—Now doubtless this rule is, in the main, and for general guidance, a good and useful one: indeed, so plain to all, that it surely needed no inculcating. But there are more things in the English language than seem to have been dreamt of in the philosophy of the rhetoricians. If this rule were uniformly applied, it would break down the force and the living interest of style in any English writer, and reduce his matter, as we just now said, to a dreary and dull monotony. For it is in exceptions to its application, that almost all vigour and character of style consist. Of this I shall give abundant illustration by-and-by. Meantime let me make some remarks on two very important matters in the construction of sentences: the requirements of *emphasis*, and the requirements of *parenthesis*; neither of which are taken into account by the ordinary rule.

248. Emphasis requires its violation.—Emphasis means the stress, or force of intonation, which the intended sense requires to be laid on certain words, or clauses, in a sentence. Very often (not always) we can indicate this by the form and arrangement of the sentence itself. Some languages have far greater capacities this way than our own; but we are able commonly to do it sufficiently for the careful and intelligent reader.

249. Now how is this done? A sentence arranged according to the rule above cited, simply conveys the meaning of its words in their ordinary and straightforward construction; and in English, owing to the difficulty often felt of departing from this arrangement, we must very generally be contented with it, at the risk of our words not conveying the fullness of the meaning which we intended. For let me explain, that whenever we wish to

indicate that a stress is to be laid on a certain word, or clause, in a sentence, we must do it by taking that word or that clause out of its natural place which it would hold by the above rule, and putting it into some more prominent one. · A substantive, for example, governed by a verb, is in a subordinate position to that verb; the mind of the reader is arrested by the verb, rather than by the substantive; so that if for any reason we wish to make the substantive prominent, we must provide some other place for it than next to the verb which governs it.

250. **In the case of words.**—Take, as an example, the words "*he restored me to mine office:*" where the words are arranged in accordance with the ordinary law, and the idea expressed is the simple one of restoration to office. But suppose a distinction is to be made between the narrator, who had been restored to office, and another man, who had been very differently treated. Of course we might still observe the rule, and say "He restored me to mine office, and he hanged him;" but the sentence becomes thus (and it is to this that I request the reader's attention) a very tame one, not expressing the distinction in itself, nor admitting of being so read as to express it sharply and decisively. Now, let us violate the rule, and see how the sentence reads: "*Me he restored unto mine office, and him he hanged.*" Thus wrote our translators of Genesis (xli. 13), and they arranged the words rightly. No reader, be his intelligence ever so little, can help reading this sentence as it ought to read.

251. And let there be no mistake about this being a violation of the rule. The words nearest connected are "*restored,*" and "*me,*" which it governs: "*hanged,*" and "*him,*" which it governs. When I take "*me*" out of its place next "*restored,*" and begin the sentence with it, letting the pronoun "*he*" come between them, I do most distinctly violate the rule, that those words which are most nearly connected in the sense should also be most nearly connected in the arrangement. I have purposely chosen this first instance of the simplest possible kind, to make the matter clear as we advance into it. Let us take another. St. Peter (Acts ii. 23) says to the Jews, speaking of our Lord, " Him, being delivered by the determinate

counsel and foreknowledge of God, ye have taken, and by wicked hands have crucified and slain." Here we have the pronoun "*Him*" placed first in the sentence, and at a considerable distance from the verbs that govern it, with the clause "being delivered by the determinate counsel and foreknowledge of God," inserted between. Yet, who does not see that the whole force of that which was intended to be conveyed by the sentence is thus gained, and could not otherwise be gained? Arranged according to the common rule, the sentence would have been, "Ye have taken Him, being delivered by the determinate counsel and foreknowledge of God, and by wicked hands have crucified and slain Him;" and the whole force and point would have been lost.

252. **And parenthesis, in the case of clauses.**— And as this necessity for bringing into prominence affects the position of words in sentences, so does it also that of clauses. A clause is often subordinate in the construction to some word or some other clause; while it is the object of the writer to bring the subordinate, not the principal, clause into prominence. And then, as we saw with regard to words just now, the clause which is inferior in constructive importance is brought out and transposed, so that the reader's attention may be arrested by it. Or perhaps the writer feels the necessity of noticing as he passes on, certain particulars which will come in flatly, and spoil the balance of the sentence, if reserved till their proper place. Such passing notices are called "*parentheses*," from a Greek word, meaning *insertion by the way;*[1] and every such insertion is a violation of the supposed universal rule of position.

253. Thus, for example, I am narrating a circumstance which, when it happened, excited my astonishment. Undoubtedly the natural order of constructing the sentence would be to relate what happened first, and my surprise at it afterwards. "I was looking at a man walking on the bank of the river, when he suddenly turned about, and plunged in, to my great surprise." But who does not see the miserable way in which the last clause drags behind, and loses all force? We therefore take this clause out of

---

[1] A correspondent can see nothing in the derivation παρεντίθημι relating to *the way*. What then does he suppose to be the force of the preposition παρά?

its place, and insert it before that to which it applies, and with which it ought to be constructed: we word the sentence thus: "I was looking at a man walking on the bank of the river, when, to my great surprise, he suddenly turned round, and plunged in." I need not further illustrate so common a transposition: I will only say that it produces instances of violation of the supposed rule of arrangement in almost every extant page of good English; and in common conversation, every day, and all day long.

254. Sometimes these insertions are such obvious interruptions to the construction, that they are marked off by brackets, and it is thus made evident that the sentence is intended to flow on as if they did not exist; but far more frequently they are without any such marks, and the common sense of the reader is left to separate them off for himself. It is impossible to write lucidly or elegantly without the use of these parenthetical clauses. Care ought of course to be taken that they be not so inserted as to mislead the reader by introducing the possibility of constructing the sentence otherwise than as the writer intended. But at the same time it may be fearlessly stated, that not one of our best writers has ever been minutely scrupulous on this point: and that there does not exist in our language one great work in prose or in poetry, in which may not be found numerous instances of possible misconstruction arising from this cause. And this has not been from carelessness, but because the writer was intent on expressing his meaning in good manly English, and was not anxious as to the faults which carping and captious critics might find with his style.

255. Lord Kames gives a rule that "*a circumstance ought never to be placed between two capital members of a sentence: or if so placed* (I suppose he means, *if it be so placed*), *the first word in the consequent member should be one that cannot connect it with what precedes.*" Any one on the look out for misunderstanding may convince himself by trial, that there is hardly a page in any English book which will not furnish him with instances of violation of this rule.

256. Examples.—Let my examples begin at home. Take a sentence which occurred in a previous portion of this work: "certain persons fall, from their ignorance, into

absurd mistakes." The parenthetical clause here is " from their ignorance." It has been proposed to amend it thus: "certain persons, in consequence of their ignorance, fall into absurd mistakes." Now this is not what I wanted to say; at least it is a blundering and roundabout way of expressing it. The purpose is, to bring the fact stated into prominence: and this is done by making the verb "*fall*" immediately follow its subject, "*certain persons.*" According to the proposed arrangement, it is the fact of what is about to be stated being a consequence of their ignorance, which is put into the place of prominence and emphasis. Very well, then: having stated that they *fall*, and being about to say *into what*, it is convenient, in order to keep the sentence from dragging a comparatively unimportant clause at its end, to bring in that clause, containing the reason of the fall, immediately after the verb itself. To my mind, the clause, in spite of the possible ambiguity, reads far better with "*from*" than with "*in consequence of*," which is too heavy and lumbering. The possibility of a ludicrous interpretation—the *falling from ignorance* as a man falls from grace, or falls from virtue, is effectually precluded in the mind of any man who happens to remember that ignorance is neither a grace nor a virtue. In contemplating the way in which our sentences will be understood, we are allowed to remember, that we do not write for idiots: and it must require, to speak in the genteel language which some of my correspondents uphold, a most abnormal elongation of the auricular appendages, for a reader to have suggested to his mind a fall from the sublime height of ignorance down into the depth of a mistake.

257. **Ellipses of auxiliary verbs.**—What is to be our rule as to the ellipses of auxiliary verbs? Under what conditions may we leave out the auxiliary of a second verb in a series of clauses, making that of the first serve for it?

258. **Examples.**—Take this sentence: "Would have been broken to pieces in a deep rut, or come to grief in a bottomless swamp." It might have been said, that this can only be filled in thus, " Would have been broken to pieces, ... or would have been come to grief in a bottomless swamp:" for a part of a complex tense means nothing without the rest of the tense. That is, I suppose,

the whole of the auxiliary verbs which belong to the first verb in a sentence must also belong to all other verbs which are coupled to that first verb. Now, is this so? I do not find that our best writers observe any such rule. In Deut. vi. 11; Israel is admonished, " *When thou shalt have eaten and be full, beware lest thou forget the Lord.*" We all know that this means : " When thou shalt have eaten and shalt be full." But, according to the above-cited view, it must be filled up, " When thou shalt have eaten and shalt have be full."

259. From Scripture.—You might, by applying to the Bible the same treatment of which I have just been giving examples, show it to be full of ambiguities, which no one in all these generations has ever found out. Take examples from one chapter, Acts xxii. In verse 4, I read, "*And I persecuted this way unto the death.*" This violates the supposed law of arrangement, and falls under the charge of ambiguity. The gospel might, according to these critics, be understood from it to be a *way unto death* instead of a way unto life. Take again verse 29, " *Then they departed from him which should have examined him.*" Now we all know what this means. It is a more neat way of expressing what would be the regularly arranged sentence, " *Then they which should have examined him departed from him.*" But here again the captious and childish critic may find ambiguity—" Then they departed—from him which should have examined him." In Rom. xv. 31, St. Paul requests the Romans to pray that he may be " delivered from them that do not believe in Judæa." According to our fidgetty friend, this ought to mean, those who refuse to assent to a geographical fact.

260. **Grammar of our authorised version.**—I must not, however, forget that some of my correspondents find it convenient to depreciate the language and grammar of our authorised version of Scripture.[1] I would recommend

[1] One gentleman says : " When I was at school, it was the habit of my tutor to give his class specimens of bad English for correction. You will be surprised to hear, that those specimens were chiefly texts from Scripture. They were given with all reverence, nevertheless. It was because the readiest examples were to be had from the Bible, that any were taken from that source at all. Again, Shakspeare is held up by you as a pattern to modern grammarians. With all respect, I cannot understand how any man, with the education that you must have re-

them to try the experiment of amending that language. They may then perhaps find that what the translators themselves once said is true. A story is told, that they had a recommendation from a correspondent to alter a certain word in their version, giving *five* sufficient reasons for the change. They are said to have replied that they had already considered the matter, and had *fifteen* sufficient reasons *against* the change. I think if my correspondents can bring themselves to consider reasonably any passage in which the English grammar of our authorised version appears doubtful, they will find themselves in the same predicament as this correspondent of the translators. I have often tried the experiment, and this has generally been the result. Mind, our present question is not that of their having adequately translated the Greek, but whether or not they wrote their own language grammatically and clearly.

261. **Of Shakspeare.**—Still, lest I should seem to be a "man of one book only," I will give from our greatest English writer, an instance (from among many) of what would be called a similar ambiguity. In the "Two Gentlemen of Verona," (act i. sc. 2,) Julia says :—

> "O hateful hands, to tear such loving words!
> Injurious wasps, to feed on such sweet honey,
> And kill the bees that yield it with your stings."

According to my correspondents, we ought to understand this as saying that the bees yield the honey by means of the wasps' stings.

262. **Best way of proceeding in regard of such rules.**—But I conceive we have had enough of these so-called universal rules. All I would say on them to my younger readers is, the less you know of them, the less you turn your words right or left to observe them, the

ceived, could venture even to insinuate such a dogma as this. Any one, with even the insufficient light which Murray affords, may detect numberless errors in every play which Shakspeare has written." This is rich indeed. One can well conceive the sort of English which was taught at my correspondent's school. And very much of the degenerate English of our day is to be traced to such instruction. I should like to have seen some of the tutor's corrected texts.

better. Write good manly English; explain what you mean, as sensible intelligent men cannot fail to understand it, and then, if the rules be good, you will be sure to have complied with them; and if they be bad, your writing will be a protest against them. See the "Edinburgh Review," quoted in par. 287.

263. **Real ambiguity.**—It is not difficult to distinguish the sentences whose arrangement I have been defending, from those in which real ambiguity arises. Take the following as examples. I found it in one of the daily papers:—" The most interesting news from Italy is that of the trial of the thieves who robbed the bank of Messrs. Parodi at Genoa, on May 1, 1862, in open daylight, which commenced at Genoa on the 5th." In a letter addressed to another paper, this sentence occurs: " I with my family reside in the parish of Stockton, which consists of my wife and daughters."

264. **How arising.**—Now both these sentences are instructive to us. We may see from them how such ambiguity really arises: viz., by the occurrence, between the antecedent and its pronoun, of another word, which naturally suggests to the mind of the hearer a connection with the following pronoun. In both these sentences this is the case. Daylight is said to commence at a certain time, as well as a trial: a parish is said to consist of certain persons, as well as a family. Hence the ambiguity: and not, as is often maintained, from the mere form of the sentence. Any one so disposed may cull sentences out of any English writer, not even excepting Lord Macaulay, and show that they *may* be understood in a certain number of hundred, or thousand, different ways. But the simple answer is, that nobody ever *will* so understand them: and, as has been seen, there are often reasons why the apparently ambiguous form should be preferred to the strictly perspicuous one, as being more forcible, putting the emphatic word or clause in the proper place, or even as avoiding stiffness and awkwardness of sound. Let your style be idiomatic, simple, natural: aim at satisfying the common sense of those who read and hear, and then, though any one who has no better employment may pick holes in every third sentence, you will have written better English

than one who suffers the tyranny of small critics to cramp the expression of his thoughts.

265. **Note after a tithe dinner.**—The following note has been sent me, received after a tithe dinner in Devonshire: "Mr. T. presents his compliments to Mr. H., and I have got a hat that is not his, and if he have got a hat that is not yours, no doubt they are the expectant ones." It would defy any analysis to detect the source of confusion here. Perhaps "*he*" and "*his*" refer to some third person, not the Mr. H. who is addressed. But I fear we must look for the clew in the notice, "after a tithe dinner." Evidently, the effects of the banquet had not passed away.

266. **Clerical advertisement.**—The following clerical advertisement from a well-known paper has been sent by a correspondent: "A married A.B., now holding a sole charge, will be disengaged on 17th September. He is an extempore preacher of the doctrines of grace in all their sanctifying influence, and now seeks another." If the hearers of the advertiser fare the same as his readers, I fear the influence, however good, would not be very effectively administered. For it really costs no little ingenuity to discover that it is not another *doctrine* nor another *influence* which he wants, but another *sole charge*.

267. **Criticism of Fechter's "Hamlet."**—Here is another specimen, in this case an extract from a criticism of Mr. Fechter's "Hamlet," in a daily paper: "His whole system consists in playing the character upside down. He does not ignore tradition, but employs it so far that it enables him to do precisely the reverse. Dress, gait, action, everything, like his pronunciation, are alike unintelligible." This is indeed a delightful specimen of confusion, and obscurity, and bad English. What is *precisely the reverse* which his employment of tradition enables him to do? The reverse of what? Is it the reverse of ignoring tradition? Does the critic mean, that he employs tradition so far that it enables him not to ignore it? Surely this is not the meaning. After feeling about in the dark some time, we arrive at a sort of suspicion, that the meaning must be, that Mr. Fechter employs tradition so far, that it furnishes him with the means of flying in

the face of tradition—of contradicting the whole scope and tenor of tradition—of doing, in fact, precisely the reverse of that which an actor would do who scrupulously followed tradition. Bad as this sentence is, it might be matched ten times over any day on the table of a reading-room.

268. **The same term in different cases.**—Can we, in an elliptic sentence, use the same term, once only expressed, as doing duty both in the nominative and accusative cases? The late famous Oxford Declaration of the Clergy described the Canonical Scriptures as "not only containing but being the Word of God." The *meaning* was sufficiently clear: but is the phrase correct? I venture to think that it is not, and that it should rather have been said "not only containing the Word of God, but themselves being the Word of God." Both precision and propriety are thus better secured.

269. Indeed we may venture to lay it down as a rule, that in sentences where several forms of speech converge, so to speak, on one term, that term is better expressed or indicated after each of them, than reserved to be expressed or indicated once only at the end of all. "He not only requested an introduction to, but received with the utmost courtesy, placed himself by the side of, and from that day kept up friendly intercourse with, my young protégé," is far better written, "He not only requested an introduction to my young protégé, but received him with the utmost courtesy, placed himself by his side, and from that day kept up friendly intercourse with him." In this sentence, the change for the better is obvious: in many others, constructed in the former manner, it may not be so plain: but that the change is for the better, if judiciously made, will I think in every case be ultimately apparent.

270. **Position of adverbs: "only."**—Much has been said by my various correspondents about the placing of adverbs and other qualifying terms[1] in respect of the verbs or nouns with which they are connected; and the dispute has turned especially on the situation of the adverb "*only,*" with regard to its verb. "*Did you see a man and a woman?*" "*No; I only saw a man.*" This is our ordi-

---

[1] See this expression justified below, paragraph 376.

nary colloquial English. Is it wrong? Of course the pedant comes down on us, and says, "Yes; it is wrong. You want your adverb '*only*' to qualify, not your act of seeing, but the number of persons whom you saw. The proper opposition to '*I only saw a man*' would be '*I saw and heard a man*,' or '*I saw and touched him.*'" So far the pedant; now for common sense. Common sense at once replies, "I beg the pedant's pardon; he says I didn't want the adverb '*only*' to qualify my act of seeing. I say, I did. For what was the act of seeing? The two things to be opposed are two acts of seeing. Seeing a man, and seeing a man and a woman. It was not the same sight. I only performed the one; I did not go further, and perform the other. I only saw a man; I did not see a man and a woman." Of course the other way is right also, and, strictly speaking, the more technically exact of the two; but it by no means follows that the more exact expression is also the better English. Very often we cannot have exactness and smoothness together. Wherever this is the case, the harsher method of constructing the sentence is, in colloquial English, abandoned, even at the risk of exactness and school rules. The adverb "*only*," in many sentences where strictly speaking it ought to follow its verb and to limit the objects of the verb, is in good English placed before the verb.

271. Let us take an example of this from the great storehouse of good English, our Authorised Version of the Scriptures. In Ps. lxii. 4, we read, "They only consult to cast him down from his excellency;" *i.e.*, their consultation is on one subject only, how to cast him down. See also Matt. xiv. 36.

272. The account of the matter before us is just this: I may use my adverb "*only*" where two things are spoken of which are affected by the same action, to qualify the one as distinguished from the other, or I may, if I will, separate the action into two parts, the one having regard to the one thing acted on, and the other having regard to the other; and I may make use of my adverb to qualify one part of the action as compared with the other. If I say, "*I will state only one thing more*," I mean, that being about to state, I will confine that action to one thing and

not extend it to any more; if I say, "*I will only state one thing more*," I mean that all I will do is, to make one statement, not more. But our gentlemen with their rules never look about to see whether usage is not justified; they find a sentence not arranged as their books say it ought to be, and it is instantly set down as wrong, in spite of the common sense and practice of all England being against them.

273. " Both."—This last-mentioned adverb is not the only word whose position is thus questioned: "*both*" is another. This word, we are told, should always be placed strictly before the former of the words to which it belongs in the sentence, not before the verb or noun which applies equally to the two. Thus, if I say "*They broke down both the door of the stable and of the cellar*," I am charged with having violated the rules of good English. The pedant would have it, "*They broke down the door both of the stable and of the cellar.*" Now, to my mind, the difference between these two sentences is, that the former is plain colloquial English: the latter is harsh and cramped, and could not have been written by a sensible man, but only by a man who thought less about conveying the sense of what he said, than about the rules by which his expression should be regulated. But let us see how the great masters of our English tongue wrote. Let us balance Shakspeare against Lindley Murray. In the "Tempest," (act i. sc. 2,) Prospero tells Miranda that the usurping Duke of Milan, her uncle,

" Having both the key
Of officer and office, set all hearts i' th' state
To what tune pleased his ear."

This is, of course, a clear violation of the rule; according to which the words ought to have run, "*having the key of both officer and office.*"

274. " The three first Gospels."—As connected with the question of the arrangement of words, I may mention that I have been in controversy, first and last, with several people,[1] while I have been engaged on my edition of the Greek Testament, about the expression "*the three first*

[1] See paragraph 472, bel w.

Gospels." My correspondents invariably maintain that this expression, which I always use, must be an oversight, and that I ought to say "*the first three Gospels.*" I should like to argue this out; and the present seems a good opportunity for doing so.

275. There are Four Gospels, as we all know. And such is the distinctive character of the three which are placed first, as compared with the one which is placed last, that it often becomes necessary to speak of the three, and the one, in two separate classes. It is in doing so that I say "*the three first Gospels,*" and my correspondents want me to say "*the first three Gospels.*" Which of the two is right? or, if both are right, which of the two is the better?

276. My view is this. The whole number is divided into two classes: the *first* class, and the *last* class. To the former of these belong three: to the latter belongs one. There are three that are ranged under the description "*first:*" and there is one that is ranged under the description "*last.*" Just in this way are the two classes spoken of in that saying of our Lord, "There are last which shall be first, and there are first which shall be last." (Luke xiii. 30.) It is not necessary that *one only* should be spoken of as first, and *one only* as last, as this quotation shows. The whole class is first, as compared with the whole other class which is last. Of twelve persons I may make two classes, and speak of the *five first,* and the *seven last.* This is a correct and logical way of speaking. The opposition between the two classes is as strict and complete, as when I say that of twelve men there are five tall and seven short. If then I wish to divide twelve men into two classes, I say, and I maintain I say rightly, *the five first* and *the seven last.* If I wish to divide the four Gospels into two classes, I say, and maintain I say rightly, the *three first* Gospels, and the last Gospel.

277. Now let us try the correctness of the other expression, "*the first three Gospels.*" Used in common talk, it would of course convey the same idea as the other. But that is not our present question. Our question is, which of the two is the more precise and correct? When I say "*the first three,*" the idea presented to the mind is, that I am going to speak of *another three,* which shall be set in

contrast to them. The proper opposition to "*a tall man*" is "*a short man*," not a short *stick*. When therefore I take twelve men, and dividing them into two classes, speak of the tall five and the short seven, I may be intelligible, but I certainly am not speaking precisely nor properly. And so when I take four Gospels, and, dividing them into two classes, speak of "*the first three*," and "*the last one*," I may be complying with technical rules, but I maintain that I am not complying with the requirements of common sense, and therefore neither with those of good English.

278. A correspondent writes:—"As to the '*three first Gospels*,' your explanation is clear. But would it be right to say, ' in the *three first weeks* of the quarter, the receipts were below the average?' and if not, why not?" In my opinion, it would be perfectly right to speak thus; and in the particular instance given, "the three first weeks" would be better than "the first three weeks," for another reason; that "*three weeks*" being a not unusual designation of the portion of time extending over three weeks, the expression, "the first three weeks" would fail to direct the attention to the receipts week by week, which appears to be the desire of the speaker.

279. Another correspondent says, "I should once have sided with your opponents as to 'the *three first* Gospels:' but I am convinced by your arguments." "I think, however," he continues, "you would not defend what we often hear from the pulpit, or even more commonly from the clerk's desk. 'In the third chapter of St. John, the three last verses, are these words:' Or, 'Let us sing the three first and the three last verses of the 92nd Psalm.'"

280. To this I answer, Why not? The "three first" verses are, the three verses whose place, with reference to the rest, is first. It is only a short way of saying, the three verses which come first: and so of the "three last." Look at our daily procession into church. What is the order? The Choristers are first: *First*, is a quality which may be predicated of them just as being in white surplices may be: they are the twelve first in order: or more briefly, they are "*the twelve first*." Then come the Lay Clerks, the twelve next in order, or in brief, "*the twelve next*." Then come the clergy, the *four*, or *seven*, or *twelve last*.

281. Hardly any good English expression gets so much wrath expended on it as this "*three first*," or "*three last*." It was but the other day that I had a whole vial of scorn poured over me because I have used it in my edition of the Greek Testament: the Reviewer being of course not aware that this is done of malice prepense, and because it is believed to be right.

282. One another.—Ought we to say, "*be kind to one another*," or "*be kind one to another*"? The latter is beyond question the more correct, and is found in the English Version of the Scriptures in such phrases as, "Be kindly affectioned one to another in brotherly love." But the former has become almost idiomatic, and the other would sound pedantic in conversation.

283. The history of the inaccuracy may be thus traced. When we say, "Love one another," "one another" is not a compound word in the objective case after the verb, but is two words, the former in the nominative, the latter in the objective case: in Latin, "Diligite alius alium:" one love another. But the ear has become so accustomed to the sound of "*one another*" pronounced together, that we have come to regard that sound as indicating a compound word, and to treat it as such after a preposition.

284. Each other—The same is the case with "each other." "Love each other," is "Love each the other:" and so when a preposition intervenes, we ought properly to say, "Each to the other." But we do not, and never shall. Idiom has prevailed, even when established in a mistake, over strict propriety.

285. Confused use of "he" and "it."—Fault has been found with me by some of my correspondents and censors, for the confused use, as they are pleased to regard it, of the personal pronouns "he" and "it." Now here is another matter on which they and I are entirely at issue. A rule is cited from Dr. Campbell, that "wherever the pronoun 'he' will be ambiguous, because two or more males happen to be mentioned in the same clause of a sentence, we ought always to give another turn to the expression, or to use the noun itself and not the pronoun: for when the repetition of a word is necessary, it is not offensive. The translators of the Bible," continues Dr. C.,

" have often judiciously used this method: I say judiciously, because though the other method be on some occasions preferable, yet, by attempting the other they would have run a much greater risk of destroying " (he means " a much greater risk, namely, that of destroying ") "that beautiful simplicity which is an eminent characteristic of Holy Writ. I shall take an instance from the speech of Judah to his brother Joseph in Egypt: ' We said to my lord, the lad cannot leave his father, for if he should leave his father, his father would die.' The words ' his father' are in this short verse thrice repeated, and yet are not disagreeable, as they contribute to perspicuity. Had the last part of the sentence run thus: 'if he should leave his father he would die,' it would not have appeared from the expression whether it was the child or the parent that would die."

286. So far Dr. Campbell, "Philosophy of Rhetoric." Now it so happens, that although Dr. Campbell has been able to find an instance to illustrate his point, this is a matter about which the translators of the Bible, and indeed the best of our English writers, *care very little;* of this, numerous instances might be produced out of our English Bible. I will content myself with two: the first from 2 Kings i. 9: "Then the king sent unto him a captain of fifty with his fifty: and he went up to him : and behold, he sat on the top of an hill." To common sense it is plain enough who is meant in each case by *he* and *him*, and I don't suppose a mistake was ever made about it: but the sentence is in direct violation of Dr. Campbell's rule. Again, in Luke xix. 3, 4, we read of Zaccheus: "And he sought to see Jesus who he was ; and could not for the press, because he was little of stature. And he ran before, and climbed up into a sycamore tree to see him: for he was to pass that way." Now here you see the pronouns "*he*" and "*him*" are used indiscriminately, sometimes of our Lord, sometimes of Zaccheus : and yet every one knows to whom to apply each of them. The caviller might find ambiguity over and over again ; and accordingly one of my censors says of this very example, " you surely do not defend the construction of these sentences?" All I can tell him is, they run thus in the *original:* and this, our

translators very well knew, is not a matter of the grammar of our language, but of all languages, belonging in fact to the laws of human thought. As to the translators having, as Dr. Campbell says, often judiciously used the other method, the expression is peculiarly unfortunate. Our translators rendered most commonly what they found in the original, and very rarely indeed would have thought of repeating the noun where the original had the pronoun. In the example from Genesis, it would have been better if they had not repeated the words "his father" the third time, but had left the sentence ambiguous, as I believe it is in the original Hebrew.

287. Quotation from "Edinburgh Review."—The "Edinburgh Review" (July, 1864), in treating with just contempt the objections of these eager discoverers of ambiguities, makes the following very sensible remarks : " If a man writes in a way which cannot be misunderstood by a reader of common candour and intelligence, he has done all, as regards clearness, that can be expected of him. To attempt more is to ask of language more than language can perform: the consequences of attempting it any one may see who will spend an hour with the Statutes at large. ' Jack was very respectful to Tom, and always took off his hat when he met him. Jack was very rude to Tom, and always knocked off his hat when he met him.' Will any one pretend that either of these sentences is ambiguous in meaning, or unidiomatic in expression ? Yet critics of the class now before us are bound to contend that Jack showed his respect by taking off Tom's hat, or else that he showed his rudeness by knocking off his own. It is useless to multiply examples; no book was ever written that could stand a hostile examination in this spirit : and one that could stand it would be totally unreadable."

288. I will add a story serving to show the usefulness, on certain occasions, of these penny-wise grammarians. The churchwardens of a parish near Bristol, having reason to make a presentation to the Bishop, met to draw it up. Churchwarden A brought the draft, beginning, "My Lord . . ." But Churchwarden B was a man of education, with the rules of grammar ever on his tongue. "My" was of course incorrect, where the "presenters" were two persons. The presentation, he maintained, ought to be

corrected; and it narrowly escaped going up to the Bishop addressed to him as "*Our Lord*..."[1]

289. Does "than" govern an accusative case?—What are we to think of the question, whether "*than*" does or does not govern an accusative case? "*than I :* " "*than me :* " which is right? My readers will probably answer without hesitation, the former. But is the latter so certainly wrong? We are accustomed to hear it stigmatised as being so; but I think, erroneously. Milton writes, (" Paradise Lost," ii. 299,)—

" Which when Beelzebub perceived, than whom,
Satan except, none higher sat."

And thus every one of us would speak: "than who" would be intolerable. And this seems to settle the question.

290. Two ways of constructing "than."—The fact is, that there are two ways of constructing a clause with a comparative and "*than.*" You may say either "*than I*" or "*than me.*" If you say the former, you use what is called an elliptical expression: *i.e.*, an expression in which something is left out;—and that something is the verb "*am.*" "He is wiser than I," being filled out, would be, "He is wiser than I am :" "He is wiser than me," is the direct and complete construction. The difference between the two usages seems to be this: and it is curiously confirmative of what has been sometimes observed, that men in ordinary converse shrink, in certain cases, from the use of the bare nominative of the personal pronoun. Where solemnity is required, the construction in the nominative is used. Our Lord's words will occur to us (John xiv. 28), "My Father is greater than I." But in ordinary conversation this construction is generally avoided, as sounding too weighty and formal. In colloquial talk we commonly say either "He is older than me," or perhaps more frequently, "He is older than I am." And so with the other personal pronouns, *he, she, we,* and *they.*

291. Dr. Latham in mentioning this construction (to which, however, he prefers the other) quotes from Prior,

" Thou art a girl, as much brighter than her,
As he is a poet sublimer than me : "

and from Swift,

" You are a much greater loser than me."

[1] See Appendix.

But he does not treat "*than whom*," an expression which leaves no choice, as not admitting of an elliptic construction, and which therefore, as above observed, seems decisive.

292. Still it is urged that "than me" cannot be right: or can only be right when "me" is necessarily in government, as in the sentence, "He likes you better than me." I can do no more in reply, than urge the necessity of saying, "than whom," to show that "*than*" can and does really govern an objective case by its own power, and therefore may govern "me," or "him," or "her," or "them," if we choose so to construct the sentence.

293. It is me.—The mention of the nominative and accusative of the personal pronoun seems not inaptly to introduce a discussion of the well-known and much controverted phrase, "It is me." Now this is an expression which every one uses. Grammarians (of the smaller order) protest: schoolmasters (of the lower kind) prohibit and chastise; but English men, women, and children go on saying it, and will go on saying it as long as the English language is spoken. Here is a phenomenon worth accounting for. "Not at all so," say our censors: "don't trouble yourself about it; it is a mere vulgarism. Leave it off yourself, and try to persuade every one else to leave it off."

294. But I cannot. I write a letter inviting a friend who is very particular on these points, to come to Canterbury. I write in some fear and trembling. All my adverbs are (what I should call) misplaced, that I may not offend him. But at last, I am obliged to transgress, in spite of my good resolutions. I am promising to meet him at the station, and I was going to write: "if you see on the platform '*an old party in a shovel*,' that will be I." But my pen refuses to sanction (to *endorse*, I believe I ought to say, but I cannot) the construction. "*That will be me*" comes from it, in spite, as I said, of my resolve of the best possible behaviour.

295. Of course it will be obvious, that in the independently constructed clause "that will be me (or I)," no difference whatever in the case of the personal pronoun can be made by its previous construction in the sentence. The mention of such an idea needs an apology: but it has

been actually maintained that the accusative is right in this clause, because the personal pronoun represents a noun governed by the verb "see.": "that will be me [you will see]."

296. Dr. Latham's opinion.—Let us see what a real grammarian says on the matter: one who does not lay down rules only, but is anxious to ascertain on what usages are founded. Dr. Latham, in his admirable "History of the English Language," (p. 586,) says, "We may .... call the word *me* a secondary nominative: inasmuch as such phrases as *it is me* = *it is I*, are common. To call such expressions incorrect English, is to assume the point. No one says that *c'est moi* is bad French, and *c'est je* is good. The fact is that, with us, the whole question is a question of degree. Has or has not the custom been sufficiently prevalent to have transferred the forms *me*, *ye*, and *you*, from one case to another? Or perhaps we may say, is there any real custom at all in favour of *I*, except so far as the grammarians have made one? It is clear that the French analogy is against it. It is also clear that the personal pronoun as a predicate may be in a different analogy from the personal pronoun as a subject."

297. And in another place, (p. 584,) he says: "What if the current objections to such expressions as *it is me* (which the ordinary grammarians would change into *it is I*), be unfounded, or rather founded upon the ignorance of this difference (the difference between the use of the pronoun as subject and as predicate)? That the present writer defends this (so-called) vulgarism may be seen elsewhere. It may be seen elsewhere, that he finds nothing worse in it than a Frenchman finds in *c'est moi*, where, according to the English dogma, *c'est je* would be the right expression. Both constructions, the English and the French, are predicative: and when constructions are predicative, a change is what we must expect rather than be surprised at."

298. The account which Dr. Latham has here given, is doubtless the right one. There is a disposition, when the personal pronoun is used predicatively, to put it into the accusative case. That this is more prevalent in the pronoun of the first person singular than in the others, may perhaps arise from the fact which Dr. Latham has else-

I

where established, that *me* is not the proper, but only the adopted accusative of *I*, being in fact a distinct and independent form of the personal pronoun. As he elsewhere expresses it, " They (*I* and *me*) are not only two words, but the names for two different ideas." But it may fairly be asked, whence arises this disposition to shrink from the use of the nominative case in the predicate? For it does not apply to all instances where the pronoun is predicative. " He said unto them, it is I: be not afraid." This is a capital instance: for it shows us at once why the nominative should be sometimes used. The Majesty of the Speaker here, and His purpose of re-assuring the disciples by the assertion that it was none other than Himself, at once point out to us the case in which it would be proper for the nominative, and not the accusative, to be used.[1]

299. " It is him," " it is her."—Dr. Latham goes on to say, after the first of my two citations, (p. 587,) " At the same time it must be observed, that the expression, *it is me = it is I*, will not justify the use of *it is him, it is her = it is he*, and *it is she*. *Me, ye, you*, are what may be called *indifferent* forms, *i.e.*, nominative as much as accusative, and accusative as much as nominative. *Him* and *her*, on the other hand, are not indifferent. The *-m* and *-r*, are respectively the signs of cases other than the nominative."

300. But is this quite consistent with the idea that the categorical use of the pronoun in the predicate may be different from that of the same pronoun as a subject? *Me* may not have been the original accusative case of *I*: but it is unquestionably the adopted accusative, in constant use as such. Where lies the difference, *grammatically*, between *it is me*, and *it is him*, or *it is her*, as far as present usage is concerned? It seems to me that, if we are prepared to defend the one, we ought in consistency also to defend the other. When, in the Ingoldsby legend, the monks of Rheims saw the poor anathematised jackdaw appear, " Regardless of grammar, they cried out, 'That's him!'" And I fear we must show an equal disregard of *what ordinarily passes for grammar*, if we would give a correct account of the

---

[1] The predicate in the *question*, " Is it I ? " (Matt. xxvi. 22), is hardly perhaps a case in point.

prevalent usages of our language. At all events, in so doing we shall be following our best writers. Cowley has,

"Say what thou wilt, Chastity is no more
Thee, than a porter is his door." [1]

301. There is one form of construction which is sometimes regarded as coming under the present question, but

[1] I venture to reprint here, as of great interest, Mr. Ellis's letter to the " Reader," of May 7, 1864 :—

"'IT'S ME.'
" *To the Editor of* 'THE READER.'
"Colney Hatch Park, 30 April, 1864.

" SIR,—In reference to your remarks on *it's me* in your notice of Dean Alford's 'Plea for the Queen's English,' I consider that the phrase *it is I* is a modernism, or rather a grammaticism—that is, it was never in popular use, but was introduced solely on some grammatical hypothesis as to having the same case before and after the verb *is*. It does not appear to have been consonant with the feelings of Teutonic tribes to use the nominative of the personal pronouns as a predicate. To them —and therefore to English people—*it is I* is just as strange as *est ego*, ἐστὶ ἐγώ, would be to Latin or Greek. These last languages require *ego sum*, ἐγώ εἰμι (Matt. xiv. 27 ; Mark vi. 50 ; John vi. 20). The predicate was here simply omitted. In Gothic we have precisely the same construction, *ik im* (John vi. 20). The English Wycliffite translations both give *I am*. But the Anglo-Saxon version, like the modern German, is not content with leaving the predicate unexpressed, and we find *ic hit eom;* High German, *ich bin es* ; literally, *I am it;* namely, *that which you see*. The Heliand paraphrase is very explicit (Schmeller's ed., p. 90, line 2), ' *Ik bium that barn Godes* ' (' I am the Son of God '). The Welsh and Gaelic try to be emphatic, the first saying *myfi ydyw* (q. d. myself am), and the second, *is mise a ta ann* (q. d. it's myself that's living). But of course we do not look to these languages as a guide to English. The Danish is very peculiar and important on account of its intimate relation with English. As in English, the dative and accusative cases of the personal pronouns now coincide in Danish, *Jeg, mig* (I, me); *Du, dig* (thou, thee) ; *Han, ham* (he, him). We find the following rule laid down in Tobiesen's *Dänische Sprachlehre* (Sternhagen's ed., 1828, p. 215) :—' After the impersonal verbs, *det er* and *det bliver* (it is), the personal pronouns *jeg, du, han* are not used in the nominative, but in the dative, as *der er mig der har gjort det* (it's me that did it) ; *det er dig, som har været mester derfor* (it's thee who was its master) ; *det bliver ham, som vi ville tale med* (it's him that we wish to speak with) ; [where also the construction of the relative and preposition is English]; and similarly in the plural : *det er os, jer, dem* (it's us, you, them).' This is perfectly explicit, and shows the same construction as the English ; but, in the Testament, the wish to be uncolloquial has apparently forced the trans-

with which, in fact, it is not concerned. I mean that occurring in such phrases as "*You didn't know it to be me*," "*I suspected it to be him.*" In these, the accusative cases, are simply in government, and nominatives would be altogether ungrammatical. The verb substantive takes the same case after it as went before it. It is in fact, in these sentences, equivalent to *as*, or *as being*. "*You didn't know it to be I*," would be equivalent to "*you didn't recognise it as I*," which of course would be wrong.

302. "**You and I,**" **accusative.**—A correspondent asks me to notice "a usage now becoming prevalent among persons who ought to know better: viz. that of 'you and I,' after prepositions governing the accusative." He gives an instance from "Bothwell," a poem by Professor Aytoun, (p. 199):

"But it were vain for you and I
In single fight our strength to try."

On the impropriety of this there can of course be only one opinion. "Perhaps," my correspondent adds, "Professor Aytoun may have read 'John Gilpin,' and, innocent himself of cockneyisms, may have supposed that it is good English to say

"On horseback after *we*."

303. "**As thee.**"—When Thomson, in "Rule Britannia," wrote "The nations not so blest as thee," was he writing correct English? I venture to think he was. *As*, like *than*, is capable of being used in two distinct constructions, the elliptic, and the complete. "*As thou*" is the elliptic

lator to depart from the usual custom when the words are given to Jesus, but he returns to it when they are echoed by Peter (Matt. xiv. 27, 28). ' *Jesus—sagde:—det er jeg,—men Ped r—sagde: Herre, dersom det er dij, ba byd mig,*' &c. ('Jesus said, It is I; but Peter said, Lord, if it is *thee*, bid me,' &c.) The conclusion seems to be that *it's me* is good English, and *it's I* is a mistaken purism. We have now, I think, come to regard the objective form of the personal pronoun as a *predicative* form, and this will justify *that's him*, although the Danes still say ' *denne er han* ' (' that's he '). We are therefore in the same condition as the French with their ' *c'est moi,*' though we have not quite reached their ' *lui n'osait pas*' ('*him* didn't dare '). "ALEXANDER J. ELLIS."

It will be curious if, after all, it should be proved that our much-abused colloquial phrase is the really good English, and its rival "a mistaken purism."

construction, requiring the verb substantive for its completion, "*as thou art.*" "*As thee,*" like "than whom," is the complete construction, in which the conjunction of comparison has a quasi-prepositional force, and governs the pronoun in the objective case. The construction cited from Sir Walter Scott by one of my critics as faulty,

> "Yet oft in Holy Writ we see
> Even such weak minister as me
> May the oppressor bruise,"

is perfectly correct: not, it is true, the usual form of expression, or the more elegant, but one to which, on purely grammatical grounds, there is no objection. The attempt which my critic makes to convict it of error by assuming it to be the elliptical form, *such . . . as me* (am), only shows how much some of us need reminding of the first principles of the syntax of our language.

304. A correspondent enquired whether Pope's lines,

> "Who shall decide when doctors disagree,
> And soundest casuists doubt, like you and me?"

involve a grammatical error—whether they ought not to end "like you and I?" Here the answer is very plain. The querist has been misled by the elliptical theory of such clauses, fancying that the verb "doubt" should be supplied at the end, and that "like you and me" must be wrong, because we cannot say "like you and me doubt." But, as we shall see further on (par. 470), "like you and I doubt" is an inadmissible vulgarism: and in consequence, the elliptical construction is here out of the question. "*Like*" (= like unto) governs both personal pronouns in the objective case. If precedents are created for this, we have them in abundance: "There was none like thee before thee" (1 Kings iii. 12): "Others said He is like him" (John ix. 9), and often. A nominative case after "like" is never found.

305. **Use of "of."**—We have said something of superfluous prepositions: let us remark on the use of prepositions themselves. The preposition "*of*" is sometimes hardly dealt with. When I read in an article in the *Times*, on a late annexation, "What can the Emperor possibly want of these provinces of Savoy?" I saw at once that the writer

must be a native of the midland counties, where your friends complain that you have not "*called of them of a long time.*" Now in this case it is not the expression, but the sense meant to be conveyed by it, that is objectionable. "What can the Emperor want of these 'provinces?" is very good English, if we mean "What request has he to make of these provinces?" But if we mean, as the *Times'* writer evidently did, "What does he *want with* the provinces?" *i.e.*, "What need has he of them?" then it is a vulgarism.

306. There is a peculiar use of prepositions, which is allowable in moderation, but must not be too often resorted to. It is the placing them at the end of a sentence, as I have just done in the words "resorted to;" as is done in the command, "Let not your good be evil spoken of;" and continually in our discourse and writing.

307. **Prepositions at the end of sentences.**—The account to be given of this is, that the preposition, which the verb usually takes after it, is regarded as forming a part of the word itself. To *speak of*, to *resort to*, are hardly verbs and prepositions, but form in each case almost one word. But let us go on. "Where do you come from?" is the only way of putting that inquiry. "Whence come you?" is of course pedantic, though accurate. "Where are you going to?" is exactly like the other question, but here we usually drop the "*to*," merely because the adverb of rest "*where*," has come to be used for the adverb of motion "*whither*," and therefore the "*to*" is not wanted. If a man chooses, as West-country men mostly do, to say, "Where are you going to?" he does not violate propriety, though he does violate custom. But let us go further still. *Going to* has not only a *local*, it has also a mental meaning, being equivalent to *intending* in the mind. And this usage rests on exactly the same basis as the other. The "*to*" of the infinitive mood is precisely the same preposition as the "*to*" of motion towards a place. "Were you going to do it?" simply means "Were you, in your mental intention, approaching the doing of it?" And the proper conversational answer to such a question is, "I was going to," or "I was not going to," as the case may be; not "I was going," or "I was not going," inasmuch as the mere verb

to go does not express any mental intention. I know, in saying this, that I am at variance with the rules taught at very respectable institutions for enabling young ladies to talk unlike their elders; but this I cannot help; and I fear this is an offence of which I have been, and yet may be, very often guilty.

308. This kind of colloquial abbreviation of the infinitive comprehends several more phrases in common use, and often similarly objected to, e.g., " *ought to*," and " *ought not to*," "*neglect to*," &c., some of them not very elegant, but all quite unobjectionable on the score of grammar. These abbreviations are very common in the West of England, and are there carried further than any reason will allow.

309. In many cases of this kind we have a choice whether the preposition shall precede or follow the object of the sentence. Thus I may say, " *the man to whom I had written*," or " *the man whom I had written to.*" In this particular instance, the former is the more elegant, and would usually be said: but this is not always so; e.g., " *You're the man I wanted to have some talk with*," would always be said; not " *You're the man with whom I wanted to have some talk*," which would sound stilted and pedantic.

310. **Present, past, and perfect tenses.**—The next thing I shall mention, not for its own sake, but as a specimen of the kind of criticism which I am often meeting with, and as instructive to those who wish to be critics of other men's language. I have said that " Dr. Donne *preaches* " so and so. My correspondent takes exception to this, and tells me that Dr. Donne has been dead some two hundred years, and therefore I ought to say Dr. Donne *preached*, and not *preaches*. This may seem mere trifling: but it is worth while to notice, that we speak thus, in the present tense, of writings permanently placed on record. Their authors, being dead, yet speak to us. It would be affected and unusual to speak otherwise of things cited from books. If we use the past tense at all, it is not the indefinite, but the perfect, which also conveys the idea of a living and acting even now. I should say, " Dr. Donne *has explained* this text thus or thus;" not " Dr. Donne *explained* this text thus or thus." This latter sentence

would bear a different meaning. If I say "Livy *writes*," or "Livy *has written*, so and so," I imply that the book containing the incident is now extant. But if I say, "Livy *wrote* so and so," I should naturally be taken to be speaking of something reported as having been written in one of the books of his history which have been lost. You may say of a sick man yet living, "He has lost much strength during the week." But the moment he is dead, you can no longer thus speak: you must say, "He lost much strength during the week." If I say, "I have seen Wales twice," I carry the period during which my assertion is true through my whole life down to the present time. If I say "I saw Wales twice," my words simply refer to the fact, and the period to which they refer is understood to have terminated. I mean, in my youth, or when I was in Cheshire, or the like. Sometimes the difference between the two tenses may convey an interesting moral distinction. If I say, "My father left me an injunction to do this or that," I leave the way open to say, "but now circumstances have changed, and I find another course more advisable:" if I say "My father has left me an injunction to do this or that," I imply that I am at this moment obeying, and mean to obey, that injunction. The perfect tense is in fact a present, relating to the effect, at the present time, of some act done in the past.[1]

311. **Their confusion.**—An important difference in meaning is sometimes made by the wrong or careless use of one of these tenses for the other. An instance of this occurs in the English Version of the Bible in the beginning of Acts xix. There we read, in the original, that St. Paul finding certain disciples at Ephesus, asked them, "Did ye receive the Holy Ghost when ye believed—when ye first became believers?" To this they answered, "We did not so much as hear whether there were any Holy Ghost." On which St. Paul asked them, "Unto what then were ye baptized?" They replied, "Unto the baptism of John." Then he explained to them that John's baptism, being only a baptism of repentance, did not bring with it the

---

[1] The confusion between these tenses is sometimes curious. "I call," says an Irish correspondent, "at the office of a gentleman who is expected every minute, and am told, 'He didn't come to-day,' or, 'He did't come yet.'"

gift of the Holy Ghost. In this account, all is clear. But the English Version, by an unfortunate mistake, has rendered the narrative unintelligible. It has made St. Paul ask the converts, "Have ye received the Holy Ghost since ye believed?" So far, indeed, all would be clear; for they certainly had not, though this does not represent what was said by the Apostle. But it is their answer which obscures the history: "We have not so much as heard," they are made to say, "whether there be any Holy Ghost." Strange indeed, that these disciples, who had probably been for years in the Church, should during that time, and up to the time when St. Paul spoke, never have heard of the existence of the Holy Spirit. Render the words accurately, and all is clear.

312. "**Was being written.**"—I am now going to speak of a combination of words which is so completely naturalised, that it would be vain to protest against it, or even to attempt to disuse it one's self. I mean, the joining together of a present and a past participle, as we do when we say "*The letter was being written,*" "*The dinner is being cooked.*" Such combinations were, I believe, not used by our best and most careful writers, until a comparatively recent date. The old and correct way of expressing what is meant by these phrases was, "*The letter was in writing,*" or "*was writing;*" "*The dinner is cooking:*" the verbs being used in a neuter sense. The objection to "*being written*" for "*in the process of writing,*" is this,—that "*written*" is a past participle, indicating a finished act. When I say "*I have written a letter,*" I mean, I have by me, or have as my act accomplished, a letter written. So that "*being written*" properly means, existing in a state of completion. "*My letter being written, I put it in the post.*" And, strictly speaking, we cannot use the combination to signify an *incomplete* action. Still, as I have said, the inaccuracy has crept into the language, and is now found everywhere, in speech and in writing. The only thing we can do in such a case is to avoid it, where it can be avoided without violation of idiom, or giving harshness to the sentence.

313. "**Shall**" and "**will.**"—The next point which I notice shall be the use of the auxiliaries "*shall*" and "*will.*" Now here we are at once struck by a curious

phenomenon. I never knew an Englishman who misplaced "*shall*" and "*will:*" I hardly ever have known an Irishman or a Scotchman who did not misplace them sometimes. And it is strange to observe how incurable the propensity is. It was but the other day that I asked a person sprung of Irish blood, whether he would be at a certain house to which I was going that evening. The answer was, "*I'm afraid I won't.*" Yet my friend is a sound and accurate English scholar and writer, and I had never before, during all the years I had known him, discovered any trace of the sister island.

314. In attempting to give an explanation of our English usage, I may premise that it is exceedingly difficult to do so. We seem to proceed rather on instinct, than by any fixed rule. Yet instinct, in rational beings, must be founded on some inherent fitness of things; and examination ought to be able to detect that fitness. Let us try to do this, though it may be difficult, in the case before us.

315. "I will."—The simplest example that can be given is "*I will.*" Now this can have but one meaning. It can only be used as expressing determination: only, where the will of the person speaking is concerned. "Wilt thou have this woman to thy wedded wife?" Answer, "I will" (in the Latin, "*volo*"). We cannot use "*I will,*" where a mere contingent future event is concerned. We cannot use "*I will*" of anything uncertain, anything about which we hope or fear. "Help me, I'll fall," if strictly interpreted, would be an entreaty to be saved from an act of wilful precipitation. "*I fear I won't*" is an impossible and unmeaning junction of terms. If it meant anything, it could only be, "I fear that, when the time comes, my power of volition will be found too weak for its work." But this is obviously not what it is intended to mean. The account then of "*I will*" seems very simple.

316. "I shall."—Now, what is "*I shall*"? In its ordinary use, it just takes those cases of things future, where "*I will*" cannot be said: those cases where the things spoken of are independent of our own will. "*Next Tuesday I shall be twenty-one*"—an event quite out of my own power. So far, all is plain. But there is a case of "*I shall*" which somewhat complicates the matter. We are

in the habit, when announcing something which we positively mean to do, to speak of it as if it were taken, so to say, out of the region of our own will, and placed among things absolutely certain ; and in such cases we turn " *will* " into "*shall*." The traveller meets with incivility, or he cannot find his luggage at the station. He breaks forth, in angry mood, "*I shall write to the ' Times ' about this*,"— and he means the station-master to conclude that his writing is as certain as if it were already done. The "*shall*" is intended to elevate the "*will*" into the category of things indisputable.

317. "You will."—So far then for "*will*" and "*shall*" when used in the first person. But how when used in the second? Let us take " *You will*." " *You will* " is used when speaking to another person of a matter entirely out of the speaker's power and jurisdiction. " *You will be twenty-one next Tuesday*." " *If you climb that ladder you will fall*." This is the ordinary use. Here again there is an exception, which I cannot well treat till I have spoken of " *You shall*."

318. "You shall."—" *You shall* " or " *You shall not* " is said to another, when the will of the speaker compels that which is spoken of. " *Thou shalt love the Lord thy God*." " *Thou shalt not steal*."

319. Exceptions.—The exceptions to both these usages may be stated thus, and they are nearly related to that of which I spoke when on the first person. A master writes to his servant, " *On the receipt of this you will go*," or " *you will please to go*," " *to such a place*." This is treating the obedience of the servant as a matter of certainty, sure to follow of course on his lord's command. The exception in the use of " *shall* " is that we may say, for instance, " *If you look through History, you shall find that it has always been so*," and the account of it seems to be, that the speaker feels as perfect a certainty of the result, as if it were not contingent, but depended only on his absolute command.

320. " Will " and " shall " in the third person.—It remains that we consider the words " *will* " and " *shall* " as applied in the third person ; said of persons and things spoken about. And here, what has already been said will

be a sufficient guide in ordinary cases. For all announcements of common events foreseen in the future, "*will*" is the word to be used. "*I think it will rain before night.*" "*To-morrow will be old May-day.*" We may sometimes use "*shall*," but it can only be in cases where our own will, or choice, or power, exercises some influence over the events spoken of: as for instance, "*The sun shall not set to-night before I find out this matter.*" "*Next Tuesday shall be the day.*" Notice, you would not say, "*Next Tuesday shall be my birthday;*" you must say, "*Next Tuesday will be my birthday;*" because that is a matter over which you have no control: but the Queen might say, "*Next Tuesday shall be my birthday;*" because she would mean, "*shall be kept as my birthday,*" a matter over which she has control.

321. **Instances of almost indifferent usage.**—There are some very delicate and curious cases of the almost indifferent usage of the two auxiliary verbs. Take this one. "*If he will look, he will find it to be so.*" Here we use the first "*will*" in the sense of "*choose to:*" "*If he please to look.*" But the second has its mere future use: "*he will find that it is so.*" Here however we might use, though it would be somewhat pedantic English, the word "*shall*" in both members of the sentence: "*If he shall look, he shall find it to be so,*" and then the former "*shall*" would be in the sense of a mere future, and the second in that sense of absolute certainty. "*I will undertake that he shall find,*" of which I spoke just now. This sentence might in fact be correctly said in four different ways:

> If he will look, he will find:
> If he shall look, he shall find:
> If he will look, he shall find:
> If he shall look, he will find.

I may mention that the almost uniform use of "*shall*" as applied to future events and to persons concerned in them, is reserved for the prophetic language of the Bible, as spoken by One whose will is supreme and who has all under his control.

322. There are certain other cases in which we may say either "*will*" or "*shall.*" In reporting what another said, or what one said one's self, we may say, "*He told me he

should go up to town to-morrow and settle it;" or we may say, "*He told me he would go up to town,*" &c. This arises from the possibility, already noticed, of using either word in speaking in the first person.

323. **Ambiguity.** — Sometimes an ambiguity arises from the fact that "*will*" and "*would*" either may convey the idea of inclination of the will, or may point to a mere future event. We have two notable instances in the English version of the New Testament. Our Lord says to the Jews (John v. 40), "*Ye will not come to me that ye might have life.*" Is He merely announcing a fact, or is He speaking of the bent and inclination of their minds? We consult the original, and the question is at once answered. What our Lord says, is this: "*Ye are not willing,*" "*ye have no mind,*" "*to come to me that ye might have life.*"

324. Again (Matt. xi. 27). "*No man knoweth the Father save the Son, and he to whomsoever the Son will reveal Him.*" Is this "*will*" a mere auxiliary for the future meaning, or does it convey the idea of *exercise of will*? Here again the original sets us right in a moment. It is, "*he to whom the Son is minded to reveal Him.*"

325. Let us take a still more remarkable case. The Pharisees said to our Lord (Luke xiii. 31), "*Get thee hence, for Herod will kill thee.*" This seems a mere future, and I have no doubt English readers universally regard it as such: but the original is "*Herod wishes,*" "*is minded,*" "*to kill thee.*"

326. The sense of duty conveyed by "*should*" sometimes causes ambiguity. Thus we have (Matt. xxvi. 35), "*Though I should die with thee, yet will I not deny thee.*" This, to the mere English reader, only conveys the sense, "*Even if it should happen that I should die with thee.*" But on consulting the original we find we should be wrong in thus understanding it. It is "*Even if it be needful for me to die with thee*" —and would have been better rendered, "*Even if I must die with thee.*" But in another clause (John xxi. 19), "*This spake He, signifying by what death He should glorify God,*" the "*should*" does not represent any necessity, but the mere future.

327. "**It would seem,**" "**it should seem.**"—Which is right, "*it would seem,*" or "*it should seem*"? asks a

Scottish correspondent. I believe both are right, but with slightly differing meanings. Both, be it observed, are expressions of very slight and qualified assent. The former, "*it would seem*," implies, "we are told that if we were to weigh all that is to be said, we should come to such or such a conclusion." The latter, "*it should seem*," conveys the meaning, with perhaps a slightly ironical tinge, that we are *required* to believe so and so. The Germans use their "*soll*," in reporting the conclusions or belief of others, in nearly the same sense.

328. Confusion of "shall" and "will."—An amusing instance of the confusion of *shall* and *will* was repeated to me by another Scottish correspondent. A young men's "Institute for Discussion and Self-improvement," is reported in a Scottish provincial paper to have met, and discussed the question, "Shall the material universe be destroyed?" My correspondent supposes that the decision was in the negative: or that if it was in the affirmative, the society cannot have proceeded to carry its resolution into effect.¹

329. Dr. Latham's account of this.—I believe Dr. Latham, in his "History of the English Language." was the first to observe that the confusion in such cases is more apparent than real. The Englishman and the Scotchman mean the same thing, but express it differently. We may say either, "the material universe *will* be destroyed," expressing merely something which will happen some day in the future: or we may say "the material universe *shall* be destroyed," in which case we put more solemnity and emphasis into our announcement, and treat it as something inevitable, pronouncing almost as if we were exercising our own will in the matter. When we turn the assertion into a question, *we* say, "Will the material universe be destroyed?" the Scotchman says, "Shall the material universe be destroyed?" He means to put, as a question, what we meant, when we used *shall* in the assertion. But be it ob-

---

¹ "I wonder," says a correspondent, "you have not given the story of the Irishman who fell into the water, 'I will be drowned, nobody shall save me.'" I have not, because I hold it to be a clumsy invention. "I'll be drowned," would be the natural exclamation of Paddy, but not "nobody shall save me," even without the emphasis which the story requires.

served, that in turning the proposition into a question, the *shall* assumes a ludicrous form, because of the deliberative aspect given to the sentence; and it looks as if the person putting the question had the option whether he would destroy the universe or not.

330. **A case in which it seems to fail.**—Five years ago I was visiting Loch Maree, in Ross-shire, with my family. We took a "trap" from the comfortable inn at Kinloch-Ewe, and lunched and sketched on the cliffs, about twelve miles down the lake. When our time was nearly up, our Highland driver appeared in the distance, shouting, " Will I yauk him?" which, being interpreted, meant to say, "Shall I harness the pony?" I hardly see how even Dr. Latham's explanation will account for the usage here.

331. I venture to insert the following remarks of a very intelligent Irish correspondent:—

"Your rules for the use of '*shall*' and '*will*' seem to me, as far as they go, the most simple and satisfactory I have ever read. But I observe:—

"I. No rule is laid down for the use of these words in interrogation. In Ireland the tendency is to make use of 'will' in *every case*. I have collected several examples from English writers which seem to me to suggest the following rules:—

"'*Will you?*' is a *request*.
"'*Shall you?*' a simple *question* as to the future event.
"'*Will he?*' a simple question.
"'*Shall he?*' means '*do you wish* that he shall.'
"'*Will I?*' is always incorrect.
"'*Shall I?*' has two meanings: 1st, it asks the simple question as to the future event, *v.g.*, 'shall I be of age next month?' 2nd, it asks, 'do you wish that *I shall?*' *v.g.*, 'shall I call you friend?'

"II. You say nothing of the use of these words in the secondary clauses of such sentences as the following:

"'He hopes that he *shall* not be thought,' &c.
"'He walked into a church knowing well he *should* find,' &c.

"Phrases of this kind occur very frequently, and, I think, almost all my countrymen would be found to use *will* and *would* instead of *shall* and *should*. I may add

that, as it seems to me nothing to be found in your book
would set them right on this point, I would propose the
following principle for such cases:—If we report in our
own words what another has said, or thought, or known, or
felt, we must use that verb which he would have used if,
speaking in the first person, he had himself related the
circumstance.

"III. There is to be found almost every day in the
Times (second column) a curious illustration of the distinction between 'shall' and 'will.' When a person advertises
for a lost article we sometimes read, 'If any person brings,
he *shall* be rewarded:' sometimes we find, 'a reward *will*
be given.' Now here your rules seem to be at fault. The
future event, namely, the giving of the reward, is dependent
on the will of the speaker in the latter case as well as in
the former. If the rule hold good, therefore, we might
say, 'A reward *shall* be given.' Yet this is never said."

332. This seems to fall under the list of exceptions
mentioned in paragraph 319; where the result is so spoken
of as not contingent but certain. "A reward *shall* be
given," is the subjective dictum of him who has so determined : "a reward will be given," is the objective future
certainty, the *determination* being lost sight of.

333. Use of superfluous particles—"doubt but
that."—We often find persons using superfluous conjunctions or prepositions in their usual talk. Two cases are
more frequent than others. One is the use of *but* after the
verb *to doubt*. "I do not doubt *but that* he will come," is
both found in print and heard in conversation. The "*but*"
is wholly unnecessary and a vulgarism. "I do not doubt
that he will come," expresses precisely the same thing, and
should be used.

334. "On to."—The same may be said of the expression
on to. "The cat jumped on to the chair;" the *to* being
wholly unneeded, and never used by any careful writer or
speaker.

335. Defence of it.—Few points mentioned in these
notes have provoked so much rejoinder as this reprobation
of "*on to*." It seems, to judge by its many defenders, to
be an especial favourite. The plea usually set up for it
is, that "*on*" without "*to*" does not sufficiently express

motion: that "the cat jumped on the chair" would imply merely that the cat, being on the chair already, there jumped. To this I have but one answer; that no doubt the words *may* mean this, to one who is disposed to invent meanings for them; but that they *do* mean this, is surely not true. "The cat jumped on the table, and began to lap the milk." Who would ever misunderstand this? Take an incident of one's schoolboy long walks. "Coachman, I'm very tired, and I shall be late in; but I've got no money in my pocket." "All right, my lad, jump on the box." Was there ever a schoolboy who would fail to comprehend this?

336. Since the publication of my first edition several correspondents have again vehemently controverted the opinion here expressed: and I have been even urged to withdraw it and confess myself in the wrong. I am afraid, therefore, that my correspondents will think me very obstinate for still maintaining my view: and saying, that I cannot conceive what signification of *motion towards* is gained by the vulgarism "*on to*," which is not already conveyed by "*on*," or at all events by "*upon*."

337. "**On to**" and "**into**."—One correspondent asks why "*on to*" is not as good English as "*into*"? I answer, because "*on*" is ordinarily a preposition of motion as well as of rest, whereas "*in*" is almost entirely a preposition of rest. To *fall on*, to *light on*, and the like, are very common; and we are thus prepared for the use of *on* to signify motion without an additional preposition.

338. "**Holding on to**."—It will be manifest, that the juxtaposition of "*on*" and "*to*" in such a sentence as this, "she continued holding on to the door of the carriage," is not an example within the scope of these remarks. The "*on*" in this case belongs to the verb: and "*holding-on to*" is equivalent to "*clinging to*."

339. "**On**" and "**upon**."—How do our usages of "*on*" and "*upon*" differ? In the very few cases where we recognise any difference, the question may be answered by observing the composition of the latter word. It almost always, as the dictionaries observe, "implies some substratum;" something that underlies the thing spoken of. But then so does also the shorter preposition in most cases.

K

There is hardly an instance to be found of which it could positively be said, that we may use the one preposition and may not use the other. Perhaps we may find one, when we say that a diver, describing his trip beneath the water, would hardly report that he "saw several rusty guns lying *upon* the bottom," but "lying *on* the bottom."

340. A correspondent sends me what he supposes to be an account of the distinction, but I believe it to be an erroneous one. "I would (should?) say, '*upon* a tower;' on the same principle, I would (should?) say, '*on* a marsh.' There would, indeed, be no harm in saying '*on* a tower;' but there would be an impropriety in saying '*upon* a marsh;' for *up*, whether we are attentive or inattentive, whether we have been a thousand times wrong or never, means somewhat high, somewhat to which we ascend. I should speak correctly if I said, 'Dr. Johnson *flew* upon me;" incorrectly, if I said, 'he *fell* upon me.'"

341. The error here seems to me to be in referring the height indicated by *up* to the motion previous to, not to the position indicated by, the action spoken of. We perhaps cannot say "*upon* the bottom;" not however because *we* do not *rise* to get there, but because the bottom, being of necessity the lowest point, has nothing beneath it with reference to which it is high. And as to my correspondent's last dictum, that "he fell upon me" would be incorrect, let him look at 1 Kings ii. 25, 34, 46, in which places it is said of Adonijah, Joab, and Shimei, respectively, that Benaiah, the son of Jehoiada, "*fell upon him* that he died."

342. To "open up."—The expression "*to open up*," is a very favourite one with our newspapers. It may have, as several of my correspondents insist, a certain meaning of its own, though I am even now unable to see, in any case where I have found it, why the simple word "open" would not be better. The meaning which it is designed to convey, seems to be, to open for the first time,— to break up and open. A railway is said to *open up* a communication between two places not so connected before. Thus used, the term may be endured, but, surely, should not be imitated. As to the instances from "Good Words," which have been produced against me as if I were respon-

sible for them, "He *opens up* in the parched desert a well that refreshes us;" "These considerations may *open up* to us one view of the expediency of Christ's departure;" I can only regard them as Scotticisms, which certainly would not have been written south of the Tweed.

343. The parallel which the defenders of the expression have drawn between *open up* and *rise up, grow up*, is hardly a just one, seeing that in these cases the adverb, or intransitive preposition, *up*, gives us the tendency in which the progressive action indicated by the neuter verb takes place; and even if it do not that, intensifies and gives precision. More apposite parallels would have been found in *rip up, tear up, pull up*, where *up* defines the active verb; a more decisive one still, in the term *to shut up*, where *up* implies the *closing* and *finality* of the act indicated; and for this reason should hardly be used with the opposite word *to open*. If we *shut up* a communication, we ought to *open* it *down* rather than *up*. Put the word with any analogous term, and its inappropriateness will be perceived. A new railway develops, expands, promotes, the traffic; but we could not say it *develops up, expands up, promotes up*, the traffic.

344. A correspondent states that in Northumberland, the expression is "*open out*." "It is universally spoken by the common people, and frequently by their superiors. Thus, a parcel is rarely said to be 'opened' without the addition 'out.'"

345. "**At best**," "**at the best**."—Which is right, "at *best*," or "at *the best?*" It is plain that this question does not stand alone; several other phrases are involved in it. It affects "at least," "at most," "at furthest," and even such very common expressions as "at first," and "at last."

346. The answer, it seems to me, is, that the insertion or omission of the definite article is indifferent. Usage has generally sanctioned its omission before the very common superlatives, "first," "last," "most," "least," "furthest;" but when we put a less usual adjective in this construction, the article seems to be required, or a possessive pronoun in its place. "The storm was at the (or "its") highest at noon;" "What is woman at her loveliest?" And we sometimes fill out the phrase with the article when we want

it to be more than usually solemn: "If he did not love his father, at the least he might have honoured him." "At the last" is found six times in the English Bible; "at last," if we may trust the Concordances, never; "at the first," twenty-eight times; "at first," never; "at the least," three times; while "at least" is found twice (1 Sam. xxi. 4, Luke xix. 42); "at the most," once (1 Cor. xiv. 27); but "at most," never.

347. "**All of them**," "**both of them**."—These expressions are often challenged. Are they right, or not? When I have a number of things, and speak of "one of them," "two of them," "the rest of them," the preposition "*of*" has what is called its partitive sense. It may be explained by "*out of*," or "*from among*." Thus, "one of them" is "one from among them;" "two of them" is two from among them;" "the rest of them" is "all from among them that do not belong to those already named." But, it is urged, "all of them" cannot be "all from among them," because there would be none left. Neither can "both of them" be said of two, because when you have taken both, there is nothing left.

348. But let us examine this. Is it so certain that the "of" in the phrases "all of them," "both of them," has the same meaning as the "of" in the phrases "one of them," "two of them," "some of them"? Let us, for "all of them," put "the whole of them," and for that, "the sum total of them," or, as our newspapers would say, "the entirety of them." Now it is manifest that any one of these is good grammar, and that the "of" does not mean "*from among*," but implies "consisting of:" is spoken of the quality, as "sum total," or "entirety," is of quantity. "The sum total of them," is as legitimate as "a pint of beer." Why not, then, "all of them," or "both of them"? The fallacy of the objection here is, the assuming for the preposition a sense which it need not have, just because it had that sense in some phrases apparently similar. In other words, the mistake was, being misled by a false analogy.

349. "**Fifty cubits high**," or "**of fifty cubits high**"? —"A gallows fifty cubits high," or, "a gallows of fifty

cubits high"? The former expression is used in Esther vii. 9; the latter in Esther v. 14. Clearly, both of these are legitimate. A gallows whose height is fifty cubits, may be said to be "fifty cubits high": it is high, and the measure of that height is fifty cubits. Thus we have "a mile wide": "ten thousand fathoms deep." Also, the same gallows may be said to be "of fifty cubits" (high, or in height): the "of" being used, as in the phrases "she was of the age of twelve years" (Mark v. 42), "of a great age" (Luke ii. 36), to indicate the class or standard of the object spoken of. The gallows is high, and belongs to that class of things whose height is fifty cubits.

350. **Adverb between "to" and the infinitive.**— A correspondent states as his own usage, and defends, the insertion of an adverb between the sign of the infinitive mood and the verb. He gives as an instance, "*to scientifically illustrate.*" But surely this is a practice entirely unknown to English speakers and writers. It seems to me, that we ever regard the *to* of the infinitive as inseparable from its verb. And when we have already a choice between two forms of expression, "scientifically to illustrate," and "to illustrate scientifically," there seems no good reason for flying in the face of common usage.

351. **"Going" and "coming."**—In a letter bearing after its address, "N. B.," I am asked whether the expression "I am *coming* to pay you a visit" is correct: whether it ought not rather to be "I am *going* to pay you a visit:" and the question is extended to the reply, "I am coming," when any one calls; which is also supposed to be incorrect, and still more so when followed by "directly." I mentioned the address of the letter to account in some measure for the inquiry; for it seems to me to be one which we Southrons should never have thought of making. In both cases, *coming* is right. In the former, we might use *going*, but it would be in the temporal sense, not in that of motion. But in the other, we could not say *going* at all, if we indicated approach to the person calling. An apology is almost required for setting down things so simple and obvious: but the doing so may serve to show what sort of usages prevail and are upheld in some portions of our realm.

352. "**Come to grief.**"—When I used, in the early part of this work, the colloquial expression *would have come to grief*, I was told by one of my censors that it ought to have been *would have gone to grief*. It is not easy, perhaps, to treat according to strict rule what is almost a slang phrase, or has but lately ceased to be one; still, I venture to think that *to come to grief* is of the two the more according to the analogy of our usage. We say *to come to an end*, not *to go to an end* (so Dan. xi. 45, "He shall come to his end, and none shall help him:" Rev. xviii. 17, "in one hour so great riches is come to nought,"); we say of a desperate young villain, that he will *come to the gallows*, not that he will *go to the gallows*. Indeed, if we chose, we might illustrate the difference between the two expressions, by saying what I fear was often true of the effect of our public executions (now happily at an end), that *going to the gallows* was but too likely to end in *coming to the gallows*.

353. **Other uses of "go" and "come."**—This use of *go* and *come* is rather curious. We say of a wrecked ship, that she *went* to pieces; but of a broken jug, that it *came* to pieces. Plants *come* up, *come* into leaf, *come* into flower; but they *go* to seed, they *go* out of flower. It may be that in this case we regard the above-ground state as that in which we ourselves are, and the being in leaf and in flower as those in which we wish them to be, and like to think of them; and so the passing into those states is a kind of approach to us: whereas the state of seed being one leading to decay, and beyond what is our own place and feeling as regards flowers, they seem to depart from us in passing into it. Thus the sun *goes* in behind a cloud, and *comes* out from behind it. But we are not consistent in speaking of the sun. He is said to *go down* in the evening; but never to *come up* in the morning.

354. And very minute shades of meaning are sometimes conveyed by the use of one or other of these verbs. You are talking about a public meeting with a friend who you know will be there. If you say to him, "I shall not *come* to the meeting," you identify him with those who get up the meeting, and imply that he is desirous you should join him there. If you say, "I shall not *go* to the meeting," you tacitly ignore the fact of his being about to attend,

and half imply that he would do well to stay away also. "Are you *coming* to church to-day?" implies that the questioner *is*; "Are you *going* to church to-day?" implies nothing as to whether he is or is not. To this latter question one might rejoin, "Yes: are you?" but not so to the former.

355. **Misuse of "whom."**—In nothing do we find more frequent mistakes in writers commonly careful, than in using the accusative case of a relative pronoun where the nominative ought to be used. A correspondent, for instance, describing what he thinks the disastrous effects of my advocacy of "*it is me*," says, "I have heard persons *whom* I knew were in the habit of using the form 'it is I,' say instead, 'it is me.'" Here, the mistake is very evident. "I knew" is merely parenthetical, put in by way of voucher for the fact—"persons who, I knew, were." The writer might have said, "*whom I knew to be*," or "*to have been;*" but as the sentence stands, *who* must be the nominative case to the verb *were*.

356. A still worse example occurred in the *Times* a short time since, in translating the Count de Montalembert's famous speech in favour of liberty of conscience. It would perhaps be hard to criticise a report of a speech; but the sentence was quoted for especial comment in the leading article, and no correction was made. It ran thus: "The gag forced into the mouth of *whomsoever lifts* up his voice with a pure heart to preach his faith, that gag I feel between my own lips, and I shudder with pain."

357. Now in this sentence, first of all it is clear that "whomsoever lifts" cannot be right. The indefinite relative pronoun ought to be the nominative case to the verb lifts, and therefore ought to be *whosoever* and not *whomsoever*.

358. But then, how about the construction? "The mouth of whosoever lifts" is an elliptical clause. Filled up, it will be "*the mouth of him whosoever lifts*," or, more completely, "*of him whosoever he be that lifts.*" In its shortened form we have the object, "*him*," omitted. But we must not visit this omission on the unfortunate relative pronoun which follows, and degrade it from its place in the sentence by making it do the work of the missing member.

359. A similar mistake is made by those who say and write, "my memory does not serve me as to whom it was." The relative is put into government after the preposition "to," it being not observed that it has no connection with that preposition. "As to" governs the whole clause that follows: memory was at fault as to [the question] who it was.

360. "**Different to.**"—A correspondent stigmatises the expression "*different to*," which he shows (I own I was not aware of it) has become very common of late. Of course such a combination is entirely against all reason and analogy. "Compare," says this writer, "any other English words compounded of this same Latin preposition, for example, '*distant*,' '*distinct*,' and it will be seen that '*from*' is the only appropriate term to be employed in connection with them." The same will be seen, I venture to add, by substituting the verb "*to differ*" in the places where "*different*," which in fact is only its participle, is thus joined. For instance, in the sentence quoted from Mr. Taylor's "Convent Life in Italy," "Michael Angelo planned a totally different façade to the existing one," make this substitution, and read it, "Michael Angelo planned a façade which totally differed to the existing one," and the error will be immediately seen.

361. "**In respect (or regard) of,**" &c.—"*In respect of*," "*in respect to*," "*with respect to:*" which of these is right? The question extends also to "*in regard of*," "*in regard to*," "*with regard to*." For *respect* and *regard*, though far from meaning the same when spoken of as feelings of the mind, yet in their primitive meaning, which is that now treated of, are identical.

362. I believe it will be found that *of* and *to* may be indifferently used after these words. Both words have the same signification; *an act of looking back at*. The former, *respect*, is a Latin word, and the expression answering to "in respect of," is used in Latin. At the same time, the natural construction of the verb from which *respect* is derived would be with the preposition *to* (*respicere ad*). There is nothing in the meaning of the word to forbid either construction—with *of*, or with *to*. The same may be said of *regard*, which is of French origin.

363. Still, if we agree on this much, it remains to be seen what preposition should be *prefixed*. "*In respect of*" is the pure Latin construction, and seems on all hands (but see below) to be admitted as pure English likewise. And the same with "*in regard of;*" "*with respect to*," and "*in respect to*," are both found: the former I think the more frequently in our best writers. But, unless I am mistaken, "*with respect of*," is not found.

364. When it was said of a sentence in these notes, that I had used "*in respect of*," for "*with respect to*," the writer surely must have been speaking without his authorities before him. It will be found in the dictionaries, that in the scanty lists there given, Spenser, Bacon, Tillotson, all use the expression complained of. It occurs in Philippians iv. 11, and Colossians ii. 16, and is certainly as much used by good modern writers as that which he wishes to substitute for it.

365. "**Inversely as.**"—What is meant when it is said that "*inversely as*" should be "*inversely to*," I am at a loss to understand. I can comprehend "*in inverse proportion to*," or "*in inverse ratio to;*" but surely by all the usages of mathematical language, from which the phrase is borrowed, one variable thing must be said to be directly or inversely *as*, not *to*, another which is compared with it.

366. "**Contrast to,**" or "**with.**"—A correspondent asks the question, "contrast *to*," or "contrast *with*"? It may be answered that both of these seem allowable. For *contrast* partakes of two ideas; that of *opposition*, and that of *comparison*. Now we oppose one thing *to* another, and we (commonly) compare one thing *with* another. Still, as the idea of opposition is, beyond question, the prevalent one, I should prefer "*contrast to*."

367. "**Dependent on,**" "**independent of.**"—I am asked why we say "dependent *on*," but independent *of*"? The answer is surely not difficult. When we make "dependent" into "independent," we not only deny that which "dependent" asserts, but we construct a different word; different in its reference and its government. The "*on*," which we use after "dependent," implies attachment and sequence; as in "hanging on," "waiting on": the "*of*," which we use after "independent," expresses

merely the relation of the thing following, as when we say "inclusive of," "exclusive of." In this case, the variation of prepositions might be still further exemplified; we say "pendent *from*," "dependent *on*," "independent *of*." A somewhat similar instance may be found in "with respect to," and "irrespective *of*."

368. "**Contemporary with**," "**a contemporary of**."—The same correspondent who proposed the last question also asks, why we say "contemporary *with*," but "a contemporary *of*"? The answer to this is to be sought from a different source. In "contemporary with," the "*with*" simply carries on the force of the preposition "*con*," or "*cum*," with which the adjective is compounded. But when that adjective is made into a substantive, it then must be connected with other substantives by the customary preposition "*of*," indicating possession or relation.

369. "**Neighbour to**," "**a neighbour of**."—A somewhat similar change takes place when substantives which may be used predicatively, are used indicatively. Thus we say "neighbour *to* him," but "a neighbour *of* him," or, as we commonly express it, "of *his*." If we keep the same preposition in the two cases, the phrase does not retain the same meaning. "He is neighbour to him," means, "He lives near him": but "He is a neighbour to him," means, "He behaves to him in a neighbourly manner."

370. The question at the end of our Lord's parable of the Good Samaritan, "Which of these three, thinkest thou, was neighbour unto him that fell among the thieves?" forms not an exception to the rule first mentioned, but rather an example of it. For the conclusion to be drawn from the parable is, that the real claim to the title of neighbour is his who acts in a neighbourly manner. So that the question does not mean, which of these three acted in a neighbourly manner to him? but which of these three had a right to be called his neighbour — neighbour to him? Then the answer naturally comes, "He that showed mercy on him."

371. **One word used for another.** I have one or two more illustrations of the blunder of using one word, when another is meant. In a well-known novel by one of our most popular writers, we read: "He had not learned

the *heart* (*sic*) of assuming himself to be of importance wherever he might find himself."
This can hardly be a misprint.

372. In another novel of the day, we read: "For these pious purposes, a visible and attractive *presentiment* of the newly promoted Saint is indispensable."
The author meant "*presentment*": "*presentiment*" being a foreboding within the mind, not a demonstration before the eyes.

373. In the *Times* of April 20, of this year [1870], we read: "The prisoners are allowed . . to receive food from their friends outside, an indulgence which has been in many instances abused by the *secretion* of tobacco and written communications in the food sent in."
Had the writer consulted his dictionary, he would have found that *secretion* means "that agency in the animal economy that consists in separating the various fluids of the body." He meant "*secreting*."

374. If our last example presented a physical curiosity, our next even surpasses it. The *Times* Law report of Feb. 13, last year [1869], told us of a plaintiff or defendant, "He, though a gentleman of property, was unhappily paralysed in his lower limbs." What a delightful idea this writer had of the usual exemption of the rich from the ills of humanity!

375. Nor does the level of physical intelligence rise in our next example,—an advertisement of Keating's Persian Insect-destroying powder. It states that "this powder is *quite harmless to animal life*, but is unrivalled in destroying fleas, bugs, flies, cockroaches, beetles, gnats, mosquitos, moths in furs, and every other species of insect." We thought we had more frequently found the converse mistake made, and the appellation "animals" applied somewhat exclusively to the unlovely genera here enumerated. The advertisement loses none of its richness as it proceeds: "Being the original importer of this article, which has found so great a sale that it has tempted others to vend a so-called article, the public are therefore cautioned to observe that the packets of the genuine powder bear the autograph of Thomas Keating."

376. **Meaning of** "**a term.**"—What is "*a term*"?

Can we call an adverb "a term"? It is said that we cannot: that an adverb is not a term, but a *word*, a *part of a term*. But the whole account to be given of "*term*," its derivation and its usage, is against this view. It comes to us proximately from the Latin *terminus*—directly from the French *terme*. Both these, when used of language, signify, not a clause, but a *word*. And so our dictionaries give the meaning of the English *term* "The word by which a thing is expressed."

377. "**I need not have troubled myself.**"—It is said that this ought to have been, "*I should not have needed to trouble myself*:" that the verb *troubled*, which I have put in the past, should have been in the present: just as the verb *need*, which I have put in the present, should have been in the past. Now in these words appears the cause of the objector's mistake. It is the very common one of confusing a *perfect* tense with a *past* one. "I need not have troubled myself" is strictly correct; being equivalent to "I need not be in the present situation of having troubled myself." Every *perfect* is in fact a *present*. "*I have troubled myself*" describes not a past action, but the *present result* of a past action. This is now so generally acknowledged even by the ordinary grammarians, that it is strange in our days to find any one who attends to the matter making a mistake about it.

378. **Caution respecting past and perfect tenses.** Seeing, however, that this has been done, it may be as well to put my readers on their guard, ever to bear in mind the distinction between the *indefinite past* and the *perfect*. I have said something on this difference in a former paragraph; it may be enough to repeat here, that while the indefinite past tense of a verb must always be constructed *as a past*, the perfect, consisting of the auxiliary "have" with the past participle of the verb, denotes present possession of the state or act described by that past participle, and must always be treated and constructed as a *present*.[1]

379. **Use of the present to signify fixed design.**

---

[1] See Dr. Latham's "History of the English Language," p. 557.

—One more point raised by way of objection may serve for our instruction. I had begun a sentence, "The next point which I notice shall be . . ." This was designated as "confusing the present and the future." Here again is a mistake as to the usage of the tenses. There is a very common use of the present, which has regard, not to actual time of occurrence, but to *design*. "Do you go abroad this year?" "I will come unto you when I shall pass through Macedonia, for I do pass through Macedonia," (1 Cor. xvi. 5). In this sense the present was used in the sentence complained of. "The next point which I notice," means, "the next point coming under notice," "the next point which I mean to notice in my lecture." It is necessary for one who would write good grammar, and remark on the grammar of others, to know the usages of the various tenses, not merely to deal with these tenses as they appear at first sight.

380. **Sentences wrongly supposed elliptic.**—"I mention it, because it may be a difficulty of many others besides him," (see below, par. 477.) This is objected to by one who fills it up thus: "it may be a difficulty of many other people, *besides being a difficulty of him*." But surely a moment's thought will convince any of us, that such a filling up, nay, that any filling up at all, is quite wrong, and beside the purpose. The pronoun "*him*" is governed by the preposition, or transitive adverb "*besides*." "Others besides him" is a clause perfect in itself, and needs no filling up whatever.

381. **Caution against rash and positive assertions about construction.**—And this may serve as a caution to us against rashness in this matter of filling up sentences, having hastily assumed them to be elliptical. One of my critics says, " We hear clergymen sometimes say . . . than *him*, than *her*, than *them!* Only place the *verb* after such words place the words *is* and *are*—and see what nonsense it makes—than *him is*, than *her is*, than *them are*."

382. Here is an instance of that against which I would caution my readers. This writer first assumes that the construction of the phrase is as he wants it to be, and then reasons on his own assumption to prove that the phrase is

wrongly expressed. The fact is, that the construction in this case does not admit of any such filling up. I have shown (in paragraphs 289 and following), by the unquestioned and unavoidable use of "*than whom*," that *than* governs an accusative case directly, without any ellipsis whatever. That the other construction, "than he is," is an admissible one, and cannot in the slightest degree affect the question whether *this one* is admissible or not. Yet I doubt not that many readers of this illogical criticism would be deceived by its rash and positive character, and imagine the point in question to be proved.

383. "Construct" and "construe."—"What do you wish us to understand by readers '*constructing*' the sentence? Writers '*construct:*' readers '*construe.*'" This is said in reference to my having written that we ought not "to mislead the reader by introducing the possibility of *constructing the sentence* otherwise than as the writer intended." And the objection is instructive, as leading to the indication of the exact meaning and difference of the two words. Supposing I am examining a class of boys, and, with reference to a given sentence, direct one of them to *construe* the sentence. He knows perfectly well what I mean. He turns the sentence into English, if it be in any other language. But suppose I tell him to *construct* the sentence. He knows, or ought to know, that I mean that he is to explain the construction of the sentence, to give an account of its concords and governments. My Censor's mistake here is, that he transfers the meaning of the verb "*construct*," when applied to building up what did not before exist, to the case of a sentence given as already existing. The word "*construing*," in the sentence quoted, would make sense, and convey a certain meaning not very far removed from that which I intended: but it would not convey that meaning itself, that of supplying a construction building up the sentence with reference to its concords and governments.

384. "Above."—A correspondent says, "You make use of the adverb '*above*' as an adjective. Can you use the correlative word '*below*' in the same sense?" The usage complained of, "the above," meaning something which has been before spoken of, is certainly not elegant, though it is

not uncommon. It may easily be avoided, by merely filling in the ellipsis, and saying " the above-mentioned."

385. **Adjectives used as adverbs.**—I must say something on the question of adjectives used as adverbs: or rather of the allowable forms of qualifying verbs. The common rule, believed in and universally applied by the ordinary teachers of grammar, is, that we must always qualify a verb by the adverbial form, and never by the adjectival. According to these teachers, such expressions as the following are wrong, " The string of his tongue was loosed, and he spake *plain*." " The moon shines *bright*." " How *sweet* the moonlight sleeps upon this bank." " Breathe *soft*, ye winds, ye waters gently flow."

386. These, we are told, ought to have been written with "*plainly*," "*brightly*," "*sweetly*," and "*softly*." But this is a case where the English language and the common grammarians are at variance. The sentences which I have quoted are but a few out of countless instances in our best writers, and in the most chaste and beautiful passages of our best writers, in which the usage occurs. On examining into it, we find that it is very much matter of arbitrary custom. Some adjectives will bear being thus used: others will not. Most of those which can be so used seem to be of one syllable; *plain, soft, sweet, right, wrong*, and the like. In all these cases it may be more precise and accurate to say *softly, sweetly, rightly, wrongly*, &c., but we certainly can, and our best writers certainly do, use these and other monosyllabic adjectives as adverbs. Still, as far as my memory serves me, they do not often thus use adjectives of more than one syllable. We may say, *He spake plain*: but we cannot so well say " He spoke *simple*," or " He spoke *delightful*." We may say, " The moon shines *bright*," but we can hardly say, " The moon shines *brilliant*." What may be the reason for this, I do not pretend to say; I only state what seems to be the fact.

387. One of my correspondents tries to make all easy, by suggesting that this adverbial use of adjectives is entirely poetical, and ought never to be allowed in prose. But, begging his pardon, this is assuming the whole question. We undoubtedly *have* the usage in prose, and have it abundantly; and this being so, to lay down a rule that it

cannot be allowed in prose, is to prejudge the matter in dispute.

388. **Two uses of adverbial qualifications—subjective and objective.**—An important consideration may be introduced into this matter, which has not, I think, yet been brought to bear on it. There may be two uses of an adverb as qualifying a verb. One of these may have respect to the action indicated by the verb, describing its mode of performance; the other may have respect to the result of that action, irrespective of its mode of performance. We may, if we will, designate these two uses respectively the subjective and the objective use. And it is to the latter of them that I would now draw the reader's attention.

389. When the adverbial term by which a verb is qualified is *objectively* used, has respect to the result, and not to the mode, of acting, there seems no reason why it should not be an adjective. Take the following: "Shall not the Judge of all the earth do *right?*" Now in these last words, "*do right*," we may take *right* either as an adverb, "do rightly," or as an adjective, "*do that which is right*," "*do justice*." In this particular case, it does not appear which of the two is intended. But take another, (Neh. ix. 33) "Thou hast done *right*, but we have done wickedly." Here it seems almost certain, from the parallelism, that *right* is meant to be used adverbially.

390. Now pass on to the other cases in which the adjective is used. "He spake plain." "That which he spake was *plain*." He spake (that which was) *plain*." Here again it is immaterial to the logical sense whether we take adjective or adverb. "They love him that speaketh right," (Prov. xvi. 13). And from these let us advance yet further to those cases where the adjectival sense is not so plainly applicable, but still may be in the thoughts. "The moon shines bright." Here it is plain, that the qualifying word *bright* refers not so much to the mode in which the moon performs her function of shining, as to the result or product of that shining: it is rather objective than subjective. "The moon is giving light, and that light is bright." "Breathe soft" is just as easily understood, "Breathe that which is soft," as "Breathe softly."

391. This after all seems to be the logical account of the usage: and by the rules of thought, not by the dicta of the ordinary grammarians, must all such usages be ultimately judged.

392. "**Looking sadly**," &c.—The account above given will at once enable us to convict of error such expressions as "looking sadly," "smelling sweetly," "feeling queerly." For in all these we do not mean to qualify the mode of acting or being, but to describe the result produced by the act or state. To "smell sweetly" is not meant to describe some sweet way of performing the act of smelling, but is meant to describe that the smell itself is sweet. And in this case the verb is of that class called neuter-substantive, *i.e.*, neuter, and akin in construction to the verb substantive "*to be.*" "*The rose smells sweet,*" is in construction much the same as "*the rose is sweet.*" "*You look sad,*" is equivalent to "*you seem to be sad.*" And so of the rest.

393. "**It would read oddly.**"—Speaking of an expression which was the subject of remark in one of my lectures, I said, "*it would read rather oddly.*" This was objected to as a violation of the rule above-mentioned. It was not really so. I here used the word "read" in an unusual sense, but at the same time one fully sanctioned by usage: in the sense of "affect the hearer when read." So that it is not, strictly speaking, a verb neuter, nor a verb substantive, but a verb anomalously used, and used in such a sense as to require the adverb rather than the adjective.

394. Still, the adjective *may* also be used, and sometimes *reads* better. Thus in an able article in the "Times" this day (Jan. 24, 1870), on the consequences to which the supporters of the grotesque figment of Papal Infallibility will stand committed, we have, "Burke's terrible account of that merciless code (the Irish penal laws) *reads moderate* by comparison with this summary of Papal Bulls."

395. "**Previous,**" or "**previously.**"—"A quarter's notice is required, previous (or, previously?) to the removal of a pupil." We may use either adjective or adverb. If the former, then it agrees with "notice:" The notice given must be anterior (= previous) by a quarter of a year, to

the removal of a pupil. If the latter, the adverb qualifies the verb "required": "In case of removal of a pupil, a quarter's notice is previously required." But the adjective, it seems to me, makes the best sentence.

396. **Usage in comparative and superlative clauses.**—What has been said hitherto applies to the positive degree of comparison only; when we pass beyond that to the comparative and superlative, another consideration comes in. All adverbs do not admit of degrees of comparison. That many do, is acknowledged. *Oftener, oftenest, seldomer*, seem to be good English words. But these exceptions are rare. We cannot say *simplier, brightlier, plainlier*. And in consequence, when we want to express comparative and superlative degrees of qualification of a verb, we commonly have recourse to one of two other constructions: we either take the resolved comparative and superlative, *more plainly, most plainly*, or we take the comparative and superlative of the corresponding adjective. Thus, for instance, we have "*well*" as the adverb of good: we cannot say "*weller*" and "*wellest;*" we do not say "*more well*" and "*most well;*" but we go back to the adjective, and we say, for our comparative and superlative adverbs, *better* and *best*. So, too, whereas we may, in the positive degree, say either "the moon shines *bright*," or "the moon shines *brightly*," we should say, in the comparative and superlative, not "the sun shines *more brightly*, and the fire shines *most brightly*," but, "the sun shines *brighter*, and the fire shines *brightest*."

397. Take another example. I originally wrote (see below, paragraph 584): "If with your inferiors, speak no *coarser* than usual; if with your superiors, no *finer*." My language was characterised as being ungrammatical, because we cannot say "*to speak coarse*." True: but, as we have seen, what cannot be done in the positive, must be done in the other degrees of comparison: and my sentence, though not the neatest possible, was strictly correct, and according to usage. In this case too, there was no choice open between the two forms, the resolved and the adjectival comparative. Had I written, "speak no more coarsely," "speak no more finely," the conjunction of "speak" with "no more" would have been awkward, as

suggesting a temporal meaning which was foreign to the construction of the sentence. And had I adopted the form of expression which my Censor recommends, "speak not more coarsely than usual," I might have escaped indeed his censure, but not the charge of having written pompous and pedantic English.

398. "A decided weak point."—Exception is taken to an expression occurring in these notes, "a decided weak point." But there can be no doubt that my Censor is wrong. A "*decidedly weak point*" is one thing; a "*decided weak point*" is another. There is a difference, according as we regard the adverb as qualifying only the adjective, or the adjective and substantive together. "There occurs in his book a remarkable prefatory announcement." Who would think of saying "a *remarkably prefatory announcement*"? Thus also in the phrase under consideration, had I written "a *decidedly* weak point," I should have spoken of *a point decidedly weak;* but writing as I did a *decided* weak point, I spoke of a *weak point of whose existence there could be no doubt.*

399. Anomalies.—If we use our powers of observation, we shall find in the usage of adjectives and adverbs, as in other usages, many things which follow no rule but that of custom, and of which it is very difficult to give any reasonable account. I mention this to shew how inadequate the laws of ordinary grammar are to regulate or even to describe our practice.

400. "Long" and "short."—Take but one example out of many; the use of the adjectives *long* and *short*, with reference to adverbial construction. *Long* is an adverb as well as an adjective. We say "How long," speaking of time. "Paul was long speaking." We have no adverb "*longly*," though we have "*widely*," "*broadly*," "*deeply*." Now observe the adjective "*short*." Its use as an adverb is hardly legitimate. Your banker asks you whether you will *take it short*, when you present a cheque to be cashed; but this use is a technical one. But what I wish to observe is, that the adverb "*shortly*" is by our usage limited to one department only of the meanings of the adjective, viz., that of *time;* and in that department, to time future. We cannot use *shortly* of time past; we

cannot use it of duration—"*he preached shortly;*" but we must use it of that which is to come, "I hope *shortly* to see you."

401. "**Just now.**"—This mention of adverbs of time reminds me of an expression which usage has assigned to time past, as it has that other to time future. "*Just now,*" in its strict meaning, imports, nearly at the present moment, whether before or after. Yet our general usage has limited its application to a point slightly preceding the present, and will not allow us to apply it to that which is to come. If we are asked "When?" and we reply "Just now," we are understood to describe an event past, not an event future.

402. In this case we have the double use of the term preserved in provincial usage. In the midland and northern counties we have such a sentence as "I'll be with you just now," which is perfectly right in logical precision, though proscribed by English usage.

403. "**Thoroughly working order.**"—Is it correct to say, "A machine is in thoroughly working order"? This might be defended as meaning, in such order as to work thoroughly. But this, I apprehend, is not the construction. Rather should we say that "working-order" is used as one word, equivalent, say, to "repair:" and in this case "thoroughly" would clearly be wrong, as an adverb can qualify only verbs and adjectives, not substantives. The wrong use has, we suppose, originated in the fact of "working," a word which will admit of advertical qualification, immediately following.

404. **Subjunctive and indicative moods in conditional sentences. The general rule.**—The use of the indicative and subjunctive moods, after conditional particles, as *if* and *whether*, is a wide subject, and one on which considerable uncertainty seems to prevail. The general rule appears plain enough: that when matter of *fact* is concerned, we should use the indicative; when matter of doubt, the subjunctive. "Whether I *be* master or you, one thing is plain." Here we have doubt: it is left in uncertainty which of the two is master. "You shall soon see whether I *am* master, or you." Here there is no uncertainty: your eyes shall see and be enlightened

as to a fact, of which the speaker at all events has no doubt.

405. Stated by Dr. Latham.—The same rule has been thus clearly laid down by Dr. Latham: "The following method of determining the amount of doubt expressed in a conditional proposition is useful: insert, immediately after the conjunction, one of the two following phrases: (1) *as is the case;* (2) *as may or may not be the case.* By ascertaining which of these two supplements expresses the meaning of the speaker, we ascertain the mood of the verb which follows. When the first formula is the one required, there is no element of doubt, and the verb should be in the indicative mood. *If (as is the case) he is gone, I must follow him.* When the second formula is the one required, there is an element of doubt, and the verb should be in the subjunctive mood. *If (as may or may not be the case) he be gone, I must follow him.*" [1]

406. Ignorance of this rule.—When a correspondent said of this sentence of mine, "If a man values his peace of mind, let him not write on the Queen's English," that I ought to have written "If a man value his peace of mind," he apparently was in ignorance of this very plain rule. For that every man does value his peace of mind, is of course, assumed, and the phrase to be supplied is the former one in Dr. Latham's rule. "If (*as is the case*) a man values his peace of mind."

407. This rule perhaps unknown to our older writers.—But this rule, satisfactory as it is for a guide, does not seem to have been known to our older writers. Our translators of the Bible notoriously do not observe it. In cases where the original (and the rule is not one belonging to English only, but to the conditions of thought) has the indicative, and the missing phrase clearly must be, "*as is the case*," they have used the subjunctive. An instance of this is found in Col. iii. 1, "If ye then *be* risen with Christ . . . ;" which according to the original ought to be "if ye then *are* risen." The fact, that those addressed are thus risen, is proved in the previous chapter, and the Apostle proceeds to ground upon it the exhorta

---

[1] "History of the English Language," p. 646.

tions that follow. "If (*as is the case*; as I have proved) ye are risen with Christ." Many more instances might be given to shew, that our translators almost universally used the subjunctive mood after conditional particles, where we should now use the indicative.

408. Sometimes they seem to use the two moods indifferently. An example is found in Job xxxi. 5-10. "If I have walked with vanity, or my foot *hath hasted* to deceit: let me," &c. "If my step *hath turned* out of the way, and my heart walked after mine eyes, and if any blot *hath cleaved* to mine hands; then let me," &c. So far is indicative. But Job goes on in the same strain, and our translators in the next place adopt the subjunctive, "If mine heart *have been* deceived by a woman .... then let," &c.

In some places, they seem to have observed the rule. "If now thou hast understanding, hear this" (Job xxxiv. 16).

409. The same irregularity appears to prevail in their construction of verbs after "though." Take as an example Col. ii. 5: "Though I be absent in the flesh." Here the Apostle is asserting his absence as a fact, and the Greek verb is in the indicative, as by the ordinary rule the English should be also: "Though (as is the fact) I am absent in the flesh."

410. **Bias formerly to the subjunctive.**—I believe it will be found, on the whole, that there is a decided bias on the part of our translators to the use of the subjunctive mood. I do not of course speak of the use of "be" as an indicative, as in 2 Kings ix. 9: "Ye be righteous." This sometimes brings in ambiguity as to which mood is actually used in a conditional sentence: as in Gen. xlii. 19, "If ye be true men." But I speak of the prevalence of the use of undoubted subjunctives, determined to be so by the auxiliary, or by the form of the verb itself.

411. **But now to the indicative.** But if there was a bias then in favour of the subjunctive, the bias is as decidedly now against it. Our conditional sentences in common talk are almost all expressed in the indicative. "I don't know whether I shall be at the committee; but if I *am*, I will mention it." This every one says. "If I *be*," would sound pedantic. We all say, "whether it is, or not,

I cannot say:" not "whether it be." And so of other conditional sentences.

412. Phenomenon to be observed.—Here then we seem to have a phenomenon, instructive to those who are more anxious to watch the actually flowing currents of verbal usage, than to build up bounds for them to run in. We have a well known logical rule, prevailing in our own and in other languages, and laid down by grammarians as to be followed. But it would seem that it never has been followed universally: that it has not regulated the language of the Book in commonest use, and yet that the language of that book speaks intelligibly to us. And more than this: for while that book violates the rule almost uniformly in one direction, we ourselves as uniformly violate it in the other.

413. Verb after "that" without an auxiliary.— While speaking upon the indicative and subjunctive moods, I may notice that the use of the bare verb without "*may*," or "*might*," or "*should*," after the conjunction "*that*," which we not unfrequently meet with in the English Version of the Bible, and in the Common Prayer-book, is not ungrammatical, nor is it to be corrected by inserting the apparently missing auxiliary verb, as I have heard some clergymen do in reading. The verb thus used was the old form of the subjunctive, now generally supplanted by the resolved form with the auxiliary. Thus when we pray "that our hearts may be unfeignedly thankful, and that we shew forth thy praise not only with our lips but in our lives," the verb "*shew*" is as truly in the subjunctive as the verb "*be*" in "that I be not ashamed," or the verb "*slip*" in "hold thou up my goings in thy paths, that my footsteps slip not." That this is so, is conclusively shown by consulting the older versions. In John xv. 2, for example, "he purgeth it, that it may bring forth more fruit," is, in Wiclif's version, "he shall purge it that it bere the more fruyt." In ver. 16, "that whatsoever ye shall ask of the Father in my name, he may give it you," is "that whatever things ye axen the fadir in my name, he give to you:" and so on, wherever the auxiliary is found in the more modern version.

414. In the daily Morning Prayer, we have, in the third

Collect, "Grant that this day we fall into no sin;" and in the first Prayer Book, in the Collect for St. Mary Magdalen's day, "Give us grace that we never presume to sin through the example of any creature."

415. A statement is sometimes made about this word, which is not in accordance with fact. I remember, a short time since, seeing in a book of instructions how to read the Liturgy, that the omission of the word "may" is only a blunder of the printers, for that it exists in the "sealed book," from which our prayer-books ought to be copied. This is true, and it is untrue. It did exist in the sealed book, but was erased by the bishops, who put the pen through it. Thus its omission was no mistake, but a deliberate act, and intended to convey a particular meaning.

416. In Psalm lxxvii. 14, the Prayer Book version has "Thou art the God that doeth wonders;" whereas the Bible version runs "Thou art the God that doest wonders." A correspondent asks, which is right? The answer I think must be, that both are right. The direct construction of the sentence in English requires the Prayer Book rendering, "Thou art the God that doeth wonders;" whereas the other can be accounted for by a not uncommon attraction of subordinate verbs into the form in which the main sentence is cast.

417. **Singulars and Plurals.** We will now pass on to another matter—the use of *singulars* and *plurals*. It is a general rule, that when a verb has two or more nominative cases to which it belongs, it must be in the plural number. But let us take care what we mean by this in each case. When I say "John and James are here," I mean "John is here, and James is here;" but when I say "*the evening and the morning were the first day*," I do not mean "the evening was the first day, and the morning was the first day," but I mean "*the evening and the morning together made up the first day*." So that here is an important difference. I may use a plural verb when it is true of both its nouns separately, and also when it is only true of them taken together. Now how is this in another example? Am I to say "*two and two are four*," or "*two and two is four*"? Clearly I cannot say *are* on the first explanation, for it cannot be true that two is four and two is four. But

how on the second? Here as clearly I may be grammatically correct in saying "two and two are four," if, that is, I understand something for the two and the four to apply to: two apples and two apples make (*are*) four apples. But when I assert the thing merely as an arithmetical truth, *with no apples*, I do not see how "*are*" can be right. I am saying that the sum of two numbers, which I express by *two and two*, *is*, makes up, another number, *four;* and in all abstract cases, where we merely speak of numbers, the verb is better singular: two and two "*is*" four, not "*are*."

418. "Twice one are two."—The last case was a somewhat doubtful one. But the following, arising out of it, is not so:—We sometimes hear children made to say, "twice one *are* two." For this there is no justification whatever. It is a plain violation of the first rules of grammar; "*twice one*" not being plural at all, but *strictly singular*. Similarly, "three times three *are* nine" is clearly wrong, and so are all such expressions; what we want to say being simply this, that three taken three times makes up, *is* equal to nine. You may as well say, "nine are three times three," as "three times three are nine."

419. Cases not understood.—There still are cases in which those who do not think about the composition of a sentence may find a difficulty as to whether a singular or a plural verb should follow two nouns coupled together by "*and*." The difficulty arises from the fact that "*and*" has many meanings. Sometimes it imports addition; sometimes it merely denotes an apposition, or simultaneous predication of two characters or qualities belonging to one and the same thing. And it is in this latter case that a difficulty arises, and a mistake is often made. Take, for instance, this sentence, where the writer is speaking of the cheapness of Bibles at the present day: "The only revelation of God's will to mankind, and the only record of God's dealings with men, is now to be obtained for a sum which a labouring man might save out of one day's wages." Now what is meant by this sentence is, "That book, which is the only revelation of God's will to men, and at the same time the only record of God's dealings with men, is now to be obtained," &c. One thing, and not two, is the subject

of the sentence. Yet in a precisely similar sentence of my own the other day, the people at the printing-office, more studious for the letter of grammar, than for the spirit of thought, corrected *is* into *are*. And observe the effect on the meaning. If I say, "The only revelation of God's will to men, and the only record of God's dealings with men, *are* to be obtained," &c., I convey the idea that I am speaking of two books, one containing the only revelation of God's will, the other, the only record of his dealings. It is obvious that the writer might have cast the sentence into another form, and having said that the Bible contains the only revelation of God's will, and the only record of God's dealings, might have gone on to say, "Both these are to be obtained," &c.; but constructed as the sentence now is, the singular verb, and not the plural, is required to express his meaning.

420. Take another case. In Psalm xiv. 7, we read, "Destruction and unhappiness *is* in their ways:" in Psalm lxxiii. 25, "My flesh and my heart *faileth*." Again, as was remarked by the critic in the "Times" of September 29th, 1863, in censuring the modernizations in the Cambridge Shakspeare, Shakspeare wrote "His steeds to water at those springs on chaliced flowers that *lies:*" and Prospero is made to say, "*lies* at my mercy all mine enemies." How are these apparent violations of grammar to be accounted for?

421. **Account of these usages.** Simply, I believe, by regarding the sense of the sentences. In each of them, one and the same act is predicated of a number of persons or things, considered as one. In the two former sentences, these things are nearly synonymous: in the two latter, they are classed together. In either case, the act is one: and this fact seems to have ruled the verb in the singular, instead of the more usual plural. It has been mentioned before in these notes, that in the Greek language a plural of the neuter gender takes after it a singular verb. The things composing it are considered as forming one mass rather than a plurality of individuals, and the verb is ruled accordingly.

422. No fault can be found with him who writes, "There have been more applications than one." The form

of the sentence, ruled by the plural noun, is of necessity itself plural. But if the words are to be transposed, "There have been more than one application," the correctness of the plural verb is not so clear. The subject of the verb is "more than one application:" and that phrase is not necessarily plural: it is a kind of abstraction, of the same kind as the literal rendering of that Scripture phrase, "more than Jonas is here." In that case, "are here" would give an erroneous sense. It would seem that "There has been more than one application," is right.

423. "**Either you or I are . . . .**" A correspondent asks which is right: "Either you or I are wrong," or "Either you or I am wrong." This it seems to me is a case where usage has gone astray knowingly, being baffled by the awkwardness of the combined construction. Nothing can be plainer than that the former of these two phrases is grammatically wrong. If "both you and I are wrong," be right, where "you and I" are coupled, "either you or I are wrong," where they are disjoined, can hardly be right. The full sentence is, "Either you (are wrong), or I [am wrong]." We may, if we please, omit the words in square brackets, and thus take the best way of expressing the proposition. But if we prefer to omit the words in curved brackets, we must somehow change the verb. "Either you or I am" is surely intolerable. This has been felt beyond our own tongue. In almost every language, whether ancient or modern, the attempt to enunciate such a sentence is attended with difficulty, and gives rise to an awkward and ungrammatical construction. An admissible form of the sentence, if grammar only were considered, would be "Either you or I is wrong," thus objectivising both, and expressing, "One of us, either you or me, is wrong;" but the sound is harsh, and usages would be violated.

424. I observe that Dr. Latham lays it down as a rule that in such clauses, 1. Whenever the word *either* or *neither* precedes the pronouns, the verb is in the third person. *Either you or I is in the wrong—neither you nor I is in the wrong.* 2. Whenever the disjunctive is simple, i.e., unaccompanied with the word *either* or *neither*, the verb agrees with the *first* of the two pronouns. *I or he am in the wrong.*

He or I is in the wrong. Thou or he art in the wrong. He or thou is in the wrong.

425. Still, I do not think usage sanctions these sentences: and usage, which in the end is the might which makes right, is that of which I am treating.

426. **Verbs with a singular nominative coupled to a plural.**—A difficulty arises as to the proper number of the verb substantive, when it couples a singular nominative case to a plural one. Two correspondents have written on this matter. One cites from a newspaper, "More curates are what we want," and asks whether "*are*" is correct. The other is a printer, and relates that on this sentence being sent for press,—"A special feature of the Reformatory Exhibition were the work-shops and work-rooms," the "Reader" in the office corrected "*were*" to "was;" upon which the Author corrected "was" back again to "were." A dispute arose in the office, some siding with the Reader, some with the Author. The former were the majority; and the minority, though they thought "were" correct, yet acknowledged that "was" would sound better.

427. And I believe that they were thus not only making an ingenuous confession, but giving the key to the whole question. In most cases of this kind, that which sounds right, is right. And that which sounds right is generally, in the examples before us, that the verb should take the number, be it singular or plural, of the preceding nominative case. "More curates are what we want." But invert the proposition, and we must say, "What we want is more curates." So in the other case, "a special feature of the exhibition was, the work-shops, and work-rooms;" but, "the work-shops and work-rooms were a special feature of the exhibition."

428. Still, this rule does not seem to have been always followed by our best writers. In the English Bible, (Prov. xiii. 8,) we have, "the ransom of a man's life *are* his riches;" and in Prov. xvi. 25, "There is a way which seemeth right unto a man, but the end thereof are the ways of death." The translators' rule seems to have been always to use the plural verb-substantive, when either of the nominatives was plural. We have in one and the same

sentence, (Prov. xvii. 6,) "Children's children are the crown of old men: and the glory of children are their fathers:" where it is plain that the occurrence of one plural, and not the order of the substantives, has ruled the number of the verb.

429. Every schoolboy will remember "Amantium iræ amoris integratio est;" in reference to which we may notice, that the Latin possesses the advantage of being able so to arrange the sentence, that the verb shall stand close to, and take the number of, the more important of the two nominative cases.

430. **Mistakes in accepting invitations.**—A curious mistake is often made in accepting invitations. In full half the notes of this kind which are sent, we see, "I shall be very happy to accept your invitation for the 9th." But the acceptance is not a thing future: the acceptance is conveyed by that very note, and your friend, when she gets it, will put you down as having accepted. The sentence is written in confusion between "I shall be very happy to come," and "I am very happy to accept," or "I accept with pleasure." And so the former half of the first sentence gets wedded to the latter half of the second.

431. This kind of confusion sometimes produces comical results. "Pat, does Mr. Flanagan live here?" "Yes, your honour, he does, but he's dead." "Why, when did he die?" "Well, your honour, if he'd lived till next Tuesday, he'd be dead a fortnight." What the man means is tolerably clear. He would say, "He'll have been dead a fortnight come next Tuesday." But in the case of a living man, any assertion of this class must be made with reserve, because he may not live till next Tuesday; so Pat puts on the reserve, and applies it to the dead, who is beyond the reach of uncertainty.

432. Answers to invitations are set thick with traps for the careless and the illiterate. Sometimes, instead of "invitation," we find a noun unknown to our language introduced, and the writer is happy to accept the kind "*invite*" of his host. Sometimes, when the invitation is declined, the poor tenses of verbs are mangled in the most ruthless manner.

Take a few forms at random: "I should be happy to come, but——" "I should have been happy to come, but——" "I should have been happy to have come, but——"

433. I believe all these are in use, one about as often as another. Let us examine them one by one.

"I should be happy to come, but I am pre-engaged." There seems, and I believe there is, no error here. The form of accepting would be, "I shall be happy to come, as I am dis-engaged:" and "should" is the strict conditional correlative of shall.

434. "I should have been happy to come, but I am pre-engaged." This is wrong, and for the following reason: "should have been" is conditional relatively to something that is past. "I should have been in Devonshire last Christmas, but I was ill." And the thing which the writer of the note is speaking of is future, not past. Had the writer said, "I should have been happy to accept your invitation, but I am pre-engaged," all would have been right; because the act of accepting or non-accepting will have belonged to the past, before the host receives the letter.

435. "I should have been happy to have come, but I am pre-engaged." This is doubly wrong. The "should have been" is wrong, as we have just seen: and "to have come" has really no sense at all. Turn it into an acceptance. What can "I shall be happy to have come," mean? Nothing surely, if not this, "I shall be rejoiced when the visit is over," which is a poor compliment to one's friend.

436. Use of certain conjunctional particles.—Care is required in the use of several conjunctional and prepositional particles. The first of these which I shall notice is "*except*." *Except* means *with the exception of*: and exempts from some previous list, or some previous predication, the substantive or substantives, or clause or clauses, before which it is placed. "*All were pleased, except Juno;*" i.e., "*with the exception of Juno,*" or, "*Juno being excepted.*" And on this account, we must take care that the person or thing excepted be one which would have been included in the previous category, if the exception had not been made.

437. Violation of this rule. This rule is violated

in the following sentence taken from a newspaper: "Few ladies, except Her Majesty, could have made themselves heard," &c. For how is the word "except" here to be understood? From what list is Her Majesty excepted, or taken out? Clearly not from among the *few ladies* spoken of. Had the sentence stood "All ladies, except Her Majesty, would have proved unequal to," &c., it would have been constructed rightly, though clumsily; what it meant to express was that "Few ladies besides Her Majesty, could have" done what was spoken of: and "*besides*" should have been the word used. *Besides* (by the side of) does not *subtract*, as *except* does, but *adds*; and thus we should have the sense required: viz., that very few ladies *added to* Her Majesty,—*besides* her,—could have done the thing spoken of.

438. **Use of "except" for "unless."**—There is a use of *except*, which was once very common, but is now hardly ever found: that, I mean, by which it stands for "*unless.*" "I will not let thee go, except thou bless me." This usage is quite legitimate: amounting in fact to saying, "In no case will I let thee go, excepted only that in which thou shalt bless me." This is found constantly throughout the English Version of the Bible, both in the Old Testament and in the New.

439. **"Without."**—*Without* is another word used in somewhat the same meaning. As in the other cases, its prepositional use has led to its conjunctional. Take the following sentence from Sir Philip Sidney: "You will never live to my age, without you keep yourselves in breath with exercise, and in heart with joyfulness." In this, "*without you keep*" is in fact a construction compounded of "*without keeping*," and "*unless*" or "*except you keep.*"

440. **"A mutual friend."**—What are we to think of the expression, "*a mutual friend*"? what is *mutual*? Much the same as "*reciprocal.*" It describes that which passes from each to each of two persons. Thus for example, when St. Paul says to the Romans (i. 12), "That I may be comforted together with you by the mutual faith both of you and me," the meaning is, in English, "by my confidence in you and your confidence in me." And that our translators meant this to be understood is clear: for they

deliberately altered the previous versions to this form. Wiclif had "bi faith that is bothe youre and myn to gidre:" Tyndale, "through the common faith which bothe ye and I have:" so also Cranmer and the Geneva Bible.

441. And *mutual* ought never to be used, unless the reciprocity exists. "The *mutual love* of husband and wife" is correct enough: but "a *mutual friend* of both husband and wife" is sheer nonsense. A *common* friend is meant; a friend that is common to both. The word *mutual* has no place or assignable meaning in such a phrase, and yet we occasionally find it used even by those who pride themselves on correct speaking.

442. "**We will write you.**" There is an expression frequently used in correspondence, principally by mercantile men: "we will *write you*," instead of "we will *write to you*;" "*write me* at your earliest convenience," instead of "*write to me*." Is this an allowable ellipsis? It is universally acknowledged that the "to" of the so-called dative case may be dropped in certain constructions: "He did me a favour;" "he sent me a birthday present;" "He wrote me a kind letter;" "The Lord raised them up deliverers." In all these cases, the object or act which the verb directly governs is expressed. But if it be omitted, the verb at once is taken as governing the personal pronoun or substantive, of which the dative case is thus elliptically expressed. Thus: "He sent me" would mean, not "He sent to me," but *he sent*, as his messenger, *me*. "The Lord raised them up," would imply, not that He raised up some person or thing *for them*, but that He lifted them up themselves.

443. And so, when we drop the substantive directly governed by the verb in the phrase, "He wrote me a letter," or "he wrote me word," and merely say "he *wrote me*," we cannot properly understand the sentence in any other way, than that "*me*" is governed by the verb "*wrote*." That this is nonsense, is not to the purpose. The construction of such a phrase necessarily halts, and is defective, not only elliptical. We should say in all cases, "*write to me*," or "*write me word*," or the like; never barely "write me."

444. "**And which.**"—Very curious blunders in construction are made by the careless use of "*and*" with the *relative pronoun*, coupling it to a sentence which will not bear such coupling. I take these two instances from one and the same page of a charitable report: "The Board offer their grateful acknowledgments for the liberal support hitherto so freely extended, *and which* has so greatly contributed to this satisfactory result." "It was feared that the untimely death of the surgeon to the hospital, occurring as it did so very shortly after its opening, *and to whose* untiring energy the Institution mainly owes its existence, might seriously affect its future prospects and position."

445. Now in both these instances the conjunction "*and*" is wholly unneeded, is indeed quite in the way of the construction. Two clauses connected by "and" must be similarly constructed. You cannot say, "Then I went home and which is quite true." Yet this is the construction of both the sentences quoted: and the fault is one of the very commonest in the writing of careless or half-educated persons.

446. In the *Times* of Nov. 11, 1863, occurred the following sentence, in the translation of M. Casimir Perrier's letter to the President of the Legislative body: "I hoped to procure the original placard which was posted on the walls of Grenoble on that occasion, *but which* I have been unable to do."

The following " Form of Order " was distributed widely by a London publisher:—"*Please send me a copy of the* SHAKESPEARE MEMORIAL, and for which *I enclose Eighteen Postage Stamps.*" I was surprised to find, that Murray's Handbooks for Italy *abound* with this vulgarism.

447. Years have passed since the preceding paragraphs were written, but the vulgarism seems as frequent as ever. This is an answer to an address presented to the Princess of Wales, and is the composition of an English nobleman:

"H.R.H. the Princess of Wales acknowledges, &c., *and for which she is profoundly recognisant.*"

I quote the following from a novel which shall be nameless: "His having been with Lorenzo at the time of his death, *and who* had wished to confess to him, raised him prodigiously in the opinion of all those who had been the admirers of that prince."

I have received a notice this very day from a London bookseller to this effect:

"A. B. C. begs to announce the above important contributions by Dr. T. to Biblical Criticism as nearly ready, *and which* he will have for sale as soon as published."

448. It would be an endless labour to give anything like an adequate number of examples from present writers. Hardly any are free from the fault. I do not hesitate to say, that it is hardly possible to take up a newspaper, a pamphlet, or a book, without finding an instance before many minutes have passed. An expression which a century ago would have been deemed intolerable, is thus fast becoming idiomatic.

449. "**The death is announced of.**"—I fear the same is likely to happen to an odious form of speech which has lately crept into our newspapers: "The death is announced of ——" "The suspension is reported of ——" And sometimes we have the sentence still further divaricated thus, "The death is announced in the Liverpool journals, at his seat in the North of Scotland, of acute bronchitis, of Mr. Blank." The source of this clumsy arrangement must, I suppose, be sought in the fact of our not being able to use the convenient impersonal form of the French, and to say, "They announce." But there are many ways in which the same thing might be better said, and among them the very simple one of keeping the plain order of the words: "The death of Mr. Blank is announced in the Liverpool journals."

In a lately published volume of verse, I found a still more remarkable form of this licence of separating words which ought to stand together: "And shall hit on some plan *to the nuisance abate*."

450. **Erroneous epithets.** Attention has been directed to the erroneous use of adjectives belonging to one bodily sense, with substantives belonging to another. We are told that a "conspicuous voice" is a not uncommon expression. I can testify to having frequently heard "a beautiful smell," and "a beautiful air." Now of course all such expressions will not bear strict investigation; but

are they therefore not allowable? Every one speaks of "beautiful music:" why may we not say, "a beautiful odour"?

451. The distinction seems to be this. Any word may be used in that which is called a metaphorical sense: *i.e.*, may be transferred from a material to a mental meaning. Thus "beautiful" being originally a word belonging to the sense of sight, may be transferred to the inward sight, and things may be called beautiful which are apprehended by the mind, with or without the aid of sense. Thus we recognise Beauty in art. Poetry, Painting, Music, are arts: the first apprehended by the eye, the ear, and the thought,—the second by the eye and the thought,—the third by the ear and the thought. In all these the mental vision sees Beauty: we may have beautiful poetry, beautiful painting, beautiful music. But smell is not an art: the mere enjoyment of wholesome air is not an art: in neither is there any scope for Beauty, and consequently of neither must "beautiful" be said. "A conspicuous voice" is even worse: it is an absolute defiance of correctness: a torturing of the machinery of one sense into the grooves of another.

452 "**Proclivities,**" what.—This torturing of words may sometimes be perpetrated where people little suspect it. The Americanism "proclivities" is sometimes a convenient word. It is used as equivalent to "tendencies." But, in reality, it does only half the work of the English term. *Clivus* being Latin for a hill, *proclivis* is an adjective signifying down-hill, while *acclivis* signifies up-hill. We have the term "acclivity" in English, meaning an upward slope. So that when we use "proclivities," we must take care that we confine it to its proper meaning. To speak, as the *Record* did last week, of a statesman having "High Church proclivities," is to make a blunder in terms. A proclivity can never carry a man up on high. The achievement of the man who used to walk up an inclined plane on a rolling globe would be far surpassed by him who through any manner of proclivities should attain to High Churchmanship. I would venture to suggest that as the American term has this defect, it would be better to discard it and employ the English one.

453. This distinction has been objected to as hypercriticism. It has been said that if we are thus precise, we ought to say "An army fled in a state of *diffusion*," instead of "*confusion*," seeing that they scatter as they flee. But surely the illustration is beside the mark. To say that an army fled in a state of diffusion, would be to say that it fled in a state of flying. By the latter words of the clause we do not want to express the same as by the former. When an army flies, *con*-fusion has plenty of examples. Discipline is confused; ranks are confused; and if the literal sense of the word is insisted on, its elements are abundantly " fused or blended together."

454. "One" joined to "his."—There is an unfortunate word in our language, which few can use without very soon going wrong in grammar, or, which is worse, in common sense. It is the word "*one*," used in the sense of the French "*on*," or the German "*man*," and meaning people in general.

> "What one has done, when one was young,
>   One ne'er will do again;
> In former days one went by coach,
>   But now one goes by train."

So far, "*one*" is pretty sure to be right. It is only when this is carried on further, that the danger arises. Suppose I wanted to put into English the saying of the French gourmand, which, by the way, I am glad an Englishman did not originally utter: "Avec cette sauce on pourrait manger son propre père;"—how am I to express myself? In other words, how am I to take up the "*one*" with the possessive pronoun, or with any possessive, in English? The French, we see, say, "With this sauce one could eat his own father." Is this an English usage (I don't mean the meal but the grammar)? I believe not, though it is becoming widely spread in current literature.

> "In such a scene one might forget his cares,
>   And dream himself, in poet's mood, away."

And one of my correspondents says, "When writing on language, grammar, and composition, *one* ought to be more than usually particular in *his* endeavours to be *himself* correct."

455. These sentences do not seem to me to be right. Having used "*one*," we must also use "*one's*" cares, and "*one's*" self. We must say, at the risk of sacrificing elegance of sound,

> "In such a scene one might forget one's cares,
> And dream one's self, in poet's mood, away."

The fact is, that this "*one*" is a very awkward word to get into a long sentence. I have sometimes seen it in our newspapers, followed not only by "*he*" and "*his*," but by "*they*" and "*their*," and "*we*" and "*our*," in all stages of happy confusion.

456. "**Didn't use**," "**hadn't used**," &c.—There is another word in our common English very difficult to keep right. It is the verb "*use*," signifying to be accustomed. "I *used* to meet him at my uncle's." When the verb is affirmatively put in this manner, there is no difficulty, and no chance of going wrong. These arise when we want to put it in the negative; to speak of something which we were not accustomed to do. And then we find rather curious combinations. I "*didn't use*," I "*hadn't used*," I "*wasn't used*." This latter would be legitimate enough, if the verb were "*used to*," meaning "*accustomed by use to*." We may say, "*I wasn't used to the practice*." But it will be plain that it is a different meaning of which I am now speaking. A friend tells me that in his part of the world the people say, "*didn't use to was:*" and a midland correspondent, that he has heard in his town, even in good society, the phrase, "*used to could*." I have a confirmation of this in a letter from Derby. My correspondent says both expressions are very common there. "I have even," he says, "heard 'used to did.' Perhaps," he adds, "the following example may be new to you. A young man speaks who has married in haste, and is repenting at leisure:

> "'And when I think on what I am,
> And what I used to was,
> I feel I've throwed myself away
> Without sufficient cause.'"

457. If you ask me what we are to say in this case, I must reply that I can answer very well on paper, but not so

well for the purposes of common talk. "*I used*" is negatived by "*I used not.*" But unfortunately, this expression does not do the work in common talk. "*I used not to see him at my uncle's,*" does not convey the idea that it was not your habit to meet him there. It rather means, that he was there, but that for some unexplained reason you did not see him. You meant to express, not something which it *was* your practice *not to do*, but something which it *was not* your practice *to do*. "*I never used*" is better, but it may be too strong. I am afraid there is no refuge but in the inelegant word "*usedn't,*" to which I suppose most of us have many times been driven.

458. "**Riding,**" "**driving.**"—*Riding* or *driving?* This question has been asked by several correspondents, in consequence of my story, told further on, of a benevolent old gentleman "*riding in his carriage.*" I am asked whether this ought not to have been "*driving,*" seeing that riding cannot properly be predicated except of persons on horseback. But there is not necessarily any such limitation of the meaning of the word to *ride*. It comes certainly from a time when the employment of wheels was almost unknown; but from centuries ago has been applied to any kind of locomotion in which a person or thing is borne, whether on an animal, or in a carriage, or as when used of a ship on the water. A *road* is a broad path on which people may *ride* on horses and in vehicles: a *road*, or *rade*, for ships, is a part of the sea where they may *ride*, or be borne at anchor. We have in Jer. xvii. 25, "Riding in chariots and on horses;" and such, as may be seen in the dictionaries, is the usage of all English writers.

459. "**I take it.**"—It is a curious symptom of our having forgotten the usages of the best age of English, that several correspondents should have objected to my having written "*I take it,*" signifying, "such is my opinion." For it is constantly found, from Shakspeare onwards, in this sense: and the sense is amply justified by other cognate usages of the verb to take: such as, *to take it well or ill, to take it in good part, to take a man for his brother*, and the like. The fact of such an objection having been made, shows the necessity for upholding our plain nervous colloquial English against the inroads of modern fine language.

It would be a loss instead of a gain if "*I take it,*" were to be superseded by "*I apprehend;*" or, as we should be sure to have it pronounced, "*I happryend.*"

460. "**The earth's revolving.**"—Another correspondent inquires respecting the construction of such sentences as the following:—"Day and night are a consequence of the earth revolving on its axis." He maintains, that here, *revolving* is a verbal noun equivalent to *revolution*, and that we ought to say, "A consequence of the *earth's revolving* on its axis." He believes that he has proved this by the test of substituting the pronoun for the earth, thus: "Day and night on our earth are a consequence of *its revolving* on its axis," where he rightly says no one would think of saying *it revolving*.

461. At first sight this appears decisive. But let us examine a little further. It is somewhat curious that, in this last sentence, we may leave out the possessive pronoun, without obscuring the sense. "Our earth enjoys day and night as a consequence of revolving on its axis." To which a rejoinder may be made, "of *what* revolving on its axis?" and the answer is "*the earth,*" not "*the earth's.*" We may, if we wish, regard *the earth revolving on its axis* as a description of an idea set before the mind. The fact indicated by that idea, viz., that the earth does so revolve, produces as a consequence day and night. Day and night, in other words, are a consequence of that fact so indicated: *i.e.*, of the *earth revolving* on her axis.

462. I believe, then, that both forms are correct in point of construction: and a writer will use one or the other, according as euphony admits or requires. In an instance which my correspondent cited, where I say that "the profusion of commas prevented the text being understood," it is plain that "the text's being understood" would have been harsh and ill-sounding. I believe that, as a general matter of choice, I rather prefer the form of the sentence to which my correspondent objects. It may be that my ears are accustomed to the Greek and Latin construction, which is according to this form and not to the other.

463. In such sentences as "on the war (or, war's) coming to an end,"—"on a difficulty (or, difficulty's) presenting itself," I believe it will be found that usage is not

uniform. We always write the possessive of pronouns in such constructions, but not always of nouns. "On his appearing,...." " on my becoming aware of it,...." "the cause of its turning sour," and the like. But if we convert these pronouns into the nouns which they represent, the usage will not be consistent with itself. We say, "On Henry's appearing..."; but we say, "the cause of the milk (not, the milk's) turning sour." I believe the difference will be found to consist in this: that we attribute possession to persons more readily than to things. But this fails, when we represent both by pronouns. That "*it*" did not always take a possessive, we have observed above, par. 12. Nor does it seem to hold, even with nouns, universally. We say equally, "On the question being put," and "On the chairman rising to put the question." So that I fear we must leave usage to its freaks.

464. – The double genitive.—A correspondent has questioned altogether the legitimacy of the double genitive (as he calls it) in such sentences as "How many hired servants of my Father's..." He would have it "of my Father," and, being a clergyman, always reads it so. In so doing, he violates not only order, but the propriety of language also. In such sentences, the " of " preceding the noun in the genitive is not one of possession, but of partition. " How many servants of my Father's " – " How many servants from among those of my Father," or if we like to call the sentence elliptical, and fill it out, " How many servants of my Father's |servants|." That this is the construction, will be seen, if we consider in what cases this form can be used. We can say, " A country house of my father's," because it is thereby implied that the father has more houses than one, and that this is one of them: we cannot say, " the country house of my father's," but must say " the country house of my father."

This form is useful as frequently conducing to perspicuity. In a phrase to which my correspondent objects, " A creation of the dean's," " one from among the dean's creations," the form which he prefers, " A creation of the dean," would at all events convey an ambiguous meaning.

465. A variety of this useful way of speaking occurs when we say, "That saying of your's," "those books of

mine," and the like. My correspondent does not, I imagine, propose to correct these phrases to, "That saying of you," "those books of me."

466. "**Predicate for predict.**"—A correspondent finds that the newspapers are in the habit of using "*predicate*" where they mean "*predict*." I have not observed this; but it may be well to say, that to *predicate* is simply to affirm this or that of anything, whereas to *predict* is to foretell a future event.

467. There are certain cases where either word might be used without a fault. And such is the very instance cited by my correspondent:—"It is impossible to predicate what the result will be." The writer very likely meant, to *predict*; but he might have intended to say, that no one can *predicate* this or that probable result. If so, he expressed himself clumsily, but did not fall into the error complained of.

468. "**If**" for "**whether**."—"*If*" for "*whether*," is another mistake which I am asked to point out. But this usage, though it may not be according to our modern habit, is found in our best writers; and I cannot see that there is anything to complain of in it. Under the word "*if*," in Johnson, we have, cited from Dryden:

"Uncertain if by augury or chance."

And from Prior,

"Doubting if she doubts or no."

We also read (Gen. viii. 8) that Noah "sent forth a dove from him, to see if the waters were abated from off the face of the ground."

469. "**Seldom or never.**"—Another of my correspondents is offended with "*seldom or never*," and prefers "*seldom, if ever.*" It seems to me that the two express the same idea in slightly differing ways, but that both are perfectly legitimate. The one is analogous to "*very little, or not at all,*" the other to "*very little, if at all.*"

470. "**Like I do.**"—"*Like*," used as an adverb, is also brought under my notice, and the complaint in this case is not without reason. "*Like I do now*," "*like he was*," "*like we are*," are quite indefensible, and are avoided by

all careful speakers and writers. The mistake has been occasioned by the legitimate use of "*like*" as an adjective at the beginning of a sentence, where it means "*like to.*" You may say, "*Like David,* I am the youngest of my family;" but you may not say, "*Like David was,* I am the youngest of my family."

471. **Nouns of number.**—*Nouns of number* are also proposed as a subject for treatment. I am supposed to have written incorrectly (par. 506), "When the band of French Guides were in this country;" and the opinion is supported by reminding me that we say "There was a large congregation," not "there were a large congregation." Most true: and from the consideration of this example we may derive something like a rule in such cases. In saying "*there was a large congregation,*" I am speaking of the assembly *as a whole.* If I were saying anything which suggested the idea of the *individuals composing it,* I should use, not the singular verb, but the plural. I should hardly say, "*the congregation was not all of the same opinion,*" but "*the congregation were not all of the same opinion.*" The slightest bias either way will influence a writer, when using such words, towards a singular or a plural verb. I should say, that in the case complained of, perhaps it was the fact of "*Guides,*" in the plural, being the word immediately preceding the verb, that induced me to put it in the plural; or perhaps the knowledge that I was about to speak of the band throughout the following sentences, as "*they,*" "*the Frenchmen,*" &c.

472. **"People" and "Persons."**—A correspondent wishes me to observe that the former of these terms signifies an aggregate of *persons,* and that we ought never to say *several people,* but always *several persons.* I own I cannot find that this distinction is entirely borne out. Bacon, as adduced by Johnson, says, "If a man temper his actions so as to content *every combination of people,* the musick will be the fuller;" in which sentence, "*people*" seems to be used for "*persons.*" Still, it is a distinction which it is worth while to remember: for doubtless it is so far just, that it represents the general import of the two words.

473. Another correspondent complains that these two words are still used as synonymous: "to me," he says, "a very offensive vulgarism. It is periodically announced by the clergyman of the church to which I go here, that there will be the usual monthly sermons for the young this afternoon, at which the attendance of 'young people' is particularly requested. Now it seems to me that 'people' is a collective noun of the singular number, and should only be used as such, never for '*persons.*' Should I be right if I said that the latter is the concrete of people?"

I must reply, that I still cannot see the distinction, nor did I find it observed by our best writers. Even supposing it to exist, usage has set in so decidedly against it, that it would be pedantry for our age to insist on reviving it. We should have to sing, "All persons that on earth do dwell," which may be a correction, but certainly is not an improvement.

474. The modern plural *folks* has been impugned. But usage has so thoroughly sanctioned it, that purism will at this time of day protest in vain. Nay, as so often where a new form has been introduced, the old form takes a different meaning from its previous one. "The Conies are a feeble folk": but we could not say, "The Conies are feeble folks." Nor, again, could we speak of the "old folk at home."

475. Another correspondent finds fault with a common method of speech in which we make the abstract noun into the concrete: "Twenty clergy walking in procession." But this surely is defensible, nay, is sometimes necessary. "Twenty clergymen walking in procession," may mean the same thing, but does not so plainly indicate that they walked where they did, because they were clergymen. After all, "twenty clergy" is only an abbreviated form of twenty of the clergy, the clerisy, or the clerical profession. In another profession, the adjective is used to perform a similar duty: we speak of calling in the "*military.*"

476. It is somewhat curious to observe the different forms which have come to designate the professions. Ministers of religion are "the clergy," soldiers are "the military," sailors hardly have a collective name, but are individually known as "Jack," or, if pluralised, "the blue

jackets;" lawyers are "the bar," or the "gentlemen of the long robe," though their robes are no longer than those of the clergy; medical men are the "faculty"; judges are "the bench," or "bigwigs." Artists, engineers, architects, seem to be as yet without collective names.

477. "I know nothing by myself," explained.—Another correspondent is puzzled by my having said that "a man who talks of Aristobūlus in the lesson, is as likely as not to preach from St. Paul's, '*I know nothing by myself,*' to show us that the apostle *wanted divine teaching,* and not to be aware that he meant he *was not conscious of any fault.*" My correspondent cannot conceive how the words can have any other meaning, than that the apostle had no knowledge of his own. His difficulty (and I mention it because it may be that of many others besides him) is that he has missed the peculiar sense of the preposition "*by,*" as here used. It bears the sense of "*of,*" in the words, "*I know no harm of him.*" This is still in the midland counties, "*I know no harm by him.*" We have a somewhat similar usage in the Prayer-book version of Ps. xv. 4, "*He that setteth not by himself,*" i.e., is not self-conceited, setteth not store by himself, as we even now say. I have heard a parish clerk pronounce these last words, "*he that sitteth not by himself,*" in allusion, I suppose, to the Squire's pew. To return to "*I know nothing by myself.*" The meaning is decided for us by the original Greek, which is simply, "I am conscious of no fault:" and it is plain that the words of the English version were so understood when they were first written; for Dr. Donne, in King James the First's time, preaches on them, and quotes them over and over again, in this sense.

478. "The three 'poys' just mentioned."—A correspondent who gives me his name vouches for the following anecdote. I own I had fancied it was an old story; but so many things related in Joe Miller have happened again within my own experience, that I must not too readily admit a doubt of my correspondent's accuracy. "My friend," he says, "happened to be present one Sabbath in a parish church some miles north of Aberdeen, the clergyman of which (a true Gael) read to his hearers a portion of the book of Daniel, containing the names 'Shadrach,

Meshach, and Abednego.' The reverend gentleman finding some difficulty in delivering himself of these vocables, resolved not to attempt the task a second time, but simply referred to '*the three "poys" just mentioned.*'"

479. I have received another and fuller account of this kind of abbreviation, certified with the name of the hearer, which is a guarantee for its accuracy. In this case the officiating clergyman said, "*same three gentlemen*," and instead of repeating the details of instruments, "sackbut, psaltery," &c., read, "*music as before.*"

480. "**Religion in the arm-chair.**"—In illustration, not of the habit of mispronouncing, but, what is worse, of misunderstanding, another correspondent assures me that he heard a man, pretending to be a teacher of the Gospel, preach on what he called "Religion in the arm-chair," his text being (1 Tim. v. 4), '*Let them learn first to show piety at home :*' where the word "*piety,*" as the margin of the English Bible would have informed him, means merely "*kindness to their relations,*" and has nothing to do with religion in the stricter sense.

481. A correspondent sends me the following. "A placard is to be seen in a certain farmyard in this county:—

"'There is a place for everything, and everything for a place. Any person offending against these rules will forfeit 2d.'"

482. "**The right man in the right place.**"—By-the-by, what are we to think of the phrase which came in during the Crimean war, "*The right man in the right place*"? How can the right man ever be in the wrong place? or the wrong man in the right place? We used to illustrate the unfitness of things by saying that the round man had got into the square hole, and the square man into the round hole; that was correct enough; but it was the *putting incongruous things together* that was wrong, not the man, nor the hole.

483. "**His wrong slippers.**"—This puts me in mind of the servant at school once coming into the schoolroom, in consequence of some interchange of slippers, and calling out, "Has any gentleman got *his wrong slippers?*" Now, if they were his, they were not wrong; and if they were wrong, they were not his.

484. In the two great hotels at Paris, a notice in the rooms was wont to proclaim among other articles of the tariff, the cost of attendance, &c., to an "ill person." This reminded one that *well* and *ill* in our modern use are only predicates, and never epithets. We can say "a person who is ill," but not "an ill person:" we can say "I am well," but not "I am in a well state of health."

485. We still retain the epithetal use in proverbs and antiquated phrases. "It's an ill wind that blows nobody any good:" "doing a man an ill turn."

486. Such adjectives seem to have half lost their adjectival force, and to have almost become adverbs. The adjectival predicative sense, be it observed, is physical only. We may say, "He behaved ill," but not, "His behaviour was ill:" "He treated him well," but not, "His treatment of him was well." For these latter respectively we must substitute "bad" and "good."[1]

487. My correspondent also sent me the following: A Mr. Crispin of Oxford announced that he sold "boots and shoes made by celebrated Hoby, London." Mr. Hoby, irate, put into the Oxford paper: "The boots and shoes Mr. Crispin says he sells of my make is a lie."

488. **Ambiguous description of men.**—Some odd *descriptions* of *men* have been forwarded me, arising from the ambiguous junction of compound words. In two or three places in London, we see "*Old and New Bookseller*"—an impossible combination in one and the same man; but of course meaning a seller of old and new books. Another tradesman describes himself as "*Gas-holder and Boiler-maker*," meaning that he makes gas-holders and boilers, but giving the idea that he undertakes to contain gas himself. We had in Canterbury a worthy neighbour, who advertised himself as "Indigenous Kentish Herbalist;" meaning, of course, not that he was born amongst us, but that he made *herbs indigenous in Kent* his study.

489. I have lying on my table a note just received, in the following words: "R. C. begs to apologise for not acknowledging P. O. order at the time (but was from home), and thus got delayed, misplaced, and forgotten."

[1] See Appendix.

490. A correspondent sends me the following note: "Mrs. A.'s compliments to Mrs. B., and begs to say that C. lived with her for a year and found her respectable, steady, and honest."

491. "**By applying.**"—"*By doing a thing,*" for "*if he will do it,*" is noticed by a friend as a common error in Scotch papers.

"Found on board the steamer 'Vulcan,' a gold locket. The owner may have it *by* giving the date when lost, and paying expenses."

"Found, in Stockwell Street, on Friday early, a gold or gold-plated Geneva watch. The owner may have the same on proving his property, *by* applying to Mr. R. B., 166, Hospital Street."

492. "**Wants cutting.**"—Is it right, a correspondent asks, to say "his hair wants cutting," "the lawn wants mowing?" I should say, undoubtedly. His hair wants a certain act performed on it. What is that process called? *Cutting.* The word is, of course, a present participle, but it is used almost as a substantive. Thus we say, "the first and second mowings of the lawn were difficult, the third was easier." Thus, too, we speak of a "flogging;" of "readings" of Shakspeare, &c. "*He wants his hair cutting*" cannot be similarly defended, nor indeed at all; it ought to be, "he wants his hair *cut.*"

493. **Deterioration of the language itself.**—But I now come, from the by-rules and details of the use of the language, to speak of an abuse far more serious than those hitherto spoken of; even the tampering with and deteriorating the language itself. I believe it to have been in connexion with an abuse of this kind, that the term "the King's English" was first devised. We know that it is a crime to clip the King's coin; and the phrase in which we first find the term which forms the subject of our essay, is, "*clipping the King's English.*" So that it is not improbable that the analogy between debasing language and debasing coin first led to it.

494. **Sources of our language.**—Now in this case the charge is twofold; that of clipping, and that of beating out and thinning down the Queen's English. And it is wonderful how far these, especially the latter, have pro-

ceeded in our days. It is well to bear in mind, that our English comes mainly from two sources; rather, perhaps, that its parent stock, the British, has been cut down, and grafted with the two scions which form the present tree:—the Saxon, through our Saxon invaders; and the Latin, through our Norman invaders. Of these two, the Saxon was, of course, the earlier, and it forms the staple of the language. Almost all our older and simpler ideas, both for things and acts, are expressed by Saxon words. But as time went on, new wants arose, new arts were introduced, new ideas needed words to express them; and these were taken from the stores of the classic languages, either direct, or more often through the French. We all remember that Gurth and Wamba complain, in "Ivanhoe," that the farm-animals, as long as they had the toil of tending them, were called by the Saxon and British names, *ox, sheep, calf, pig*; but when they were cooked and brought to table, their invaders and lords enjoyed them under the Norman and Latin names of *beef, mutton, veal*, and *pork*. This is characteristic enough; but it lets us, in a few words, into an important truth. Even so the language grew; its nerve, and vigour, and honesty, and manliness, and toil, mainly brought down to us in native Saxon terms, while all its vehicles of abstract thought and science, and all its combinations of new requirements as the world went on, were clothed in a Latin garb. To this latter class belong all those larger words in *-ation* and *-ations*, the words compounded with *ex* and *in* and *super*, and the like.

495. It would be mere folly in a man to attempt to confine himself to one or other of these two main branches of the language in his writing or his talk. They are inseparable; welded together, and overlapping each other, in almost every sentence which we use. But short of exclusive use of one or the other, there is a very great difference in respect of the *amount* of use between writers and speakers. He is ever the most effective writer and speaker, who knows how to build the great body of his discourse out of his native Saxon; availing himself indeed of those other terms without stint, as he needs them, but not letting them give the character and complexion to the whole.

496. **Process of degeneration : whence mainly arising. In what consisting.**—Unfortunately, all the tendency of the lower kind of writers of modern English is the other way. The language, as known and read by thousands of Englishmen and Englishwomen, is undergoing a sad and rapid process of deterioration. Its fine manly Saxon is getting diluted into long Latin words not carrying half the meaning. This is mainly owing to the vitiated and pretentious style which passes current in our newspapers. The writers in our journals seem to think that a fact must never be related in print in the same terms in which it would be told by word of mouth. The greatest offenders in this point are the country journals, and, as might be expected, just in proportion to their want of real ability. Next to them comes the London penny press; indeed, it is hardly a whit better; and highest in the scale, but still by no means free from this fault, the regular London press—its articles being for the most part written by men of education and talent in the various political circles. The main offence of the newspapers, the head and front of their offending, is, the insisting on calling common things by uncommon names ; changing our ordinary short Saxon nouns and verbs for long words derived from the Latin. And when it is remembered that this is very generally done by men for the most part ignorant of the derivation and strict meaning of the words they use, we may imagine what delightful confusion is thus introduced into our language. A Latin word which really has a meaning of its own, and might be a very useful one if confined to that meaning, does duty for some word, whose significance extends far wider than its own meaning ; and thereby to common English hearers loses its own proper force, besides utterly confusing their notions about the thing which its new use intended to represent.

497. **Dialect of our journals.**—Our journals seem indeed determined to banish our common Saxon words altogether. You never read in them of a *man*, or a *woman*, or a *child*. A man is an "*individual*," or a "*person*," or a "*party ;*" a woman is a "*female ;*" or if unmarried, a "*young person*," which expression, in the newspapers, is

N

always of the feminine gender; a child is a "*juvenile*," and children *en masse* are expressed by that most odious term, "*the rising generation*." As to the former words, it is certainly curious enough that the same debasing of our language should choose, in order to avoid the good honest Saxon *man*, two words, "*individual*" and "*party*," one of which expresses a man's *unity*, and the other, in its common untechnical use, belongs to man *associated*. And why should a *woman* be degraded from her position as a rational being, and be expressed by a word which might belong to any animal tribe, and which, in our version of the Bible, is never used except of animals, or of the abstract, the sex in general? Why not call a man a "*male*," if a woman is to be a "*female*"?

498. " Party."—The word *party* for a man is especially offensive. Strange to say, the use is not altogether modern. It occurs in the English version of the apocryphal book of Tobit vi. 7, " If an evil spirit trouble any, one must make a smoke thereof before the man or the woman, and the party shall be no more vexed." And in Shakspeare ("Tempest," act iii. sc. 2):

"STEPHANO: How now shall this be compassed? Canst thou bring me to the party?

"CALIBAN: Yea, yea, my lord: I'll yield him thee asleep, where thou may'st knock a nail into his head."

And a correspondent quotes from Archbishop Ussher that, relating how he had been obliged to rebuke one of his clergy, he writes, " I sent for the party, and upon conference had with him, I put him in mind," &c. I once heard a venerable dignitary pointed out by a railway porter as "*an old party in a shovel*." Curious is the idea raised in one's mind by hearing of "*a short party going over the bridge*." Curious also that raised by an advertisement sent me; " Wanted, *a party* to teach a young man dancing *privately*. Apply, &c."

499. **Technical sense of** " party."—I have said that *party*, in its common untechnical use, signifies *man associated*. But we must remember that it has a technical use also. " I don't think," says a correspondent, " that party must mean '*man associated*,' but that it means one or more persons as regarded in relation to one or more others:

and that by following out this, the passages in 'Tobit' and the 'Tempest' may be cleared, without giving any countenance to bagman's English. The *parties* (partes) in a lawsuit may be each a single person: and a clergyman who gives out a notice about 'these *parties* being joined together,' although he is wrong in departing from the Prayer-book, does not seem to me incorrect in language."

500. This view seems to be borne out by other examples of this use of "party," in English authors. In Beaumont and Fletcher's " Wit at Several Weapons," (act ii. sc. 3,) we have,—

" Whatsoever things have past between the lady
And the other party " . . .

And again,—

" Are things of no moment betwixt parties and parties ? "

Also in " The Captain," (act iii. sc. 3,)—

" My brother will be here, and——
What ?
The other party.
What party ? "

But such examples furnish no justification of "*party*," as applied to a single person where no other is concerned.

501. " Proceed."—The newspaper writers never allow us to *go* anywhere, we always *proceed*. A man going home, is set down as "an individual *proceeding* to his *residence*."

502. " Partake."—We never *eat*, but always *partake*, even though we happen to eat up the whole of the thing mentioned. In court, counsel asks a witness, "Did you have anything to eat there ? " " Yes." " What was it ? " " A bun." Now go to the report in the paper, and you'll be sure to find that " witness confessed to having *partaken of* a bun*,*" as if some one else shared it with him.

503. " Locality."—We never hear of a *place;* it is always a *locality*. Nothing is ever *placed*, but always *located*. " Most of the people of the place" would be a terrible vulgarism to these gentlemen; it must be " *the majority of the residents in the locality*."

504. " Apartments."—Then no one lives in *rooms*, but

always in "*apartments.*" "*Good lodgings*" would be far too meagre; so we have "*eligible apartments.*"

Besides being a vulgarity, this is also an impropriety. An *apartment* is properly, not one room, but a set of rooms: the portion of the house which is set apart for one occupant, or family of occupants. In foreign towns, this is the English use of the word still, as it is the uniform foreign use.

505. **An euphuistic blacksmith.**—I witnessed the other day a curious example of the use of fine words. A blacksmith was endeavouring to persuade the smoke of my kitchen range to go up the chimney instead of filling the room. He tried to explain to me the conditions under which this might be done; and to my astonishment added, "You may always measure the success of an apparatus of this construction, by the *incandescence of the ignited material.*"

506. "**Evince.**"—No man ever *shews* any feeling, but always "*evinces*" it. This "*evince,*" by the way, is one of the most odious words in all this catalogue of vulgarities, for such they really are. Everybody "*evinces*" everything. No one *asks*, but "*evinces a desire.*" No one is hurt, but "*evinces a sense of suffering.*" No one thanks another, but "*evinces gratitude.*" I remember, when the French band of the "Guides" were in this country, to have read in the "Illustrated News," that as they *proceeded*, of course, along the streets of the *metropolis* (we never read of *London* in polite journals), they were *vehemently* (everybody does everything vehemently) cheered by the assembled *populace* (that is the genteel name for the people). And what do you suppose the Frenchmen did in return? Of course, something very different from what Englishmen would have done under similar circumstances. But did they toss up their caps, and cry, *Vive l'Angleterre?* The "Illustrated News" did not condescend to enter into such details; all it told us was, that they "*evinced a reciprocity*"!

507. "**Commence.**" – Again, we never *begin* anything in the newspapers now, but always *commence*. I read lately in a Taunton paper, that a horse "*commenced kicking.*" And the printers seem to think it quite wrong to violate this rule. Repeatedly, in drawing up handbills for charity

sermons, I have written, as I always do, "Divine service will *begin* at so and so;" but almost always it has been altered to "*commence;*" and once I remember the bill being sent back after proof, with a "*query, commence?*" written against the word. But even *commence* is not so bad as "*take the initiative*," which is the newspaper phrase for the other more active meaning of the verb to *begin*.

508. "Eventuate."—Another horrible word, which is fast getting into our language through the provincial press, is to "*eventuate.*" If they want to say that a man spent his money till he was ruined, they tell us that *his unprecedented extravagance eventuated* in the total dispersion of his property.

509. "Avocation."—"*Avocation*" is another monster patronised by these writers. Now *avocation*, which of itself is an innocent word enough, means the being called *away* from something. We might say, "He could not do it, having avocations elsewhere." But in our newspapers, *avocation* means a man's calling in life. If a shoemaker at his work is struck by lightning, we read, that "*while pursuing his avocation, the electric fluid penetrated the unhappy man's person.*"

510. "Persuasion."—"*Persuasion*" is another word very commonly and very curiously used by them. We all know that *persuasion* means the fact of being *persuaded*, by argument or by example. But in the newspapers, it means a sect or *way of belief*. And strangely enough, it is most generally used of that very sect and way of belief, whose characteristic is this, that they refuse to be persuaded. We constantly read of the "*Hebrew persuasion*," or the "*Jewish persuasion.*" I expect soon to see the term widened still more, and a man of colour described as "*an individual of the negro persuasion.*"

511. "To sustain."—Not only our rights of conscience, but even our sorrows are invaded by this diluted English. In the papers, a man does not now *lose his mother:* he *sustains* (this I saw in a country paper) *bereavement of his maternal relative.* By the way, this verb *to sustain* is doing just now a great deal of work not its own. It means, you know, to endure, to bear up under; to *sustain* a bereavement, does not properly mean merely to undergo or suffer

a loss, but to behave bravely under it. In the newspapers, however, "*sustain*" comes in for the happening to men of all the ills and accidents possible. Men never break their legs, but they always "*sustain a fracture*" of them; a phrase which suggests to one the idea of the poor man with both hands holding up the broken limb to keep it straight.

512. "**To experience.**"—Akin to *sustain* is the verb to *experience*, now so constantly found in our newspapers. No one *feels*, but *experiences a sensation*. Now, in the best English, *experience* is a substantive, *not a verb at all*. But even if it is to be held (see above, paragraph 229), that the modern dialect has naturalized it, let us have it at least confined to its proper meaning, which is not simply to *feel*, but to have *personal knowledge of by trial*.'

513. "**To accord.**"—Another such verb is to "*accord*," which is used for "*award*," or "*adjudge*." "*The prize was accorded*," we read, "*to so and so*." If a lecturer is applauded at the end of his task, we are told that "*a complete ovation was accorded him*."

514. "**To entail.**"—*Entail* is another poor injured verb. Nothing ever *leads* to anything as a consequence, or brings it about, but it always *entails* it. This smells strong of the lawyer's clerk; as does another word which we sometimes find in our newspapers, *in its entirety* instead of *all* or *the whole*.

515. "**Desirability**," "**displenishing**."—*Desirability* is a terrible word. I found it the other day, I think, in a leading article in the *Times*. And a correspondent sent me a quotation from the *Standard*, in which *displenishing* occurs.

516. "**Reliable.**" *Reliable* is hardly legitimate. We do not *rely a man*, we *rely upon a man*; so that reliable does duty for *rely-upon-able*. "*Trustworthy*" conveys all the meaning required.

517. "**Allude.**" *Allude to* is used in a new sense by the journals, and not only by them, but also by the Government offices. If I have to complain to the Post-Office that a letter legibly directed to me at Canterbury has been missent to

¹ I read the other day in the *Times*, that the weather had experienced a change!

Caermarthen, I get a regular red-tape reply, beginning "The letter *alluded to* by you." Now I did not *allude to* the letter at all; I *mentioned* it as plainly as I could.

518. **Innovations in talk.**—I have had an amusing letter from which I extract the following: " All you say is indeed most true: I grieve over the changes and innovations in our language I hear daily around me, especially among young people. Young people say '*Thanks*' now, never 'Thank you.' I am sick of '*abnormal*,' and '*æsthetic*,' and '*elected*' for 'chosen,' all used most absurdly by modern writers. '*Advent*' for 'coming' I hate; it seems a sacred word, which ought to be only used for our Saviour's coming. Why has '*people*' now an *s* added to it? It never used to have; we do not yet say '*sheeps*;' and both are nouns of multitude. I can't bear to be asked at dinner if Mr. Blank shall *assist* me to anything, instead of help, and yet both mean much the same, but the former smacks of 'the commercial gent.' I dare say I could think of many more follies and vulgarisms, but I shall tire you. I wish you to write a third article on the subject. Excuse an old-fashioned single woman (not a *female*) having plagued you with this letter."

519. "**Thanks.**" We had better take in order the words complained of. "*Thanks*" for "Thank you," seems to deserve better treatment than it meets with at our good Priscilla's hands. It is, first, of respectable parentage and brotherhood: having descended from classic languages, and finding both examples in our best writers,[1] and present associates in the most polished tongues of Europe. And then, as generally used, it serves admirably the purpose of the generation now coming up, who are for the most part a jaunty, off-handed set, as far as possible removed from the prim proprieties of our younger days. "Thank you" was formal, and meant to be formal: "Thanks" is both a good deal more gushing for the short time that it takes saying, and also serves the convenient purpose of nipping off very short any prospect of more gratitude or kindly remembrance on the part of the young lady or gentleman from whose mouth it so neatly and

---

[1] It occurs fifty-five times in Shakspeare: and, in the formula "Thanks be to God," four times in the English Bible.

trippingly flows. Let "thanks" survive and be welcome; it is best to be satisfied with all we are likely to get.

520. "**Abnormal.**"—"*Abnormal*" is one of those words which have come in to supply a want in the precise statements of science. It means the same as "irregular;" but this latter word had become so general and vague in its use, that it would not be sure to express *departure from rule*, which "abnormal" does. Thus far its use is justified, and even the old-fashioned lady could hardly complain: but the mischief is that the apes of novelty have come to substitute it for "irregular" in common talk: and Miss, at home for the holidays, complains towards the end of breakfast, that "the post has become quite abnormal of late." The effect of this, as of fine talk in general, will be to destroy the proper force of the word, and drive future philosophers to seek a new one, which in its turn will share the like fate with its predecessor.

521. "**Æsthetic.**—"*Æsthetic*," again, has its proper use in designating that which we could hardly speak of before it came into vogue. Unfortunately our adjective, formed from the substantive "sense," had acquired an opprobrious meaning: and the attempt to substitute sensuous for it had altogether failed. There was no remedy but to have recourse to the Greek, the language of science, and take the word we wanted. If it has suffered in the same manner as the last, it is no more than might have been expected: but I do not remember to have heard it used, where any other word would serve the turn.

522. "**Elect.**" "**Advent.**"—"*Elect*" for choose is one of our modern newspaper fineries: and it is not to be denied that "*Advent*" is rapidly losing its exclusively sacred reference. I am not sure that this is to be regretted, as the popular mind will thus become aware, without explanation, what is meant by the solemn season when it comes round.

523. "**Peoples.**"—The adding of "s" to "people" has been rather a convenience. We always spoke of the English people, the French people, the German people: why then should we not say, the European *peoples?* At all events, it is better than what is now "newspaper" for it, "nationalities."

524. "**Assisting**" at dinner.—"Assisting" at dinner

is of course what the single lady characterises it as being,
—and even worse. I don't imagine the respectable class
whom she somewhat uncourteously snubs would be flattered
by the idea that they can descend to any expression so
simply detestable. Another correspondent says, "I have
been often amused by a host, requesting her guest (this
gender is unkind), to *assist himself.*" The construction in
which the unfortunate verb finds itself in this usage, is
somewhat curious. The challenge runs, " Mr. Blank, shall
I assist you to beef?" The impression of those who are
unacquainted with the vulgarism would be, that "to
beef" was a verb, meaning to eat beef, or, as very refined
people say, to "partake of beef."

525. They do the thing somewhat differently over the
water. An English gentleman for the first time seated at
the table of an American family, was thus accosted by the
lady of the house: " Mr. Smith, sir, do you feel beef?"

526. "Aggravate."—I have been requested to enter a
protest against the use of "aggravate" in the sense of
"irritate." My correspondent asks, "Has it any other
origin than the coinage of some Mrs. Malaprop?" To
which I answer that the Latin "aggravo" has the sense
of to "irritate," and therefore my protest must be somewhat modified. At the same time, Shakspeare's usage of
this word "aggravate" would uphold a meaning down-
right opposite. Thus in "Henry IV.," (Part ii., act ii.
sc. 4,) the Hostess says, "Good Captain Peesel, be quiet:
it is very late, i' faith : I beseek you now aggravate your
choler." And in "A Midsummer Night's Dream," (act i.
sc. 2,) " I will aggravate my voice so, that I will roar you
like any sucking dove." And in "The Merry Wives of
Windsor," (act ii. sc. 2,) " I will aggravate his style," *i.e.*
from being called knave, will make him be called knave
and something worse. In all these places the word seems
to mean to *load*, to put a weight upon. This may take
place either in the direction of abatement, as in our two
former instances : or of augmentation, as in the latter, and
in the only other place where he uses the word, " Richard
II.," (act i. sc. 1,)

" Once more, the more to aggravate the note,
With a foul traitor's name stuff I thy throat."

From this meaning, certainly, the modern sense of to irritate is a departure: but in the presence of Pliny's saying that wounds "aggravantur," are irritated, when the murderer comes into presence, I do not think we have any right to find fault with it.

527. "In our midst." To say *in our midst, in their midst*, for in the midst *of us*, or *of them*, is, to my mind, objectionable. No doubt it can claim some justification by the analogy of "at their head," "in their rear," and the like. But the analogy does not quite hold. In those phrases the substantive is at least a plain concrete term: but the word *midst* is not so: there is no such thing as *a midst*, and *the midst* or *middest*, indicates a point relatively to some objects equidistant from it, just as *the first* and *the last* are used with reference to objects following and preceding respectively. In all these cases, not the possessive pronoun, but the possessive case of the personal pronoun, should be used: the first *of them*, the last *of us*, *in the midst of them*, or *of us*.

528. **Examples of the deterioration.**—I send a sentence to a paper to the following effect:—"When I came to the spot, I met a man running towards me with his hands held up." Next day I read, "When the very rev. gentleman arrived in close proximity to the scene of action, he encountered an individual proceeding at a rapid pace in the opposite direction, having both his hands elevated in an excited manner."

529. This is fiction; but the following are truth. In a Somersetshire paper I saw that a man had had his legs burned by sitting for warmth, and falling asleep, on the top of a lime-kiln. The lime was called the "*seething mass*" (to "*seethe*" means to *boil*, and "*sod*," or "*sodden*," is its passive participle); and it was said he would soon have been a *calcined corpse*, which, I take it, would have been an unheard-of chemical phenomenon.

530. In the same paper I read the following elegant sentence: "Our prognostications as regards the spirit of the young men here to join the Stogursey rifle corps proves correct." The same paper, in commenting on the Hopley case, speaks through a whole leading article of *corporal* punishment. I may mention that, in this case, the

accused person figures throughout, as so often in provincial papers, as a "*demon incarnate,*" and "*a fiend in human shape.*"

531. In travelling up from Somersetshire I find the directors of the Great Western Railway thus posting up the want of a schoolmaster at their board: "£5 reward. Whereas the windows of the carriages, &c. Whoever will give *information as shall lead to conviction*, shall receive the above reward;" as being used for *which*: "*the man as told me.*"

532. The South-Eastern directors seem to want the schoolmaster also. On the back of the tickets for the fast trains, we read the following precious piece of English grammar:—"This ticket is not transferrable, only available for the station named thereon." This implying, of course, that using it for the station named on it, is *part of the process* of transferring it to some other person.

533. On a certain railway the following intelligible notice appears:—"Hereafter, when trains moving in an opposite direction are approaching each other on separate lines, conductors and engineers will be required to bring their respective trains to a dead halt before the point of meeting, and be very careful not to proceed till each train has passed the other."

534. A wonderful public notice from the East London Waterworks, dated 1868, was sent me: "Detector pipes may be used to guard against and shew overflow from defective ball valves and ball cocks, provided they are placed so that the water flowing therefrom may be seen outside the house if possible, and fixed to the satisfaction of the company." Here, by the ordinary rules of construction, it is the water which is to be "fixed to the satisfaction of the company."

535. In the *Morning Chronicle's* account of Lord Macaulay's funeral occurred the following sentence:— "When placed upon the ropes over the grave, and while being gradually lowered into the earth, the organ again pealed forth." Here, of course, on any possible grammatical understanding of the words, it was the *organ* which was placed over the grave, and was being lowered into the earth. Akin to this was the following notice, sent to my

house the other day by a jeweller:—"The brooches would have been sent before, but have been unwell."

536. In a narrative of one of Mr. Glaisher's balloon ascents, we read that, "After partaking of a hearty breakfast, the balloon was brought into the town amidst the cheers and congratulations of the major part of the inhabitants." They may well have applauded a balloon which had performed so unheard-of a feat.

537. In Lecky's "History of European Morals," (ii. 197,) we read: "Another hermit, being very holy, received pure white bread every day from heaven; but, being extravagantly elated, the bread became worse and worse, till it became perfectly black."

538. Here is an advertisement from a manufacturer of iron netting: "This netting answers perfectly as a fence against rabbits, tied to iron standards, stapled to wooden stakes, fastened to iron or wire fencings put along at the foot of a hedge (merely tied to the bushes), or cut up into small pieces, and put round single plants, &c." It is well the Society for Preventing Cruelty to Animals did not get hold of the advertiser.

539. In a leading article of the *Times*, not long since, was this beautiful piece of slipshod English:—

"The atrocities of the middle passage, which called into action the Wilberforces and Clarksons of the last generation, were not so fully proved, and were certainly not more harrowing in their circumstances, than are the iniquities perpetrated upon the wretched Chinese."

540. Here you will observe we are by the form of the sentence committed to the combination of "were not so fully proved . . . than." This is a fault into which careless writers constantly fall: the joining together two clauses with a third, whose construction suits the latter of them, but not the former. "He was more popular, but not so much respected as his father." Nothing can be easier than to avoid the fault. Transpose your third clause, letting it follow your first, and constructing it without reference to your second. "He was more popular than his father, but not so much respected." The mind of the hearer easily fills up the ellipsis after "respected," and the sentence sounds well. Thus the *Times'* writer might have said,

"were not so fully proved as are the iniquities perpetrated upon the wretched Chinese, and were certainly not more harrowing in their circumstances."

541. There is another way, making the sentence correct indeed, but exceedingly clumsy. We *may* say, "He was more popular than, but not so much respected as, his father." But to my mind, this is almost worse than the incorrect sentence. It exhibits punctiliousness in all its stolidity, without any appreciation of the sound, or effect, of the sentence.

542. **Excuse of hasty writing.**—And just let me, as I pass, notice one defence which has been deliberately set up for English of this kind. It has been said that one who sits in his study, writing at leisure, may very well find time to look about him and weigh the structure of his sentences; but that the contributors of articles to the daily press are obliged to write always in a hurry, and have no such opportunities of consideration.

. 543. Now this plea either fails in its object of excusing the practice complained of, or it proves too much. It fails, if it does not assign sufficient cause for the phenomenon: if, as I believe, it is not mere haste which causes a man to write such English as this, but deficiency in his power of putting thoughts into words: it proves too much, if it really does sufficiently excuse the writers; for if such writing is the inevitable result of the hasty publication of these critiques, why is not more time given for their production, and why are not more pains bestowed on them? For surely it is an evil, for a people to be daily accustomed to read English expressed thus obscurely and ungrammatically: it tends to confuse thought, and to deprive language of its proper force, and by this means to degrade us as a nation in the rank of thinkers and speakers.

544. **More examples.**—I am indebted for the following to a correspondent:—"To MILLERS.—To be let, a windmill, containing three pair of stones, a bakehouse, corn shop, and about five acres of land, dwelling house, and garden,"

545. In the *Times*, a few days since, an advertisement thus ended: "If dead, his wife or children may apply."

546. Here is another rich morsel:—

"Notice. An advertisement headed Evans and Co., merchants, Shanghae, appears in the London *Daily Telegraph* of June 4th, intimating I was about, or had left, China. I beg to state, I never authorised H. Evans, baker and biscuit maker, to state I had, or intended leaving Shanghae—John Deverill."

547. Really ambiguous sentences are to be found even in our most careful writers. One would think that Miss Austen, if anyone, would not be caught tripping in this matter. But I read in "Pride and Prejudice," (ch. xxviii., pt. i.): "Mr. Collins and Charlotte appeared at the door, and the carriage stopped at the small gate, which led by a short gravel walk to the house, amidst the nods and smiles of the whole party." And again, (ch. xiii., pt. ii.): "Elizabeth hesitated, but her knees trembled under her, and she felt how little could be gained by an attempt to pursue them." I also find in the same novel, (ch. xx., pt. ii.): "Each felt for the other, and of course for themselves." In this case the correction is easy, as the two persons were Jane and Elizabeth: "Each felt for the other and of course for herself:" but had the genders been different, it would have been impossible to write the sentence in this form at all.

548. I find the following sentence in Thackeray's "Virginians," (part iv.):

"He dropped his knife in his retreat against the wall, which his rapid antagonist kicked under the table."

A letter in the *Pall Mall Gazette* about a fortnight ago (Oct. 23, 1866), begins, "Sir, I have been spending this autumn in the vicarage of a pleasant village in Blankshire, famous for its cricket, which I have rented during the parson's holiday."

In a review in the same paper of Aug. 24, 1866, we read as follows:

"We defy any sensible bachelor anxious to change his condition, to read Lady Harriett Sinclair's book without drawing a painful contrast in his mind between a future passed with that gifted lady, and with (the writer means, and one passed with) the fast, very fast young women *with whom* he rides in the morning, plays croquet and drinks tea in the afternoon, *sits by* at dinner, and dances with at night, but wisely abstains from marrying."

549. One of the commonest of newspaper errors is to use a participial clause instead of one with a verb, leaving the said clause pendent, so that in the reader's mind it necessarily falls into a wrong relation. Thus we had in the *Times* the other day, in the description of the York congress, assembled under the presidency of the Archbishop: "His Grace said, &c., and after pronouncing the benediction, the assembly separated." And again, in the account of the Queen's visit to open the Aberdeen waterworks, " In 1862, the Police Commissioners, headed by the Provost, set themselves in earnest to the work of obtaining a new Police and Water Act, and, succeeding in their labours, the splendid undertaking opened to-day is the result."

550. Mistakes in the arrangement of words and clauses are found in high quarters not less frequently than of old. In the *Times*, not long since, a paragraph is headed, "The Late Queen's Huntsman," when "The Queen's Late Huntsman" is intended. A correspondent sends the following from a letter describing the great hurricane at Calcutta in 1864: "The great storm wave which passed up the lower Hooghly, is said to have been of the height of a man at a distance of ten miles from the bed of the river."

551. The ignorant use of one word for another continues to give rise to curious mistakes. A letter to a newspaper says, "There is in the parish of Helmingham, Suffolk, an ancient graveyard of human skeletons, bearing much resemblance to, *if not identical with*, that mentioned in your impression on Thursday last as being recently discovered on the farm of Mr. Attrim at Stratford-on-Avon."

In this sentence let me notice that "as being discovered" is also wrong. The writer meant, "as having been discovered."

552. The secretary of a railway publishes in the *Times* the following notice. I suppose he is an Irishman. "The *present* service of trains between Three Bridges and East Grinstead, and the coach now running between Uckfield and Tunbridge Wells, is *now* discontinued."

553. In the leading article of the *Times* the same day, appeared this sentence: "To our mind it was impossible to entertain any doubt on the subject, at least not since the intimation conveyed by the American minister." You will observe that there is here a "not" too much. The writer meant "at least since the intimation," &c.

554. A correspondent sends me a very rich example of this confusion of ideas. It occurs in a leading article of the *Standard*: "The progress of science can neither be arrested nor controlled. Still less, perhaps, in this hurrying nineteenth century, can we expect to persuade men that, after all, the most haste may finally prove the worst speed, and that as a rule it must be of less importance to arrive at your journey's end quickly than it is not to arrive at all." Of course the writer meant, "than it is to make sure of arriving at all."

555. It is astonishing what different things people sometimes say from those which they intended to say. There was a letter a short time since, in one of the London papers, concerning a matter which the writer believed to be no credit to the Church. In his opening sentence he intended to announce this. But he made a very comical mistake. He asked the editor of the paper to allow him *to make a statement which was no credit to the Church*. And having done this, he signed himself "A Priest of the Province of Canterbury." So that, as far as appeared from the letter, a clergyman had made a discreditable statement. It was the old story, of one going out to commit murder, and committing suicide by mistake.

556. The last-mentioned correspondent also points out the curious difference which is made in the meaning of one and the same word in a sentence, when variously introduced by other words. Thus, if I say of one in India, "He will return for two years," I am rightly understood as meaning that the length of his stay at home will be two years. But if I say, "He will not return for two years," then I do not, by the insertion of the negative, reverse the former proposition, *i.e.*, mean that the length of his stay at home will not be two years, but I imply something quite different; *viz.*, that two years will elapse

before his return. By the insertion of the "not," the preposition "for," retaining its meaning of "during," "for the space of," ceases to belong to the length of time during which he will "*come*," and belongs to the length of time during which he will "*not come*."

557. My correspondent offers another example, which was originally given by the writer of the article on my little book in the Edinburgh Review for June, 1864. "Jack was very respectful to Tom, and always took off his hat when he met him." "Jack was very rude to Tom, and always knocked off his hat when he met him." You will see that "his hat" in the former sentence is Jack's, but in the latter sentence it is Tom's. There is absolutely nothing to indicate this but the context. "Will anyone pretend," says the Reviewer, "that either of these sentences is ambiguous in meaning, or unidiomatic in expression? Yet critics of the class now before us [*i. e.*, those who proceed on the assumption that no sentence is correct, unless the mere syntactical arrangement of the words, irrespective of their meaning, is such, that they are incapable of having a double aspect] are bound to contend that Jack showed his respect by taking off Tom's hat, or else that he showed his rudeness by knocking off his own."

558. And this is important, as showing how utterly impossible it is for every reference of every pronoun to be unmistakeably pointed out by the form of the sentence. Hearers and readers are supposed to be in possession of their common sense and their powers of discrimination: and it is to these that writers and speakers must be content to address themselves.

559. In a report of a charitable society I read of "a desideratum which is entirely absent from the present building." Now the intelligent committee meant to specify some pressing want which was felt in their present building: some needful accommodation of which it was destitute. But they have expressed precisely the contrary meaning. If a *desideratum* (understanding the word not as classically translated, but as commonly used) is *absent*, the thing wished for is present.

560. **Confusion of abstract and concrete.**—The

following sentence, occurring in a hotel advertisement, may serve to illustrate a very common mistake: "Its nightwatchman enables gentlemen to be called at any time, and, hourly patrolling the building, adds greatly to the comfort and security of all." Now we are sensible of an absurdity here. But what is the mistake? It is not, you see, that some word, which to any ordinary reader has but one application, *may* be so combined as to bear other applications: but the incongruity is inevitable. A man who hourly patrols the building enables gentlemen to be called at any time: *i.e.*, by some arrangement which he makes, puts it in their power to be called, by somebody. Whereas the intention plainly was to notify that, owing to the fact of a night-watchman being employed, gentlemen can be called at any time by the night-watchman. The mistake is one easy to understand, though called by rather a hard name. It is the confounding of the abstract with the concrete. The fact of the night-watchman being employed is in its nature abstract: is a consideration apart from persons and things which put it forth in action. This fact is independent of the particular man employed as night-watchman, and is the source of the advantages arising from it, whoever may happen to be so employed.

561. **Inflated language in prayers.**—I have received more than one letter from a gentleman who is much troubled by the inflated language of a book of prayers used in a school of small and ignorant boys. It would not become me to bring forward as subjects for mirth, sentences and phrases whose meaning is so solemn: I can only deal with the complaint in a general way. And in doing so, I may say that there can hardly be a graver offence in the compilers of books of devotion, than this of using hard words and inflated sentences. If there is one essential requisite in a written prayer, it is, that it provide as much as possible for every word being understood and felt by those that are to use it. My correspondent tells me that the writer of whom he complains invariably uses *felicity* for happiness, *avocations* for employments, and the like. If I might presume to counsel the teachers of schools and heads of families, I would say, cast aside every book of prayers which offends in this way. The simple and well-

known collects of the Prayer-book, or even your own sense of the wants of your school or household, will furnish you with better, because more easy and real language of devotion, than these high-flown manuals. And in default of either of these resources, I may venture to say that a school or a family rising from the reverent utterance of the Lord's prayer only, will have really *prayed* more, than one which has been wearied with ten minutes of a form such as that of which my correspondent complains.

562. **Nicknames and expressions of endearment.**—Another criticism which I cannot help making, is on the practice of using, in general society, unmeaning and ridiculous familiar nicknames or terms of endearment. A more offensive habit cannot be imagined, or one which more effectually tends to the disparagement of those who indulge in it. I find myself, after the departure of the ladies from the dining-room, sitting next to an agreeable and sensible man. I get into interesting conversation with him. We seek a corner in the drawing-room afterwards, and continue it. His age and experience make him a treasure-house of information and practical wisdom. Yet, as talk trieth the man, infirmities begin to appear here and there, and my respect for my friend suffers diminution. By-and-by, a decided weak point is detected: and further on, it becomes evident that in the building up of his mental and personal fabric there is somewhere a loose stratum which will not hold under pressure. At last the servants begin to make those visits to the room, usually occurring about ten o'clock, which begin with gazing about, and result in a rush at some recognised object, with a summons from the coachman below. I am just doubting whether I have not about come to the end of my companion, when a shrill voice from the other side of the room calls out, "Sammy, love!" All is out. He has a wife who does not know better, and he has never taught her better. This is the secret. The skeleton in their cupboard is a child's rattle. A man may as well suck his thumb all his life, as talk, or allow to be talked to him, such drivelling nonsense. It must detract from manliness of character, and from proper self-respect: and is totally inconsistent with the good taste, and consideration, even in

the least things, for the feelings of others, which are always present in persons of good breeding and Christian courtesy. Never let the world look through these chinks into the boudoir. Even thence, if there be real good sense present, all that is childish and ridiculous will be banished; but at all events keep it from the world. It is easy for husband and wife, it is easy for brothers and sisters, to talk to one another as none else could talk, without a word of this minced-up English. One soft tone, from lips on which dwells wisdom, is worth all the "loveys" and "deareys" which become the unmeaning expletives of the vulgar.

563. **Talking nonsense to children.**—And as we have ventured to intrude into the boudoir, let us go one step further up, and peep into the nursery also. And here again I would say, never talk, never allow to be talked, to children, the contemptible nonsense which is so often the staple of nursery conversation. Never allow foolish and unmeaning nicknames to come into use in your family. We all feel, as we read of poor James I., with his "Steenie" for the Duke of Buckingham, and "Baby Charles" for his unfortunate son, that he cannot have been worthy to rule in England. We often find foolish names like these rooted in the practice of a family, and rendering grown-up men and women ridiculous in the eyes of strangers. And mind, in saying this, I have no wish to proscribe all abridgments, or familiar forms of names for our children, but only those which are unmeaning or absurd. I hold "Charley" to be perfectly legitimate: "Harry" is bound up with the glories of English history: Ned, and Dick, and Tom, and Jack, and Jem, and Bill, though none of them half so nice as the names which they have superseded, are too firmly fixed in English practice and English play, ever to be banished. Kate has almost become a name of itself; few maidens can carry the weight of Eleanor, whereas there never was a lass whom Nelly did not become. The same might be said of Milly and Amelia, and of many others. But the case of every one of such recognised nicknames differs widely from that, where some infantine lisping of a child's own name is adopted as the designation for life: or where a great rifleman with a bushy beard is called to

hold his mamma's skein of wool by the astounding title of "Baby."

564. **Sir J— M— and the tired nurse.**—All perhaps do not know the story of the kind old gentleman and his carriage. He was riding at his ease one very hot day, when he saw a tired nursemaid toiling along the footpath, carrying a great heavy boy. His heart softened: he stopped his carriage, and offered her a seat: adding, however, this: "Mind," said he, "the moment you begin to talk any nonsense to that boy, you leave my carriage." All went well for some minutes. The good woman was watchful, and bit her lips. But alas! we are all caught tripping sometimes. After a few hundred yards, and a little jogging of the boy on her knee, burst forth, "Georgy porgy! ride in coachy poachy!" It was fatal. The check-string was pulled, the steps let down, and the nurse and boy consigned to the dusty footpath as before.

565. The story is true. The person mainly concerned in it was a well-known philanthropic baronet of the last generation, and my informant was personally acquainted with him. A similar story, a correspondent reminds me, is told of Dr. Johnson.[1]

566 **Extract from the** Leeds Mercury **on importation of foreign phrases.**—As I was sending these sheets to the press, I received a copy of the Leeds Mercury containing a leading article under the title of "English for the English," which touches on an abuse of our language unnoticed in these pages, but thoroughly deserving of reprobation. It is so appropriate to my present subject that I shall venture to cite a large portion of it almost as it stands.

567. "While the Dean," the writer says, "took so much trouble to expose one danger with which our mother tongue is threatened, he took no notice whatever of another peril which to us seems much more serious. He dealt only with the insubordinate little adverbs and pronouns of native growth, which sometimes intrude into forbidden places, and ignored altogether the formidable invasion of foreign nouns, adjectives, and verbs which promises ere long to

[1] See Appendix.

transform the manly English language into a sort of mongrel international slang. A class of writers has sprung up who appear to think it their special business to 'enrich' the language by dragging into it, without any attempt at assimilation, contributions from all the tongues of the earth. The result is a wretched piece of patchwork, which may have charms in the eyes of some people, but which is certainly an abomination in the eyes of the genuine student of language."

568. "We need only glance into one of the periodical representatives of fashionable literature, or into a novel of the day, to see how serious this assault upon the purity of the English language has become. The chances are more than equal that we shall fall in with a writer who considers it a point of honour to choose all his most emphatic words from a French vocabulary, and who would think it a lamentable falling off in his style, did he write half a dozen sentences without employing at least half that number of foreign words. His heroes are always marked by an *air distingué*; his vile men are sure to be *blasés*; his lady friends never merely dance or dress well, they dance or dress *à merveille*; and he himself when lolling on the sofa under the spirit of laziness does not simply enjoy his rest, he luxuriates in the *dolce far niente*, and wonders when he will manage to begin his *magnum opus*. And so he carries us through his story, running off into hackneyed French, Italian, or Latin expressions, whenever he has anything to say which he thinks should be graphically or emphatically said. It really seems as if he thought the English language too meagre, or too commonplace a dress, in which to clothe his thoughts. The tongue which gave a noble utterance to the thoughts of Shakespere and Milton is altogether insufficient to express the more cosmopolitan ideas of Smith, or Tomkins, or Jenkins!"

569. "We have before us an article from the pen of a very clever writer, and, as it appears in a magazine which specially professes to represent the 'best society,' it may be taken as a good specimen of the style. It describes a dancing party, and we discover for the first time how much learning is necessary to describe a 'hop' properly. The reader is informed that all the people at the dance belong

to the *beau monde*, as may be seen at a *coup d'œil;* the *demi-monde* is scrupulously excluded, and in fact everything about it bespeaks the *haut ton* of the whole affair. A lady who has been happy in her hair-dresser is said to be *coiffée à ravir*. Then there is the bold man to describe. Having acquired the *savoir faire*, he is never afraid of making a *faux pas*, but no matter what kind of conversation is started plunges at once *in medias res*. Following him is the fair *débutante*, who is already on the look-out for *un bon parti*, but whose *nez retroussé* is a decided obstacle to her success. She is of course accompanied by mamma *en grande toilette*, who, *entre nous*, looks rather *ridée* even in the gaslight. Then, lest the writer should seem frivolous, he suddenly abandons the description of the dances, *vis-à-vis* and *dos-à-dos*, to tell us that Homer becomes tiresome when he sings of Βοῶπις πότνια Ἥρη twice in a page. The supper calls forth a corresponding amount of learning, and the writer concludes his article after having aired his Greek, his Latin, his French, and, in a subordinate way, his English."

570. "Of course, this style has admirers and imitators. It is showy and pretentious, and everything that is showy and pretentious has admirers. The admixture of foreign phrases with our plain English produces a kind of Brummagem sparkle which people whose appreciation is limited to the superficial imagine to be brilliance. Those who are deficient in taste and art education not unfrequently prefer a dashing picture by young Daub to a glorious cartoon by Raphael. The bright colouring of the one far more than counterbalances the lovely but unobtrusive grace of the other. In a similar way, young students are attracted by the false glitter of the French-paste school of composition, and instead of forming their sentences upon the beautiful models of the great English masters, they twist them into all sorts of unnatural shapes for no other end than that they may introduce a few inappropriate French or Latin words, the use of which they have learned to think looks smart. Of course, the penny-a-liners are amongst the most enthusiastic followers of the masters of this style. They not only think it brilliant, but they know it to be profitable, inasmuch as it adds considerably to their ability

to say a great deal about nothing. The public sees a great deal in the newspapers about ' *recherché* dinners ' and ' sumptuous *déjeûners* ' (sometimes eaten at night), and about the *éclat* with which a meeting attended by the ' *élite* of the county ' invariably passes off; but they get but a trifling specimen of the masses of similar rubbish which daily fall upon the unhappy editors. The consequence of all this is that the public is habituated to a vicious kind of slang utterly unworthy to be called a language. Even the best educated people find it difficult to resist the contagion of fashion in such a thing as conversation, and if some kind of stand is not made against this invasion, pure English will soon only exist in the works of our dead authors."[1]

571. "But it is not only on literary grounds that we think the bespanglement of our language with French and other foreign phrases is to be deprecated. Morality has something to say in the matter. It is a fact that things are said under the flimsy veil of foreign diction which could not very well be said in plain English. To talk in the presence of ladies about disreputable women by the plain English names which belong to them is not considered to display a very delicate mind, but anybody may talk about the *demi-monde* without fearing either a blush or a frown. Yet the idea conveyed is precisely the same in the one case as in the other; and inasmuch as words can only be indelicate when they convey an indelicate idea, we should think that the French words ought to be under the same disabilities as the English ones. In like manner, things sacred are often made strangely familiar by the intervention of a French dictionary. Persons whose reverence for the Deity is properly shown in their English conversation by a becoming unwillingness to make a light use of His holy Name, have no hesitation in exclaiming *Mon Dieu!* in frivolous conversation. The English name

---

[1] A correspondent says, " In your next edition pray dispose of those Gallicisms which are becoming too prevalent : ' The king *assisted at* the ceremony :' ' My brother has come to *pass* a few days with me : ' instead of the English *was present* and *to spend.*" For the former of these there is, I believe, no excuse. But the latter usage, " passing time," is surely found in all periods of our literature ; and the good English substantive " *pastime* " is a voucher for it.

for the Father of Evil is not considered to be a very reputable noun, but its French synonym is to be heard in 'the best society.' Far more telling illustrations than these could easily be found, but we have no inclination to seek them. Ideas which no decent person would ever think of expressing before a mixed company are certainly often spoken and written in French, and in our opinion they do not lose a particle of their coarseness by being dressed up in foreign clothes. We think, therefore, that the interests of morality as well as of pure taste concur in calling upon those who have influence with the public to set their faces against this vicious style."

572. I need not say that with every word of this I heartily concur. It is really quite refreshing to read in a newspaper, and a provincial one too, so able and honest an exposure of one of the worst faults of our daily and weekly press.

573. Among recent adoptions of French phrases and words is this, which occurred in "Regulations for Prisons," from the Home Office, printed in the *Times* of February 28, 1868: "windows giving on the yard," meaning, of course, *opening* on the yard. This instance is instructive as illustrating perhaps the way in which such new senses of words creep in. It looks very much as if the phrase had been originally a bald version of the French expression, overlooked in an official document which itself was beholden to a French origin.

574. **Use of expletives.**—I am tempted to add some remarks on the use, in speaking and writing, of terms which either seem to be, or really are, unneeded by the sense. To prohibit the use of expletives altogether, would perhaps seem hard. In conversation, they seem to help the timid, to give time to the unready, to keep up a pleasant semblance of familiarity, and, in a word, to grease the wheels of talk; in writing, we often want them to redress the balance of a halting sentence, when any other way of doing so would mar the sense; or to give weight to a term otherwise feeble, or to fill out a termination which, without them, would be insignificant in sound. For these reasons, the occasional use of expletives must be tolerated; and that style of speaking or writing which

should abandon them altogether would appear to us harsh and rugged.

575. "**You see**," "**you know**."—I said, the *occasional* use. Moderation ought to be observed: and where it is not, there is just ground for complaint. The man is properly found fault with who interlards his talk at every turn with "You see," and "You know." Both these terms have their use, and if that use be disregarded in an indiscriminate profusion of them, they will become vapid and meaningless. They serve, when used as quasi-expletives, just to keep the hearer up to the mark of the knowledge you are imparting to him, and should be used only as applying to facts or ideas of which he is, or should be, already in possession.

576. "**Well**," "**why**."—There are other expletives which serve merely to indicate the sequence of the course of talk, or the frame of mind in which it is continued. A simple question is asked; and your friend's answer begins with "*Well*." Little as the word means, it just does this service: it puts the respondent *en rapport* with the questioner: he intends by it to say that he does not absolutely repudiate the inquiry: that, so far, is *well*, and that we have common ground up to this point. Or the first word of the answer is "*Why*,—" a particle, of which the meaning is not quite so easy to assign; but I suppose it gives a kind of dubitative aspect to what follows: introduces a deliberative and not quite certain reply; or perhaps slightly rallies the querist on some obvious element in the reply which his question shows him to have overlooked. "What would you do first, if you were to fall down?" "Why get up again, of course." So that the use of such prefatory particles is, I conceive, by no means to be proscribed. It should however in the main be confined to oral communication or dramatic dialogue, and not be admitted in the style of a writer.

577. "**At all**."—Yet even in written composition there are certain expressions more or less nearly approaching to expletives, the use of which cannot well be prohibited. I am challenged by one of my correspondents, who gives a list of sentences in which I have used the expression "*at all*," to say what difference in the meaning of any of them

there would be if the words were struck out. My answer must be, in accordance with the foregoing remarks, that the difference in meaning would perhaps not be great, but it would be quite enough to justify the use of the words, as any intelligent reader may at once perceive. "Thou hast not delivered thy people *at all*" (Exod. v. 23), is surely very distinct, at all events in the feeling of utter desolation expressed, from "Thou hast not delivered thy people." "If thou do *at all* forget the Lord" (Deut. viii. 19), makes the hypothesis much more complete than it would be without the qualifying words. Or, to take another notable example, where the difference would seem to be less than in the others, "God is light, and in Him is no darkness *at all*" (1 John i. 5), who does not see that by the words "*at all*" every possibility of even the least shade of darkness existing in Him is altogether excluded? So that, when my correspondent designates these words as a feeble expletive, which adds nothing to the meaning of the sentence to which it is attached, I cannot agree with his opinion, nor do I think that the majority of my readers will.

578. If the origin of the phrase is to be sought for, I know not any other than may be found in the requirements of speech itself. What the Apostle, in the original Greek of 1 John i. 5, expressed by the strong double negation, σκοτία ἐν αὐτῷ οὐκ ἔστιν οὐδεμία, we could not in English render by "there is not in Him no darkness," because in our language the doubling of a negation destroys instead of strengthening it: we had recourse to another way of expressing total exclusion, "there is in Him no darkness *at all;*" "*at all*," i.e., taking the assertion even up to the measure of all,—"*altogether*,"—providing for, and taking into consideration, every supposable exception, every qualifying circumstance. The preposition "*at*," in this phrase, has the same sense as in "*at least*," "*at best*," and the like.

579. "**And the like.**"—This is also designated by my correspondent as a feeble expletive, and indeed as an "*Irishism*." No doubt it may be so used as to *become* an expletive; but I am not conscious of having so used it: at least, in every one of the sentences which he quotes,

it does full service, as shortly comprehending other examples of the same kind as those already cited.

580. "The first foundation."—I am asked whether an expression which I had used, "the *first foundation* of an institution," can be right, seeing that an institution can have but one foundation? The reply is to be sought in the general use of expletive, *i.e.*, superabundant words, together with others which already express the meaning required. Thus we have, "O that they would consider their *latter end*," when "their end" would, strictly speaking, have been sufficient. Thus also we say, "the utmost end of the earth," "the first beginning of creation"; the expletive prefix in each case tending to give precision and emphasis, and showing that it is on the fact reasserted by it, that the stress of the sentence is laid.

581. A notable and very solemn instance of this usage is found in the title, "the most Highest," given to the Almighty in the Prayer-book version of the Psalms (Ps. ix. 2; xiii. 6; xxi. 7; etc.). In the Bible version the expression seems not to occur, the "Most High," or, "the Highest," being its equivalent. But we have a reduplication of the same kind in Acts xxvi. 5: "After the most straitest sect of our religion I lived a Pharisee." In this place, it is difficult to account for it, as it represents only the simple superlative in the original text. King James's translators seem merely to have retained it from the older English versions, Tyndale's, Cranmer's, and the Geneva Bible.

582. "From hence," "from thence."—These expressions are of very frequent occurrence. We have in the English Version of the Bible "from hence," in Gen. i. 25; Deut. ix. 12; Jer. xxxviii. 10; Luke iv. 9, xvi. 26; etc.: "from henceforth," 2 Chron. xvi. 9; Luke v. 10; etc.: "from thence," almost always, with very few exceptions: "from thenceforth," 2 Chron. xxxii. 23; John xix. 12. Shakspeare has "from henceforth" only thrice out of forty-one times that he uses the adverb. Usage has now stamped its mark on the expletive preposition, I think, in ordinary converse. It is true we thus reduplicate the force of the adverb, but such reduplications are constantly found in idiomatic language.

583. **Unmeaning exclamations.**—Let me say a word on expletives of another kind: exclamations of surprise, or of any other feeling, which taken by themselves carry no meaning. It is perhaps impossible to avoid them altogether: speech will break out when emotion is excited: and " *You don't say so,*" or " *Indeed!*", or " *Dear me!* " is sometimes heard even from persons best able to give an account of what they say. Yet it may not be amiss to remember, that idle words are seldom quite harmless; and to impress on ourselves, that the fewer we use of such expletives the better. This was strikingly brought before me during intercourse with Italians one winter in Rome. I had observed that my Italian friends often in their talk uttered some sounds very like our " dear, dear," and at first I thought that my ear must have deceived me. But I soon found that it was so: and that sometimes the exclamation even took the form of "*dear me!*" The explanation of course is obvious. The Italians were exclaiming " *Dio, Dio!* " and the fuller form was " *Dio mio!* " And the reflection arising from it was as obvious: *viz.*, that it thus seems probable that our unmeaning words, " *dear, dear!* " and " *dear me!* " are, in fact, nothing but a form of taking the sacred Name in vain, borrowed from the use of a people with whom we were once in much closer intercourse than we now are. Thus it would seem that the *idle* word is not quite free from blame.

584. **Concluding advice.**—But it is time that this little volume drew to an end. And if I must conclude it with some advice to my readers, it shall be that which may be inferred from these examples, and from the way in which I have been dealing with them. Be simple, be unaffected, be honest in your speaking and writing. Never use a long word where a short one will do. Call a spade a spade, not *a well-known oblong instrument of manual industry;* let home be *home*, not a *residence;* a place a *place,* not a *locality;* and so of the rest. Where a short word will do, you always lose by using a long one. You lose in clearness; you lose in honest expression of your meaning; and, in the estimation of all men who are qualified to judge, you lose in reputation for ability. The only true way to shine, even in this false world, is to be modest and un-

assuming. Falsehood may be a very thick crust, but in the course of time, truth will find a place to break through. Elegance of language may not be in the power of all of us; but simplicity and straightforwardness are. Write much as you would speak; speak as you think. If with your inferiors, let your speech be no coarser than usual; if with your superiors, no finer. Be what you say; and, within the rules of prudence, say what you are.

585. Avoid all oddity of expression. No one ever was a gainer by singularity in words, or in pronunciation. The truly wise man will so speak, that no one may observe how he speaks. A man may show great knowledge of chemistry by carrying about bladders of strange gases to breathe; but he will enjoy better health, and find more time for business, who lives on the common air. When I hear a person use a queer expression, or pronounce a name in reading differently from his neighbours, the habit always goes down, in my estimate of him, with a *minus sign* before it; stands on the side of deficit, not of credit.

586. Avoid likewise all *slang* words. There is no greater nuisance in society than a talker of slang. It is only fit (when innocent, which it seldom is) for raw schoolboys, and one-term freshmen, to astonish their sisters with. Talk as sensible men talk: use the easiest words in their commonest meaning. Let the sense conveyed, not the vehicle in which it is conveyed, be your object of attention.

587. Avoid in conversation all singularity of accuracy. One of the bores of society is the talker who is always setting you right; who, when you report from the paper that 10,000 men fell in some battle, tells you it was 9,970; who, when you describe your walk as two miles out and back, assures you it wanted half a furlong of it. Truth does not consist in minute accuracy of detail, but in conveying a right impression; and there are vague ways of speaking, that are truer than strict fact would be. When the Psalmist wrote, " Rivers of waters run down mine eyes, because men keep not thy law," and when the Redeemer said, " If these held their peace, the stones would immediately cry out," it was not facts that were stated, but truths deeper than fact, and truer.

588. "The talker who is always setting you right." Yes, and there is another, and an even more formidable bore. And that is, the man who is for ever *capping* your saying with something that may bring credit to *himself*, or excite wonder, or in some way take the wind out of your sails. You mention some unfortunate mistake which you have made: your friend replies with some wise rule by which he tells you he has always escaped such a misfortune. You have seen some remarkable sight: he, at some friend's, has seen a much more remarkable one of the same kind. I remember hearing a talker of this kind complained of, who always adduced, if a thing happened to be praised, a brother of his, as possessing one of the same kind, far grander, or more beautiful, or more costly. I suggested to the complainants to try him with *double yellow violets*, and wait the result. The capper was capt, and subsided.

589. Talk to please, not yourself, but your neighbour to his edification. What a real pleasure it is to sit by a cheerful, unassuming, sensible talker; one who gives you an even share in the conversation and his attention; one who leaves on your memory his facts and his opinions, not himself who uttered them, not the words in which they were uttered.

590. All are not gentlemen by birth; but all may be gentlemen in openness, in modesty of language, in attracting no man's attention by singularities, and giving no man offence by forwardness; for it is this, in matter of speech and style, which is the sure mark of good taste and good breeding.

591. Conclusion.—These stray notes on spelling and speaking have been written more as contributions to discussion, than as attempts to decide in doubtful cases. The decision of matters such as those which I have treated is not made by any one man or set of men; cannot be brought about by strong writing, or vehement assertion: but depends on influences wider than any one man's view, and taking longer to operate than the life of any one generation. It depends on the directions and deviations of the currents of a nation's thoughts, and the influence exercised on words by events beyond man's control Grammarians

and rhetoricians may set bounds to language: but usage will break over in spite of them. And I have ventured to think that he may do some service who, instead of standing and protesting where this has been the case, observes, and points out to others, the existing phenomena, and the probable account to be given of them.

APPENDIX.

On paragraph 31 and following :—

I observe that in a new notice, the London, Chatham, and Dover Railway Company announce to their passengers the stations at which *Feet-warmers* may be procured. The old notice had *Foot-warmers*. The change is a step into barbarism. If carried out, it would introduce *Hands-cuffs*, and *Eyes-glasses*. Did it never strike the corrector, that *foot* in composition is generic, as in "foot-stool," "foot-rot"? Fancy a man having lived long enough in a neighbourhood to have gained his "*feeting*."

On paragraph 288 :—

In the "Times" of March 12, 1870, appeared the following letter :

"ARCHIEPISCOPAL GRAMMAR.

"TO THE EDITOR OF THE 'TIMES.'

"Sir,—I have taken the enclosed letter of the Archbishops of Canterbury and York to the Archbishop of Armagh, from the 'Times' of this day. Can any one imagine that two Archbishops could write such bad grammar, which any schoolboy should be ashamed of?

"The Archbishops begin with a pronoun singular 'my' ('My Dear Lord Archbishop'), and then go on with a plural pronoun 'we' and 'our' throughout the letter, until their Graces come to the conclusion, when they combine the plural and singular together, by saying, 'We are, my dear Lord Archbishop.'

"Surely 'my dear' means dear to me. Who is 'me' when two persons are writing and signing the letter?

"Does not the Editor of the 'Times' think it is quite time that an Education Bill was brought in by the Government?

"Yours faithfully,

"A SUBSCRIBER TO THE 'TIMES.'

"March 10."

This is just a specimen of the knowledge of usage, and of the slashing style, of these censors of those who know better than themselves. Of course I need not say that "their Graces" were perfectly right, and their slap-dash censor was in the wrong. After I had tried to explain this in the "Times," I had a letter, suggesting that the incongruity ought to have been avoided by wording the address "Dear Lord Archbishop" (!).

I need hardly remind the reader that other languages besides our own have the same habit of regarding "my lord" as a term by itself, and invariable. Thus we have "I Monsignori," designating a class of prelates at Rome.

Our own lords of the privy council designate themselves in their correspondence as "My Lords." And lastly, as another correspondent reminds me, the Archbishops had high authority for their address: for in Gen. xlii. 10, we read of Joseph's brethren, "And they said unto him, Nay, my lord: but to buy food are thy servants come."

On paragraph 293 and following :—

It might have been stated that Chaucer uses a curiously varied form of "it is me," in the "Shipman's Tale," about the middle :—

"Qui est la (q. he), Peter, it am I."

On paragraph 474 :—

The word "*riches*" is frequently the object of a misstatement. In a critique, not long since, it was said as a set-off against some defects of an author, "he at least appears to be aware that '*riches*' is properly a singular, being derived from the French '*richesse*.'" But begging the critic's pardon, this is not so. The singular noun in French, "*la richesse*," is abstract, and signifies abundance,—rich-ness (if we had such a word). When the concrete, riches, "*biens*," "*possessions*," is signified, the French use "*les richesses*": from which, and not from the singular, our "*riches*" is derived. The usage of "*riches*" in the English Bible is plural :—"He heapeth up riches, and cannot tell who shall gather them," Ps. xxxix. 6: "Riches make themselves wings," Prov. xxiii. 5; and in many other places.

On paragraph 486 —

I omitted to notice, while on this part of my subject, that

epithetal and predicative possessive pronouns are curiously distinguished. "That is my hat:" but, "That hat is mine." "This is your book:" but, "This book is yours." And so with "*her*" and "*hers*," "*their*" and "*theirs*," "*thy*" and "*thine*." The usage is traceable in provincial dialects in the case of "his," which is not varied in good English:

> He that prigs what isn't *his'n*,
> When he's cotched, is sent to prison.

And also in "her'n," which we might once have similarly illustrated,

> She that prigs what isn't *her'n*,
> At the treadmill takes a turn.

On paragraph 564 :—

In reference to this paragraph I have received the following letter:

"Edinburgh, 3rd April, 1869.

"Rev. Sir,

"As one of those who read with pleasure at the time, and who has hardly, for a single day since, forgot the lesson of the story you told in 'Good Words' some years ago about the kind old gentleman and the nursemaid on the hot summer-day, when the conditions of a favour from the former to the latter were so suddenly broken by the escape of 'Georgy-porgy ride in coachy-poachy' from the nurse, I take the liberty of sending you the enclosed verses which appeared in to-day's 'Scotsman.' They are rather pretty, exceedingly Scotch, and an exact picture of what goes on in many a home here between parent and child."

"BONNIE BAIRNIE."

AIR—"*Bonnie Scotland, I adore thee.*"

> Bonnie bairnie, how I love it,
> None can rob its daddy of it;
> Many a one my bairn may covet,
>   Bonnie, bonnie bairnie.

> Wi' its wee bit nosey-posey,
> Cheeky-peekies red and rosy,
> And its bosey, cosey-osey,
>   Bonnie, bonnie bairnie.

Wi' its bonnie brow brow brenty,
And its mouthie-pouty dainty,
Made for kissie-wisses plenty,
    Bonnie, bonnie bairnie.

Wi' its e'enie-peenies glancin',
And its leggie-peggies dancin',
Like a horsie-porsey prancin',
    Bonnie, bonnie bairnie.
Kittlie-wittly my bit pussie,
Creepie-crappy up the housie,
Cuddlie-wuddly, my ain mousie,
    Bonnie, bonnie bairnie.

Ridie-pidey pownie-owney,
Fallie-pally down, down, downy,
Mendie-pendy, crackie-crownie,
    Bonnie, bonnie bairnie.
Toesie-posey, feetie-peety,
Handie-pandy, goodie-sweety,
Nicie-picey, catie-peaty,
    Bonnie, bonnie bairnie.

Cockie-locky, henie-peney,
Duckie-pucky, kitty-wrenie,
"Cow wow-wow-ie"—nowie, thenie,
    Bonnie, bonnie bairnie.
Bedie-pedy, cosie creep in,
Hushy-bushy, bairnie sleepin',
Guardian angels watches keepin'
    Ower my bonnie bairnie.

INDEX.

⁎ *The references are to the pages, not to the paragraphs.*

"A" or "an" before a vowel, 33, 34.
"A" and "aw," words ending in, 35.
"Abarcy," 87.
Abel, 46.
"Aberuncate," 87.
"Abhorred" and "abhored," 22.
"Able" for "Abel," &c., 46.
"Abnormal,' 183, 184.
"Abolishable," 87.
"Above, the," 142.
Abstract and concrete, confusion of, 193.
Abstract for concrete, 171.
"Abstringe," 87.
"Abstrude," 87.
"Abundant," "reluctant," &c., 10.
Adverbial qualifications, two uses of, 144.
"Accord," to, 182.
Accusative and nominative cases, 103.
Accusative case, does "than" govern it? 111; "them" and the, 142.
"Acervate," 87.
"Acetosity," 87.
Achaiens, 44.
"Acquaintances," or "acquaintance," 17.
Addison referred to, 12, 59.
Adjectives and adverbs, 144, 174.
Adjectives used as adverbs, 143.
"Adjugate," 87.
"Adjustible," 87.
"Admetiate," 87.
"Adminicle," 87.

Admiration, notes of, 76.
"Advent," 183, 184.
Advertisement, clerical, 102.
Advertisements, errors in, 189.
Adverb between " to " and the infinitive, 133.
Adverbs and adjectives, 174.
Adverbs, position of, 104; superseded by adjectives, 143.
Advice, concluding, 205.
"Advolation," 87.
"Æsthetic," 183, 184.
Affirmative turned to negative, 93.
Affirmatives and negatives, contradictory, 63.
"Aggravate," 135.
"Ain't," 71.
Alexandria, 44.
Alford, Dean, his Greek Testament, 74, 105; his "Queen's English," 82; at Rome, 205; and his critics, viii, 110; other references, 38, 40, 42, 43, 47, 85, 112, 127, 129. *See also under* "Queen's English," &c.
"All," "always," &c., 23.
"All of them," 132.
"Allude," to, 182.
"Almighty," 23.
"Alms," 39.
"Also," 23.
"Also," with commas, 73.
Ambiguity, real, and supposed, examples of, 97-101; how arising, 101.
Ambiguous descriptions of men, 171.
"Alms," pronunciation of, 39.

American pronunciation, 49.
Americanisms, 6, 85, 163.
"Am, I," and "I be," 149.
"Among" and "amongst," 53.
"Amplify," 38.
"Anathematise," or "anathematize"? 25.
"And" and relative pronouns, 161.
"And" and singular and plural verbs, 153.
"And the like," 203.
"And which," 161.
"An ear," "a year," 38.
"Animals" and "insects," 139.
Anomalies, 147.
"Apartments," 179.
"Apostasy" or "apostacy," 11.
Apostrophe after a plural noun, 14.
Apostrophe of the genitive singular, 12.
Apostrophe, what is the? 13.
"Archiepiscopal Grammar," letter on, 209.
Arcturus, 48.
Aristobulus, 42, 44, 172.
"Arn't," 71.
Arrangement of words in sentences, 93; rule for, 94; its violation required by emphasis, ibid.
"As" and "so," 70.
"As" and "to," 137.
"As being discovered," 191.
"As" used for "which," 187.
Aspirate following "a" and "an," 34.
Aspirate in the Bible, 31.
Aspirate in "hospital," 33.
Aspirate, misuse of, 30.
"Assertor," 37.
"Assisted at" the ceremony, 200.
"Assisting" at dinner, 183, 184.
"Assurance" or "insurance," 11.
Asyneryitus, 44.
"At all," 202, 203.
"At best," or "at the best"? 131.

"At first," &c., 131.
"At least," or "at the least"? 131.
"Attain" (to) one's —th year, 91.
"Attornies" or "attorneys," 16.
Attraction, 58, 64, 151, 152.
Austen, Miss, 190.
Author, the. See under Alford, Dean.
Auxiliary verbs, ellipses of, 98, 151; indifferent use of, 124.
Auxiliary verbs "shall" and "will," 121.
"Avocations," 181, 194.
Aytoun, Prof., 116.

Bacon, Lord, 52, 59, 72, 137, 170.
Bailey's Dictionary, 87.
"Battle," 46.
"Be, I," and "I am," 149.
Beaumont and Fletcher, 179.
"Beautiful music," &c., 162.
"Beautiful smell, a," 162.
"Beg (I) to," 84.
"Being written, was," &c., 121.
"Bellpull," 23.
"Belltower," 23.
"Belong," "belong Leeds," &c., 85.
"Benefitted," or "benefited," 22.
Berridge, Mr., and Johnny Stittle, 43.
"Besides" and "except," 159.
"Best, at," "at the best," 131.
Bible, the, grammar of, 99; other references to, 5, 16, 20, 25, 28, 33, 35, 45, 61, 69, 76, 77, 95, 99, 101, 108, 117, 120, 124, 130, 132, 133, 134, 150, 151, 152, 154, 156, 159, 166, 169, 178, 183, 203, 204, 206. See also New Testament.
Blacksmith, an euphuistic, 180.
Blair, Dr., his rules, 94.
"Blessed" and "blest," 49.
"Blow," does an organ? 88.
"Bonnie Bairnie" (nursery song), 211.
Bootmakers, the rival, 174.

INDEX. 215

Bores, talking, 207.
"Both," position of, 105.
"Both of them," 132.
"Brewery," 26.
Bull, Thomas Palmer, 40.
"But," use of between epithets, 69.
"But that," 128.
"Buttery," 26.
"By " and " of," 172.
"By and by," or " by and bye"? 78.
"By applying," &c., 175.
"By doing a thing," &c., 175.
"By-end," 78.
"By, passing," &c., 78.
"By-play," 78.
"By the by," or " by the bye"? 78.
"Bye-ball," 78.

"Cæsar," 27.
"Calcined," 180.
"Calm," 39.
"Calves' head" or "calf's head," 16.
Cambridge, Johnny Stittle of, 43.
"Came into flower," 134.
"Came to pieces," 134.
"Cameleopard," 23, 38.
Campbell, Dr., his " Philosophy of Rhetoric," quoted, 108.
"Capping" in conversation, 207.
Caprice of idiom, 56.
Case, nominative and accusative, 103.
"Castle," 46.
"Cattle" or "chattel," 46.
"Canterise" or "canterize"? 25.
"Caviller," "cavilling," 22.
Censors, grammatical, 210.
"Centre," 77.
"Centre-line," &c., 77.
"Cemetery," 27.
"Cincture," 67.
"Chattel" and " cattle," 46.
Chatterton's imposture, 4.
Chaucer, 210.
"Chemistry," 27.

"Cherubim," 28.
"Chickens " or " chicken," 19.
Children, talking nonsense to, 196, 211.
Children's names, 196.
"Choose," 24.
"Chose," 24.
"Chough," pronunciation of, 41.
Churchwarden, story of an educated, 110.
Classification of both sexes together, 72.
Clauses, the arrangement of, in sentences, 96.
Clerical advertisement, a, 102.
"Clergy," 171.
Clergy, anecdotes of the, 172; their bad reading, 53, 79, 89; errors of, 192; their ignorance, 41, 45, 47; pronunciation of "ed " by, 48.
"Close," 24.
"Clue " and "clew," 28.
"Coal, to," 87.
Coleridge, 83.
"Coleridge," pronunciation of, 40.
Collects, the, 194.
Colloquial contractions, 71.
Colon and semicolon, 76.
Colosse, 43.
"Come to grief," 134.
"Come to the gallows," 134.
"Coming " and "going," 133, 134.
Commas, excess of, 73; after "now," 74; between two adjectives, ibid.; too few, 75.
"Commence," 180.
Common Prayer. See Prayer Book.
Common sense wanted, 193.
Common sense and the pedant, 104.
Comparatives and superlatives, 81, 146.
Compositors and punctuation, 73.
Concrete and abstract, confusion of, 193.
"Confectionery," 27.

"Confusion" and "diffusion," 164.
Confusion of abstract and concrete, 193.
Confusion of ideas, 192.
"Congregation was," or "congregation were"? 170.
Conjunctional particles, use of certain, 158.
Conjunctions, 40, 69, 128.
"Conspicuous voice, a," 162.
"Construct" and "construe," 142.
Construction, careless, 188; caution against rash assertion about, 141; and idiom, 54; and usage, *ibid.*
"Contemporary with," "a contemporary of," 138.
Contractions ("ain't," &c.), 71.
"Contrast to," or "contrast with," 137.
"Control," or "controul," 9.
"Controller," or "comptroller," 9.
Conversation, 206.
Core, or Korah, 43.
Corrections, ingenious, 51.
Correspondents and censors, viii, 83, 127. *See also* "Queen's English," &c.
"Cough," pronunciation of, 41.
"Could, used to," 165.
"Covetous," 45.
Cowley, 92, 115.
"Cowper," pronunciation of, 40.
Crispin and Hoby, the rival boot-makers, 174.
"Criticise," or "criticize," &c., 25.
Criticism, in a newspaper, 46; of Mr. Fechter's "Hamlet," 102.
Critics of English, the small, 102, 110.
Cruden's "Concordance," 31.
"Cruelly," 23.
"Cubit high, fifty." *See* "Fifty cubits high."
"Cucumber," pronunciation of, 40.
"Cupboard" and "cubboard," 37.

"Curător," 36.
"Cursed," &c., 49.
"Cutlery," 26.
"Cutting, wants," 175.

Daniel, the Book of, 89.
"Dare," "dared," and "dares," 23.
Dash, the, in punctuation, 77.
"Deanery," 26.
"Dear me!" "Dear, dear!" &c., derivation of, 205.
"Death (the) is announced of," 162.
"Decanal," &c., 37.
"Decided (a) weak point," 147.
"Dependent," or "dependant," 11.
"Dependent on" "independent of," 137.
Derby usage, 165.
Derivations, ingenious, 51.
"Desideratum, a," 193.
"Desirability," 182.
Deterioration of our language, 175; process of, 177; examples of, 186. *See also* English, &c.
"Devil," 46.
"Devilry," 27.
Devonshire usage, 60.
"Dew," pronunciation, 36.
Dialect of our journals, 177.
Dialects. *See* under names of counties; *also* under Midlands, West-country, &c.
Dickens, Charles, 22, 32.
Dictionary words *versus* English, 87.
"Did [to] me a favour," 160.
"Didn't use," &c., 165.
Difference of utterance in singing, 49.
"Different," &c.
"Different to," 136.
"Diffusion" and "confusion," 164.
"*Domine!*" and "dear me!" 205.
"Diocess," or "diocese," 26.
Diphthongs, 27; shall we drop them? 28.

"Displenishing," 182.
"Disputer"and "disputant,"37.
Division of a word between lines, 21.
"Do? How d'ye," 56.
"Doest" and "doeth," 152.
"Doeth" and "doest," 152.
"Dogmatise," or "dogmatize"? 25.
Donaldson, Dr., on *s* and *z*, 25.
Donne, Dr., 172.
"Dose," 24.
Double letters, in past participles, 22; in compound words, 23.
Doubling the final letter, 22.
"Dough," pronunciation of, 41.
"Driving," or "riding"? 166.
Dryden, 9, 169.
Duel caused by a blunder in language, 55.
"Duty," pronunciation of, 36.

"Each other," 108.
"Earth's (the) revolving," &c., 167.
"Ecstasy," or "extasy," 11, 38.
"Ed," pronunciation of, 48.
Edinburgh Review, on some of Dean Alford's critics, 110, 193; respecting the confused use of "he" and "him," *ibid.*
"Either you or I," &c., 155.
"-El" or "-il," terminations, 46.
"Eldest" and "oldest," 82.
"Elect," to, 183, 184.
Ellipses of auxiliary verbs, 98.
Elliptical usages, 56.
Elliptical sentences, 93, 103, 141.
Ellis, Mr. A. J., on "It is me," &c., 115.
"Emergency," 67.
"Empress," 53, 72.
Emphasis, requirements of, in arranging words, 94; in clauses, 96.
Emphatic reading, 52.
"Enclose" or "inclose," 11.
"Enclosure," 66.
Endearment, expressions of, 195.

"Endeavour ourselves," 79.
"Endorse" or "indorse," 11.
English, the best, 104; deterioration of, 186; the dictionary writers' and "the Queen's English," 2; interlarded with French, &c., 198; Latin in, 87; Saxon in, 176; spoken and written, 57.
"English for the English," 197.
English Grammar. *See* Grammar, &c.
English language, 3, 54. *See* also "Queen's English," Language, &c.
English style, the best, and Kames' rules for, &c., 97, 101.
"Enough," pronunciation of, 41.
"Enquire" or "inquire," 11.
"-Ent" and "-ant," 10.
"Entail" to, 182.
"Entirety, in its," 182.
Epænetus and Sophænetus, 47.
Epithets, erroneous, 162.
Epœnetus, 44.
Epsilon, 45.
"Ery," "ary," and "ry" terminations, 26.
"Ethel," 46.
Euphony, claims of, 167.
Euphuistic blacksmith, an, 180.
"Eventuate," 181.
"Ever so," or "never so"? 62.
"Evil," 46.
"Evince," 180.
Exact expression not always the better English, 104.
"Except" and "besides," 158.
"Except" for "unless," 159.
Exclamation, notes of, 76.
Exclamations, unmeaning, 205.
"Excuse," "excuse not," 63.
Excuse of hasty writing in newspapers, 189.
"Experience," to, 88, 182.
Expletives, use of, 201.
Expressions of endearment, 195.
"Extasy," or "Ecstasy," 11.

F. W., a correspondent, 83.
Fact and truth, 206.

"Fall on," to, &c., 129, 130.
"Fallacy," 38.
Fallacy in the axiom, that of two ways one must be wrong, 88.
Farmyard, placard in a, 173.
"Favor," or "favour," 6.
Fechter's Hamlet, criticism of, 102.
"Feet-warmers," or "foot-warmers," 209.
"Felicity," 194.
"Female," for "a woman," 178.
Feminine substantives, 72.
"Fifty cubits high," &c., 132.
Figurative use of words, 78.
Fine language, the inroads of, 166.
"First" and "former," 81.
"First," the, "the last," &c., 186.
"First foundation," &c., 204.
"Fishery," 26.
"Fissure," 67.
"Fitted" and "fited," 22.
"Flies" (carriages), or "flys," 12.
"Flys" (carriages), or "flies," 12.
"Folk" and "folks," 171.
"Foot-warmers," or "feet-warmers," 209.
Foreign words, use of, in English composition, 197.
"Former" and "first," 81.
"Foundry," 26.
"Fraternise," or "fraternize"? 25.
French, vocabulary and spoken, 87.
French, &c, interlarding English with, 198.
"From," "of," and "on," 137.
"From hence," "from thence," 201.
"Ful one," 23.

"Gallbladder," 25.
Gallici-ans, 200.
"Gallnut," 23.

"Gas-holder and Boiler-maker," 174.
"Genesis, the book," or "the book of Genesis"? 89.
Genitive, the double, 168.
Genitive singular, the apostrophe of the, 12.
"Georgy porgy," &c., 197, 211.
"Get, could not," 85.
"Gifted men," "gifted pens," &c., 85.
"Giving [i.e., opening] on the yard," 201.
"Go to seed," 134.
"Going" and "coming," 133, 134.
"Going, where are you"? and "going to," 118.
"Good-looking," or "well-looking"? 80.
"Good Words," 1863, this work originally published there, 18, 42, 131, 211.
"Goose," 24.
"Gospels, the first three," or "the three first"? 105.
"Governess," 72.
"Grammar, Archiepiscopal," letter on, 209.
Grammar, of the Bible, 99; English books of, some, vii, 86, 94, 105; rules of, vii, 83; and idiom, 1; and usage, 54. See also Rule v. usage, &c.
Grammarian, the strict, 65.
Grammarians, "penny-wise," 110.
Grammatical anomalies, 147.
"Greater" and "greatest," 82.
Greek language, 57, 58, 184.
"Grovelling," 22.

H after "a" and "an," 34; dropping, 36; misuse of, 30. See also Aspirate.
"Had as lief," 71.
"Had as soon," 71.
"Had rather," 71.
"Hadn't used," &c., 165.
"Halfpenny," 37.
"Hallo!" and "Halloop!" 51.

"Hamlet," Mr. Fechter's, criticism of, 102.
"Handrailing," noun, 88.
Hare, Archdeacon, on "honor," &c., 6.
Hasty writing, excuse for, 189.
"Have [there] been more applications than one," and "there *has* been more than one application," 154.
"Hawk and a hand-saw," *i.e.*, "herneshew," 50.
"He" and "it," confused use of, 108.
"He, it is," or "it is him"? 114.
"Head, to," 87.
"Heart" for "art," 139.
"Hell fire," 23.
"Hen[n], only one in Venice," 35.
"Hence, from," 204.
"Henceforth, from," 204.
"Her'n," "his'n," &c., 211.
Herbalist, an "Indigenous Kentish," 174.
"Heritor," 36.
"Herne Hill," "Herne Bay," &c., 50.
"Herneshew," 50.
"Heron," pronunciation of, 50.
"Heronry," 26.
Higginson's (E.), English Grammar, viii, 86.
Hill, Rowland, and Johnny Stittle, 43.
"Him, it is," "it is her," 114.
"His," "his'n," and "her'n," 211.
"His," "one," joined to, 164.
"History," a, "an historian," 34.
"Holding on to," 129.
"Holy" and "wholly," 45.
Home talk, 195.
"Homœopathy," 27.
"Honor" or "honour,' 6.
"Hose," 21.
"Hospital," the aspirate in, 33.
"Hough" and "ough," pronunciation, 41.

Houghton, Lord, pronunciation of his name, 41.
"How d'ye do?" 56.
"However," with commas, 73.
"Humble," "umble," &c., 31.

"I am," and "I be," 149.
"I be," and "I am," rule as to, 149.
"I, it is," or "it is me"? 112, 210.
"I need not have troubled myself," 140.
"I shall," 122.
"I take it," 166.
"I, than," or "than me"? 111.
"I will," 122.
"Idear," &c., 35.
Ideas, confusion of, 192.
Idiom, 54 ; caprice of, 56 ; example of from the Greek 57.
Idiom and Construction, 54 ; and grammar, 1.
Idiomatic address, 55.
Idiomatic expressions, 162.
"If" for "whether," 269.
"If I be," &c., 149.
Ignorance of the clergy, 48. *See also* Clergy.
"I know nothing by myself" explained, 42, 172.
"-ll" or "-el" terminations, 46.
"Ill" and "well," 174.
"Ill turn, an," &c., 174.
"Illustrated London News," 24, 180.
"Immergency," 67.
"In" and "on," 129.
"In" and "with," 136.
"In" or "en" in "inquiry," &c., 11.
"In our midst," &c., 186.
"In respect (or regard) of," &c., 136.
"Inclose," or "enclose," 11.
Incongruity, 194.
"Indeed!" 205.
"Independent of," "dependent on," 137.

Indicative moods in conditional sentences, 149.
"Individual," 177.
"Indorse" or "endorse," 11.
"Inferior," "superior," 82.
Infinitive and "to," 133.
Inflated language in prayers, 194.
"Ingoldsby Legends," 114.
"Inimical," pronunciation of, 45.
"Initiative, take the," 181.
Innovations in talk, letters concerning, 183.
"Insects" and "animals," 139.
Instinct in language, 122.
"Insurance" or "assurance," 11.
"Into" and "on to," 129.
"Inversely as," 137.
Invitations, mistakes in accepting and answering, 157, 158.
"Invite" for "invitation," 158.
Irish correspondent on "shall" and "will," 127.
Irish misuse of "shall" and "will," 122, 126; and of "which?" for "what?" 62.
Irish use of "that," "those," &c., 59.
"Irregular," 184.
"It" and "he," confused use of, 108.
"It" and "its," 5, 167.
"It is him," "it is her," 114.
"Irrespective of," 137.
Italian talk, 205.
Italic type, a and o in, 27.
"Ivanhoe," 176.
"Ize" or "ise" (in utilize, &c.), 25.

"Jack was very respectful to Tom, and always took his hat off when he met," &c., 193.
Jacobites, "mole" toasted by, 50.
James I., 196.
Jeweller, notice by a, 180.
"John Gilpin," 116.
Johnny Stittle. See Stittle.

Johnson, Dr., 169, 170, 197; his Dictionary, 67.
Journals, dialect of our, 177. See also Newspapers, &c.
"Jovially," 23.
"Juvenile, a," 178.

Kames, Lord, his rule, 97.
Keating's Insect-destroying powder, advertisement of, 139.
"Kindnesses, many," or "much kindness," 16.
"King's" includes "Queen's," 72.
"King's English, the," 175.
"Know (I) nothing of myself" (St. Paul's) explained, 42, 172.
"Know no harm by him," 172.
"Know-ledge" and "knolledge," 49.
Korah, or Core, 43.

L in "alms," "psalms," "calm," 39.
Language, our, deterioration of, 175; sources of, ibid. See also English, "Queen's English," &c.
Languages, analogy of, vii.
"Last" and "latter," 81.
Latham, Dr., 111; his English Grammar, viii; his History of the English Language, 5, 73, 113, 126, 140, 149; his opinion on "It is me," 113; on "overflow," 26; his account of "shall" and "will," 126; his rule in subjunctive moods, 149; his rule about "either you or I," 155; on the termination "ery," &c., 26; on "which," 68.
Latin in English, 87.
"Latter" of more than two; "Last" of only two, 81.
"Laundry," 26.
"Lay" and "lie," 11.
"Leave, to," absolute, 81.
"Lechery," 27.

Lecky's "History of European Morals," 188.
Leeds Mercury, extract from on the importation of foreign words, 197.
Leicestershire usage, 51.
"Lesser" and "less," 64.
"Lie" and "lay," 11.
"Light on," to, &c., 129.
"Like" and the nominative, 117.
"Like" as an adverb, 169.
"Like, and the," 203.
"Like he was," 169.
"Like I do," 169.
"Like we are," 169.
"Livy writes," or "Livy wrote"? 120.
"Locality," 179.
"London, the city," or "the city of," 88.
"Long" and "short," anomalies in the usage of, 147.
Longley, Archbishop, 48.
"Looking sadly," &c., 245.
"Loose" and "lose," 23.
"Lord, my," "Our Lord," &c., 110, 210.
Lord's Prayer, the, 195.
"Lose" and "loose," 23.
"Lovéd" and "lov'd," &c., 48.
"Lovey," "dearey," &c., in home talk, 195.

M——, Sir J., and the tired nurse, 197.
"Mabel," 46.
Macaulay, 101.
Magazine writing for the "best society," 198.
"Manifold," or "many-fold"? 37.
Manning, Mr. Sergeant, on the "Possessive Augment in English," &c., 13.
"Me," "ye," and "you," 114.
"Me, it is," and "it is I," 112, 210.
"Me, than," or "than I"? 111.
"Means," 17.
"Medicine," 38.
"Mentioned," 183.

"Mercies," or "mercy," 17.
"Meseems," 65.
"Messrs. Jackson," or "Messrs. Jacksons"? 13.
"Messrs. Jackson's works," or "Messrs. Jacksons' works"? 13.
Metaphorical adjectives, 163.
"Methinks," 65.
"Mewses" and "mews," 18.
Midlands, use of "by" in the, 172; other Midland usages, 5, 118, 148, 165.
"Midst, in our," 186.
"Military," 171.
Milldam, 23.
Miller, Joe, 172.
"Millstone," 23.
"Millstream," 23.
Milton, 5, 83, 86, 88, 111.
"Mine" and "my," 33, 211.
"Minister," 37.
Mispronunciation of Scripture names, 41.
"Misses Brown, the," or "the Miss Browns"? 15.
Mis-spelling in newspapers, 24.
"Mistaken," ambiguous sense of, 79.
Mistakes, in accepting invitations, 157; of one word for another, 139.
Misuse of the aspirate, 30.
"Mole" and "mouldy-warp," 50.
Mole, toasted by Jacobites, 50.
"Moneys," or "monies," 16.
"Moneyed," or "monied," man, 84, 88.
Moods, rule as to, 149.
"More than probable," 65.
Morning Chronicle, quoted, 187.
"Most Highest," &c., 204.
Mouldy-warp, 50.
"Mowing, wants," 175.
"Much," "this much," &c., 61.
"Music as before," 173.
Murray's Handbooks, 161.
Murray, Lindley, balanced with Shakespeare, 105.
"Mutual friend, a," 159.

"My Lord," the address "Our Lord," &c., 110, 210.
"Mystify," 38.

N in Venice, 35.
"Naabis" = (?) "navvys," 7.
Names, compound, their plurals, 15.
Names, pronunciation of, 40.
Napoleon III., his "Life of Julius Cæsar," 51.
"Nationalities," 184.
"Navvy" and "navigator," 8.
"Need" and "needs," 20.
Negative, affirmative turned to, 93.
Negatives and affirmatives, contradictory, 63.
"Neglect to," &c., 119.
"Neighbour" and "neighbor," 6, 7.
"Neighbour to," and "a neighbour of," 138.
"Net," or "nett"? 22.
"New," comma after, 74.
New Testament, the, references to, 5, 35, 74, 92, 95, 99, 104, 106, 109, 111, 114, 115, 117, 120, 125, 132, 133, 134, 137, 138, 141, 149, 150, 151, 159, 203, 204, 206. See also under Bible.
"New Whig Guide," 84.
"News," 18.
Newspaper criticism, 46; newspaper English, 84, 101, 130, 139, 159, 162, 165, 177, 201.
Newspapers, excuse for slipshod writing in, 189; mis-spelling in, 24.
"Never so," or "ever so"? 62.
"Nicknames," 195.
"No" and "yes" the same, 63.
Nominative and accusative cases, 103.
Nonsense, talking, to children, 196.
"Noose," 24.
Northern counties, usage in the, 5, 118.
"Nor" and "or" in a negative sentence, 91.

"Nose," 24.
"Not," redundant, 192; varying use of, 192.
"Notes of admiration" [129].
Nouns, abstract and concrete, 171; collective, 170; made into verbs, 87; of number, 170.
Novels, modern, &c., use of foreign phrases in, 198.
Novels, popular, mistakes in, 139.
"Now, just," 148.
Nursery talk, 196, 211.

"Oasis," 46.
Objective and subjective words, 90; of adverbs, 144.
"Objector," 37.
"Obnoxious," 91.
Oddity of expression, avoid it, 206.
"Oddly, it would read," 145.
"Of," improper use of, 117.
"Of," preposition, 89.
"Of," "on," and "from," 137.
"Of" and "to," 136-138.
"Of" in "all of them," &c., 132.
"Of" in "of fifty cubits high," &c., 132.
"Oftener," "oftenest," 146.
"Old and New Bookseller," 174.
"Oldest" and "eldest," 82.
"Oldest inmate," 64.
Omicron, 45.
Omission of "u" in words in "our," 6.
"On" and "upon," 129.
"On," "of," and "from," 137.
"On to," 128; compared with "into," 129.
"On the chairman rising to," &c.? 168.
"One," "a one," or "an one"? 35.
"One" joined to "his," 164.
"One another," 108.
Onesimus, 44.
"Only," position of, 104.
"Open out," to, 131.
"Open up," to, 131.
"Optative," 37.

"Or" and "nor" in a negative sentence, 91.
Oral and vocal sounds, 39.
"Orator," 37.
"Orion," 48.
"-Ough," pronunciation of, 41.
"Ought to" and "ought not to," 119.
"Our," terminations in, 6.
"Our Father which," or "who art"? 69.
"Overflown" for "overflowed," 26.
Oxford, Declaration of the Clergy, 103.

Pagliardini, Sig., vii.
Pall Mall Gazette, quoted, 190.
"Palmistry," 27.
Parenthesis, definition and requirements of, 94, 96.
Parish clerk, a, 172.
Parliament, speakers in, 36.
"Partake" for "eat," 179.
Participles, 175; and verbs, 191.
Particles, conjunctional, 158; "if," "whether," &c., 149; superfluous, use of, 128.
"Party, a," 178; technical sense of, *ibid*.; examples of the use of, 179.
"Pass a few days with," 200.
"Passbook," 23.
"Password," 23.
"Pastime," 23.
Patrobas, 44.
Pedant, the, and common sense, 104.
"Pendent from," 137.
Pendent participial clauses, absurdity of, 191.
"Penny-a-liners," English, 199. *See also* Newspaper English, &c.
"People" and "persons," 170.
"Peoples," 183, 184.
"Person," 177.
"Person, a young," 178.
"Persons" and "people," 170.
"Persuasion," 181.

"Pewed," a church, 87.
"Phantasy," 38.
"Pharaoh," not "Pharoah," 24.
Phenomenon to be observed in usage of subjunctive and indicative, 151.
"Philadelphia," 44.
Philemon, 43.
Phonetic News, the, 9.
Phonetic spelling, 9.
"Piety," 173.
"Piggery," 26.
"Pilgrimess," &c., 72.
"Pillbox," 23.
"Pinery," 26.
"Plain" for "plainly," 143.
"Pleiades," 48.
"Plough," pronunciation of, 41.
Plural and singular of nouns of number, 170.
Plurals, the apostrophe and, 14; of compound names, 15; and singulars, 152.
Pope, 9, 59, 117.
"Portress," 72.
"Pose," 24.
Possessive, marking the, 167.
"Possessive Augment in English," &c., Mr. Sergeant Manning's work on, 13.
Possessive case, "On the chairman rising to," &c.? 168; "one" joined to "his," 164. *See also* Apostrophe, &c.
Possessive pronouns, 211.
"'Poys,' the three," 172.
Prayer Book, the, references to, 14, 25, 28, 32, 61, 72, 79, 93, 151, 152, 172, 195, 204.
Prayer, the Lord's, 69.
Prayers, inflated language in, 194.
"Predicate" for "predict," 169.
Preposition "of," 89.
Prepositions, 117, 128; at the end of sentences, 118.
Present tense, use of the, to signify fixed design, 140.
Present, past, and perfect tenses, 119; confusion of, 120; caution respecting, 140.

"Presentiment" for "presentment," 139.
"Previous," or "previously"? 145.
"Princess," or "princéss," 52.
Printers, their liking for commas, 73; their corrections, 156, 180.
Prior, 111, 169.
"Proceed," 179.
"Proclivities," what? 163.
Professions, collective names of the, 171.
"Progress," to, 85.
"Projector," 37.
"Prophecy," or "prophesy," 38.
Pronouns, idiomatic, 55; and nouns, 108; possessive, 211; "whom," &c., 135.
Pronunciation, 30; of names, 40; in Somersetshire, 38; sticklers for, 37.
"Psalms," 39.
Punch, the barber in, his misuse of h, 31.
Punctuation, 73-77; standard of, 77.

"Qualify," 38.
"Queens" included in "Kings," 72.
"Queen's English," what? vii, 2; this work, 1, 175, 207; the critics of this work, 110, 129. *See also* Critics, Correspondents, &c.
"Quitted," or "quited"? 22.

"Rack" and "wrack," 51.
Railway and other public notices, 187.
"Read oddly, it would," 115.
Reader, The, quoted, 115.
Reading, emphatic, 52; on stilts, 49.
"Rebelled" and "rebeled," 22.
"Record," 36.
Record, The, quoted, 163.
"Reflector," 37.

"Reliable," 182.
"Religion in the arm-chair," 173.
Religion in the Isle of Skye, 39.
"Remains" and "remainder," 18.
"Replace," 66.
"Respect, in," or "in regard" of, 136.
"Revelation," not "Revelations" of St. John, 45.
"Revenue," pronunciation of, 40.
"Reverend" and "reverent," 90.
"Reviler" and "caviller," 22.
Rhetoricians, their rules destructive of the best English style, 97.
"Riches," a plural, 210.
"Ride," "road," &c., 166.
"Riding," or "driving"? 166.
Right: That which sounds right is right, as a rule, 156.
"Right man in the right place, the," 173.
"Rising generation, the," 178.
Rogers, Dr. Goddard, 40.
Romans in the Thames, 51.
"Rose," 24.
"Rough," pronunciation, 41.
"Round man in the square hole," &c., 173.
"Royally," 23.
Rule *versus* usage, vii, 1, 41, 88, 97, 143, 147, 151, 208. *See also* Usage.
Rules of constructing sentences, so called, 93; best way of proceeding in regard of such rules, 100.
"Rule Britannia," 116.
"Ruri-decânal," 37.
Russian, a, on the rules of English Grammar, 83.

S in "loose," "choose," &c., 24.
S or z in "ise," &c., 25.
"Sacrament," 49.
St. Davids, Bishop of, 73.

"St. George, the parish of," and "the parish of St. George's," 89.
St. John, the Revelation of, 46.
St. Paul, his "I know nothing by myself," 42, 43, 172; his list of salutations, 47.
St. Peter, detection of, by his speech, 5.
"Samaria," 44.
"Sanitary" and "sanatory," 24.
"Savior," or "Saviour," 6.
"Scotch," or "Scottish," 26.
Scott, Sir Walter, 117.
Scotticisms, 131. *See also* under Scottish.
"Scottish" and "Scotch," 26.
Scottish, misuse of "shall" and "will," 122, 126; nursery song, "Bonnie Bairnie,"211; usages, 133, 175; use of "that," "those," &c., 59.
Scripture names, mispronunciation of, 41.
"Secretion" for "secreting," 139.
"Seething," 186.
"Seldom, or never," "seldom, if ever," 169.
"Seldomer," 146.
Selucia, 44.
Semicolon and colon, 76.
"Senator," 37.
Sennacherib, 44.
"Sent [to] me a letter," 160.
Sentences, construction of, 54; elliptical, 93; arrangement of words in, *ibid.*; wrongly supposed elliptic, 141.
"Seraphim," "seraphin," "seraphs," &c., 28.
"Set," or "sett"? 22.
"Setteth not by himself, He that," 172.
"Shadrach, Meshach,and Abednego," 172.
Shakspeare balanced against Lindley Murray, 105; his grammar, 99, 100, 105; references to his works, 5, 9, 20, 26, 29, 52, 59, 65, 86, 154, 166, 178, 183, 185, 204.

Shakspeare, the Cambridge edition of, 154.
"Shall" and "should," 158.
"Shall" and "will," confusion of, 121-126; rules for the use of, 127.
"Shall I," 122.
"Shall you," 123.
"She, it is," or "it is her"? 114.
"Shew" and "show," 25.
"Shines bright" for "shines brightly," &c., 143.
"Short" and "shortly," 147.
"Should" and "shall," 158.
"Should," "would," &c., 125.
"Should have been happy to," 158.
"Should seem," or "would seem"? 125.
"Show" and "shew," 25.
"Shrubbery," 26.
"Shutting to," or "shutting too"? 22.
"Shut up," to, 131.
Sidney, Sir Philip, 9, 159.
Simeon, Rev. Charles, and Johnny Stittle, 43.
Singing, difference of utterance in, 49.
Singular and plural of nouns of number, 170.
Singulars and plurals, cases of not understood, 152, 153; account of usage, 154.
Skye, Isle of, religion there, 39.
Slang words, avoid, 206.
"Slippers, his wrong," 173.
Shipshod writing in newspapers, excuse for, 189.
"So" and "as," 70.
"Society, the best," writing for, 198.
"Soft" for "softly," 143.
Somersetshire, dialect, 66; pronunciation, 38.
Sophænetus and Ephænetus, 47.
"Sough," pronunciation of, 41.
South Kensington Museum, 24.
Spelling, 6; phonetic, 9.

Spenser, 137.
Spoken and written language, 57.
"Spoonfuls," or "spoonsfull," 16.
Standard, The, quoted, 182, 192.
"Staircasing," noun, 88.
"Stationary" and "stationery," 27.
Stittle, Johnny, of Cambridge, 43.
Stops not unimportant, 75. *See also* Punctuation.
Style, the best English, 97; written and talking, 202.
Subjunctive and indicative moods in conditional sentences, 148; bias once to the former, 150; but now to the indicative, *ibid.*
Subjective and objective use of adverbs, 144.
Subjective and objective words, 90.
"Such an one," or "such a one," 35.
"Summons," 19.
"Superior," "inferior," 82.
Superlative and comparative clauses, 146.
"Sustain," to, 181.
"Sweet" for "sweetly," 143.
Swift, Dean, 59, 90, 111.
Syntactical perfection impossible, 193.

"Take heed how (hoo) ye hear," 39.
"Take it, 1," 166.
"Take your choice," in pronunciation, 46.
"Talented," 83.
Talk, home, 195; innovations in, 183; nursery, 196.
Talking bores, 206.
Talking nonsense to children, 196.
Taylor's "Convent Life in Italy," 136.

"Teddington," instance of ingenious derivation, 51.
"Tendencies," 163.
"Tenor," or "tenour," 9.
Tenses, 119; perfect and past, 140.
"Term," what is a? 139.
Term in nominative and accusative cases, 103.
Terminations "cry" and "ry," 26.
Thackeray, 192.
"Thames, the river," not "the river of Thames," 90.
Thames, tide of the, 51.
"Than," 188; and the accusative case, 142; does it govern an accusative? 111; two ways of constructing, *ibid.*
"Than I," or "than me"? 111.
"Thanks," for "thank you," 183.
"That," triple meaning of, 60.
"That," verb after, without auxiliary, 151.
"That" and "this," 59.
"That" and "those," 59.
"That" for "which," &c., 68.
"That ill" = "so ill," 62.
"Thee, as," in "Rule Britannia," 116.
"Thence, from," 204.
"They," "you," and "them," 55.
"This" and "that," 59.
"This" and "these," 59.
"This much," "that much," 61.
Thomson, 116.
"Thoroughly working order," 148.
"Those kind of things," 58.
"Them," "you," and "they," 55.
"Though," pronunciation of, 41.
"Three first Gospels," or "first three Gospels"? 105, 108.
"Three boys' just mentioned, the," 172.
"Through," pronunciation of, 41.
"Tigeress," 53.
Tillotson, 107.

Times, The, quoted, 20, 24, 117, 135, 139, 145, 161, 182, 188, 191.
Timotheus, 44.
Tithe dinner, note after a, 102.
"To" and "as," 137.
"To" and "of," 136, 137, 138.
"To" and "too," 20, 78.
"To" and "with," 137.
"To" followed by an adverb, 133.
"To-day," "to-night," 60.
"To-year"="this year," 60.
"To, on," or "on"? 128.
"To scientifically illustrate," &c., 133.
"Too" and "to," 20, 78.
"Too," with commas, 73.
"Trafalgar," pronunciation of, 40.
"Travelling," 22.
"Treachery," 27.
"Treat of," to, or to "treat"? 88.
Trench, Archbishop, 34.
"Troubled myself, I need not have," 140.
"Trough," pronunciation of, 41.
Truth and fact, 206.
"Tuesday," pronunciation, 36.
"Twice one is [not are] two," 153.
"Two and two *are* four," or "two and two *is* four"? 152.

U, omitting, in terminations "our," 6.
U pronounced as "oo," 36.
"Umble," &c., 31.
"Unless," "except" used for, 159.
Unmeaning exclamations, 205.
"Upon" and "on to," 129.
Urbane and Urban, 45.
Usage, 46, 90; freaks of, 168; must prevail, 53; we must wait upon, 28, 37, 64; and construction, 54; and rule, 1, 41, 80, 143, 147, 151, 156, 208. *See also* Rule.
Usages, elliptic, 56.
"Use" and "used," 165.

Use of expletives, 201.
"Use, didn't," "hadn't used," &c., 165.
"Usedn't," 166.
Ussher, 178.
Usage, indifferent, of auxiliary verbs, 124.
"Utilise or utilize"? 25.
"Utmost end," &c., 204.

"Venery," 27.
Venice, only one hen[n] in, 35.
"Venison," 38.
"*Venite exultemus*," 44.
Verb, after "that," without auxiliary, 151; made from noun, 87; neuter-substantive, 145; with a singular nominative coupled to a plural, 156; and participle, 191.
"Very," and "very much," 80.
"Very pleased," &c., 80.
"Victual," 37.
"Vinery," 26.
"Vinyard" and "vineyard," 37.
Vocal and oral sounds, 39.
Vulgarisms, 180.

W——, Mr. F., M.P., 85.
Walker's "Pronouncing Dictionary" at fault, 46.
"Wallflower," 23.
"Wants cutting," 175.
"Warn't," 71.
"Was being written," 121.
"Was, used to," 165.
"Washhouse," 23.
"Watchhouse," 23.
"Welcome," 23.
"Well," 202.
"Well" and "ill," 174.
"Well," "wel-fare," &c., 23.
"Well-looking," or "good-looking"? 80.
"Went to pieces," 134.
West-country talk, 118.
"What?"="which"? 63.
"What was...!" "what was not...!" 63.
"Whether I am," &c., 149.

"Whether," "if" for, 169.
"Which, and," 161.
"Which," "as" used for, 187.
"Which," English, Scotch, and Irish, 34.
"Which," pronunciation of, 33.
"Which?" "what?" 63.
"Which," "who," 68.
"Whilk," 68.
"Who" and "which," 68.
"Who' and "whom," 39.
"Wholly" and "holy," 45.
"Whom," misuse of, 135.
"Whomsoever" and "whosoever," 135.
"Why," 202.
"Wicklow, the county," not "the county of Wicklow," 90.
Wighill, Yorkshire, 85.
"Will," ambiguity in, 125.
"Will" and "shall," 121-128; rules for the use of, 127.
"Will," "would," and "should," 125.
"Will, I," 122.
"Will, you," 123.
"Witchery," 27.
"With" and "in," 136.
"With" and "of," 138.
"With" and "to," 137.
"Withhold," or "withold," 23.
"Without" for "unless," 159.
"Wolf, wolf!" cry of, 51.
Word, one used for another, 139, 191.
Word, the same in different cases, can it be used in an elliptic sentence? 103.
Words, division of, between lines, 21; terminating in "-cry" or "-ry," 26, 27; torturing, 163; unmeaning, 205; use simple, 205.
Words, superabundant. *See* Expletives.
Words which ought to stand together, 162.
Words and phrases, foreign, 197.
"Would" and "should," 125.
"Would seem," or "should seem"? 125.
"Wreck," "wrack," and "rack." 52.
"Write you, we will," for "we will write to you," 160.
Writing, hasty, excuse for, 189.
Written and spoken language, 57.

"Ye," "you," and "me," 114.
"Yes" and "no" the same, 63.
"You," "thou," and "they," 55.
"You," "ye," and "me," 114.
"You and I," accusative, 116.
"You don't say so," &c., 205.
"You know," 202.
"You shall," &c., 123.
"You see," 202.
"You will," 123.

Z or s in "ize," &c., 25.
"Zabulon," 44.

CATALOGUE OF
BOHN'S LIBRARIES.

N.B.—It is requested that all orders be accompanied by payment. Books are sent carriage free on the receipt of the published price in stamps or otherwise.

The Works to which the letters 'N. S.' (denoting New Style) are appended are kept in neat cloth bindings of various colours, as well as in the regular Library style. All Orders are executed in the New binding, unless the contrary is expressly stated.

Complete Sets or Separate Volumes can be had at short notice, half-bound in calf or morocco.

New Volumes of Standard Works in the various branches of Literature are constantly being added to this Series, which is already unsurpassed in respect to the number, variety, and cheapness of the Works contained in it. The Publishers have to announce the following Volumes as recently issued or now in preparation:—

Seneca's Minor Works. Translated by Aubrey Stewart, M.A. [*In the press.*

Elze's Life of Shakespeare. Translated by L. Dora Schmitz. [*See p. 4.*

Dunlop's History of Fiction. With Introduction and Supplement, bringing the Work down to recent times. By Henry Wilson. [*Immediately.*

Letters and Works of Lady Mary Wortley Montagu. [*Ready, see p. 7.*

Heaton's Concise History of Painting. [*In the press.*

Lucian's Dialogues of the Gods, the Sea Gods, and the Dead.

Strickland's Lives of the Tudor and Stuart Princesses. [*Ready, see p. 9.*

Mme. de Staël's Corinne. [*Immediately.*

Josephus's Works. Edited by the Rev. A. R. Shilleto. [*In the press.*

Johnson's Lives of the Poets. [*In the press.*

Schopenhauer's The Fourfold Root and The Will in Nature. [*In the press.*

June, 1888.

BOHN'S LIBRARIES.

STANDARD LIBRARY.

317 *Vols. at* 3*s*. 6*d. each, excepting those marked otherwise.* (56*l*. 1*s. per set.*)

ADDISON'S Works. Notes of Bishop Hurd. Short Memoir, Portrait, and 8 Plates of Medals. 6 vols. *N. S.* This is the most complete edition of Addison's Works issued.

ALFIERI'S Tragedies. In English Verse. With Notes, Arguments, and Introduction, by E. A. Bowring, C.B. 2 vols. *N. S.*

AMERICAN POETRY. — *See Poetry of America.*

BACON'S Moral and Historical Works, including Essays, Apophthegms, Wisdom of the Ancients, New Atlantis, Henry VII., Henry VIII., Elizabeth, Henry Prince of Wales, History of Great Britain, Julius Cæsar, and Augustus Cæsar. With Critical and Biographical Introduction and Notes by J. Devey, M.A. Portrait. *N. S.*

— *See also Philosophical Library.*

BALLADS AND SONGS of the Peasantry of England, from Oral Recitation, private MSS., Broadsides, &c. Edit. by R. Bell. *N. S.*

BEAUMONT AND FLETCHER. Selections. With Notes and Introduction by Leigh Hunt.

BECKMANN (J.) History of Inventions, Discoveries, and Origins. With Portraits of Beckmann and James Watt. 2 vols. *N. S.*

BELL (Robert).—*See Ballads, Chaucer, Green.*

BOSWELL'S Life of Johnson, with the TOUR in the HEBRIDES and JOHNSONIANA. New Edition, with Notes and Appendices, by the Rev. A. Napier, M.A., Trinity College, Cambridge, Vicar of Holkham, Editor of the Cambridge Edition of the 'Theological Works of Barrow.' With Frontispiece to each vol. 6 vols. *N.S.*

BREMER'S (Frederika) Works. Trans. by M. Howitt. Portrait. 4 vols. *N.S.*

BRINK (B. T.) Early English Literature (to Wiclif). By Bernhard Ten Brink. Trans. by Prof. H. M. Kennedy. *N. S.*

BRITISH POETS, from Milton to Kirke White. Cabinet Edition. With Frontispiece. 4 vols. *N. S.*

BROWNE'S (Sir Thomas) Works. Edit. by S. Wilkin, with Dr. Johnson's Life of Browne. Portrait. 3 vols.

BURKE'S Works. 6 vols. *N. S.*

— **Speeches on the Impeachment** of Warren Hastings; and Letters. 2 vols. *N. S.*

— **Life.** By J. Prior. Portrait. *N. S.*

BURNS (Robert). Life of. By J. G. Lockhart, D.C.L. A new and enlarged edition. With Notes and Appendices by W. S. Douglas. Portrait. *N. S.*

BUTLER'S (Bp.) Analogy of Religion; Natural and Revealed, to the Constitution and Course of Nature; with Two Dissertations on Identity and Virtue, and Fifteen Sermons. With Introductions, Notes, and Memoir. Portrait. *N. S.*

CAMÖEN'S Lusiad; or the Discovery of India. An Epic Poem. Trans. from the Portuguese, with Dissertation, Historical Sketch, and Life, by W. J. Mickle. 5th edition. *N. S.*

CARAFAS (The) of Maddaloni. Naples under Spanish Dominion. Trans. by Alfred de Reumont. Portrait of Masaniello.

CARREL. The Counter-Revolution in England for the Re-establishment of Popery under Charles II. and James II., by Armand Carrel; with Fox's History of James II. and Lord Lonsdale's Memoir of James II. Portrait of Carrel.

CARRUTHERS. — *See Pope, in Illustrated Library.*

CARY'S Dante. The Vision of Hell, Purgatory, and Paradise. Trans. by Rev. H. F. Cary, M.A. With Life, Chronological View of his Age, Notes, and Index of Proper Names. Portrait. *N. S.*
This is the authentic edition, containing Mr. Cary's last corrections, with additional notes.

CELLINI (Benvenuto). Memoirs of, by himself. With Notes of G. P. Carpani. Trans. by T. Roscoe. Portrait. *N. S.*

CERVANTES' Galatea. A Pastoral Romance. Trans. by G. W. J. Gyll. *N. S.*

—— **Exemplary Novels.** Trans. by W. K. Kelly. *N. S.*

—— **Don Quixote de la Mancha.** Motteux's Translation revised. With Lockhart's Life and Notes. 2 vols. *N. S.*

CHAUCER'S Poetical Works. With Poems formerly attributed to him. With a Memoir, Introduction, Notes, and a Glossary, by R. Bell. Improved edition, with Preliminary Essay by Rev. W. W. Skeat, M.A. Portrait. 4 vols. *N. S.*

CLASSIC TALES, containing Rasselas, Vicar of Wakefield, Gulliver's Travels, and The Sentimental Journey. *N. S.*

COLERIDGE'S (S. T.) Friend. A Series of Essays on Morals, Politics, and Religion. Portrait. *N. S.*

—— **Aids to Reflection. Confessions** of an Inquiring Spirit; and Essays on Faith and the Common Prayer-book. New Edition, revised. *N. S.*

—— **Table-Talk and Omniana.** By T. Ashe, B.A. *N.S.*

—— **Lectures on Shakspere and** other Poets. Edit. by T. Ashe, B.A. *N.S.*
Containing the lectures taken down in 1811-12 by J. P. Collier, and those delivered at Bristol in 1813.

—— **Biographia Literaria; or, Bio**graphical Sketches of my Literary Life and Opinions; with Two Lay Sermons. *N. S.*

—— **Miscellanies, Æsthetic and** Literary; to which is added, THE THEORY OF LIFE. Collected and arranged by T. Ashe, B.A. *N.S.*

COMMINES.—*See Philip.*

CONDÉ'S History of the Dominion of the Arabs in Spain. Trans. by Mrs. F—ter. Portrait of Abderahmen ben Moavia. 3 vols.

COWPER'S Complete Works, Poems, Correspondence, and Translations. Edit. with Memoir by R. Southey. 45 Engravings. 8 vols.

COXE'S Memoirs of the Duke of Marlborough. With his original Correspondence, from family records at Blenheim. Revised edition. Portraits. 3 vols.
. An Atlas of the plans of Marlborough's campaigns, 4to. 10s. 6d.

—— **History of the House of Austria.** From the Foundation of the Monarchy by Rhodolph of Hapsburgh to the Death of Leopold II., 1218-1792. By Archdn. Coxe. With Continuation from the Accession of Francis I. to the Revolution of 1848. 4 Portraits. 4 vols.

CUNNINGHAM'S Lives of the most Eminent British Painters. With Notes and 16 fresh Lives by Mrs. Heaton. 3 vols. *N. S.*

DEFOE'S Novels and Miscellaneous Works. With Prefaces and Notes, including those attributed to Sir W. Scott. Portrait. 7 vols. *N. S.*

DE LOLME'S Constitution of England, in which it is compared both with the Republican form of Government and the other Monarchies of Europe. Edit., with Life and Notes, by J. Macgregor, M.P.

DUNLOP'S History of Fiction. With Introduction and Supplement adapting the work to present requirements. By Henry Wilson. 3 vols. [*In the press.*

ELZE'S Life of Shakespeare; Translated by L. Dora Schmitz. [*In the press.*

EMERSON'S Works. 3 vols. Most complete edition published. *N. S.*
Vol. I.—Essays, Lectures, and Poems.
Vol. II.—English Traits, Nature, and Conduct of Life.
Vol. III.—Society and Solitude—Letters and Social Aims—Miscellaneous Papers (hitherto uncollected)—May-Day, &c.

FOSTER'S (John) Life and Correspondence. Edit. by J. E. Ryland. Portrait. 2 vols. *N. S.*

—— **Lectures at Broadmead Chapel.** Edit. by J. E. Ryland. 2 vols. *N. S.*

—— **Critical Essays contributed to** the 'Eclectic Review.' Edit. by J. E. Ryland. 2 vols. *N. S.*

—— **Essays: On Decision of Charac**ter; on a Man's writing Memoirs of Himself; on the epithet Romantic; on the aversion of Men of Taste to Evangelical Religion. *N. S.*

—— **Essays on the Evils of Popular** Ignorance, and a Discourse on the Propagation of Christianity in India. *N. S.*

—— **Essay on the Improvement of** Time, with Notes of Sermons and other Pieces. *N. S.*

—— **Fosteriana:** selected from periodical papers, edit. by H. G. Bohn. *N. S.*

STANDARD LIBRARY.

FOX (Rt. Hon. C. J.)—*See Carrel.*

GIBBON'S Decline and Fall of the Roman Empire. Complete and unabridged, with variorum Notes; including those of Guizot, Wenck, Niebuhr, Hugo, Neander, and others. 7 vols. 2 Maps and Portrait. *N. S.*

GOETHE'S Works. Trans. into English by E. A. Bowring, C.B., Anna Swanwick, Sir Walter Scott, &c. &c. 13 vols. *N. S.*
Vols. I. and II.—Autobiography and Annals. Portrait.
Vol. III.—Faust. Complete.
Vol. IV.—Novels and Tales: containing Elective Affinities, Sorrows of Werther, The German Emigrants, The Good Women, and a Nouvelette.
Vol. V.—Wilhelm Meister's Apprenticeship.
Vol. VI.—Conversations with Eckermann and Soret.
Vol. VII.—Poems and Ballads in the original Metres, including Hermann and Dorothea.
Vol. VIII.—Götz von Berlichingen, Torquato Tasso, Egmont, Iphigenia, Clavigo, Wayward Lover, and Fellow Culprits.
Vol. IX.—Wilhelm Meister's Travels. Complete Edition.
Vol. X.—Tour in Italy. Two Parts. And Second Residence in Rome.
Vol. XI.—Miscellaneous Travels, Letters from Switzerland, Campaign in France, Siege of Mainz, and Rhine Tour.
Vol. XII.—Early and Miscellaneous Letters, including Letters to his Mother, with Biography and Notes.
Vol. XIII.—Correspondence with Zelter.

—— **Correspondence with Schiller.** 2 vols.—*See Schiller.*

GOLDSMITH'S Works. 5 vols. *N.S.*
Vol. I.—Life, Vicar of Wakefield, Essays, and Letters.
Vol. II.—Poems, Plays, Bee, Cock Lane Ghost.
Vol. III.—The Citizen of the World, Polite Learning in Europe.
Vol. IV.—Biographies, Criticisms, Later Essays.
Vol. V.—Prefaces, Natural History, Letters, Goody Two-Shoes, Index.

GREENE, MARLOW, and BEN JONSON (Poems of). With Notes and Memoirs by R. Bell. *N. S.*

GREGORY'S (Dr.) The Evidences, Doctrines, and Duties of the Christian Religion.

GRIMM'S Household Tales. With the Original Notes. Trans. by Mrs. A. Hunt. Introduction by Andrew Lang, M.A. 2 vols. *N. S.*

GUIZOT'S History of Representative Government in Europe. Trans. by A. R. Scoble.

—— **English Revolution of 1640.** From the Accession of Charles I. to his Death. Trans. by W. Hazlitt. Portrait.

—— **History of Civilisation.** From the Roman Empire to the French Revolution. Trans. by W. Hazlitt. Portraits. 3 vols.

HALL'S (Rev. Robert) Works and Remains. Memoir by Dr. Gregory and Essay by J. Foster. Portrait.

HAUFF'S Tales. The Caravan—The Sheikh of Alexandria—The Inn in the Spessart. Translated by Prof. S. Mendel. *N. S.*

HAWTHORNE'S Tales. 3 vols. *N. S.*
Vol. I.—Twice-told Tales, and the Snow Image.
Vol. II.—Scarlet Letter, and the House with Seven Gables.
Vol. III.—Transformation, and Blithedale Romance.

HAZLITT'S (W.) Works. 7 vols. *N.S.*
—— **Table-Talk.**
—— **The Literature of the Age of Elizabeth** and Characters of Shakespeare's Plays. *N. S.*
—— **English Poets and English Comic Writers.** *N. S.*
—— **The Plain Speaker.** Opinions on Books, Men, and Things. *N. S.*
—— **Round Table.** Conversations of James Northcote, R.A.; Characteristics. *N. S.*
—— **Sketches and Essays,** and Winterslow. *N. S.*
—— **Spirit of the Age;** or, Contemporary Portraits. To which are added Free Thoughts on Public Affairs, and a Letter to William Gifford. New Edition by W. Carew Hazlitt. *N. S.*

HEINE'S Poems. Translated in the original Metres, with Life by E. A. Bowring, C.B. *N. S.*

—— **Travel-Pictures.** The Tour in the Harz, Norderney, and Book of Ideas, together with the Romantic School. Trans. by F. Storr. With Maps and Appendices. *N. S.*

HOFFMANN'S Works. The Serapion Brethren. Vol. I. Trans. by Lt.-Col. Ewing. *N. S.* [*Vol. II. in the press.*]

HUGO'S (Victor) Dramatic Works: Hernani—Ruy Blas—The King's Diversion. Translated by Mrs. Newton Crosland and F. L. Slous. *N. S.*

—— **Poems,** chiefly Lyrical. Collected by H. L. Williams. *N. S.*
This volume contains contributions from F. S. Mahoney, G. W. M. Reynolds, Andrew Lang, Edwin Arnold, Mrs. Newton Crosland, Miss Fanny Kemble, Bishop Alexander, Prof. Dowden, &c.

HUNGARY: Its History and Revolution, with Memoir of Kossuth. Portrait.

HUTCHINSON (Colonel). Memoirs of. By his Widow, with her Autobiography, and the Siege of Lathom House. Portrait. *N. S.*

IRVING'S (Washington) Complete Works. 15 vols. *N. S.*

—— **Life and Letters.** By his Nephew, Pierre E. Irving. With Index and a Portrait. 2 vols. *N. S.*

JAMES'S (G. P. R.) Life of Richard Cœur de Lion. Portraits of Richard and Phil'p Augustus. 2 vols.

—— **Louis XIV.** Portraits. 2 vols.

JAMESON (Mrs.) Shakespeare's Heroines. Characteristics of Women. By Mrs. Jameson. *N. S.*

JEAN PAUL.—*See Richter.*

JONSON (Ben). Poems of.—*See Greene.*

JUNIUS'S Letters. With Woodfall's Notes. An Essay on the Authorship. Facsimiles of Handwriting. 2 vols. *N. S.*

LA FONTAINE'S Fables. In English Verse, with Essay on the Fabulists. By Elizur Wright. *N. S.*

LAMARTINE'S The Girondists, or Personal Memoirs of the Patriots of the French Revolution. Trans. by H. T. Ryde. Portraits of Robespierre, Madame Roland, and Charlotte Corday. 3 vols.

—— **The Restoration of Monarchy** in France (a Sequel to The Girondists). 5 Portraits. 4 vols.

—— **The French Revolution of 1848.** 6 Portraits.

LAMB'S Charles) Elia and Eliana. Complete Edition. Portrait. *N. S.*

—— **Specimens of English Dramatic** Poets of the time of Elizabeth. Notes, with the Extracts from the Garrick Plays. *N. S.*

—— **Talfourd's Letters of Charles** Lamb. New Edition, by W. Carew Hazlitt. 2 vols. *N. S.*

LANZI'S History of Painting in Italy, from the Period of the Revival of the Fine Arts to the End of the 18th Century. With Memoir of the Author. Portraits of Raffaelle, Titian, and Correggio, after the Artists themselves. Trans. by T. Roscoe. 3 vols.

LAPPENBERG'S England under the Anglo-Saxon Kings. Trans. by B. Thorpe, F.S.A. 2 vols. *N. S.*

LESSING'S Dramatic Works. Complete. By E. Bell, M.A. With Memoir by H. Zimmern. Portrait. 2 vols. *N. S.*

—— **Laokoon, Dramatic Notes, and** Representation of Death by the Ancients. Frontispiece. *N. S.*

LOCKE'S Philosophical Works, containing Human Understanding, with Bishop of Worcester, Malebranche's Opinions, Natural Philosophy, Reading and Study. With Preliminary Discourse, Analysis, and Notes, by J. A. St. John. Portrait. 2 vols. *N. S.*

—— **Life and Letters,** with Extracts from his Common-place Books. By Lord King.

LOCKHART (J. G.)—*See Burns.*

LONSDALE (Lord).—*See Carrel.*

LUTHER'S Table-Talk. Trans. by W. Hazlitt. With Life by A. Chalmers, and LUTHER'S CATECHISM. Portrait after Cranach. *N. S.*

—— **Autobiography.**—*See Michelet.*

MACHIAVELLI'S History of Florence, THE PRINCE, Savonarola, Historical Tracts, and Memoir. Portrait. *N. S.*

MARLOWE. Poems of.—*See Greene.*

MARTINEAU'S (Harriet) History of England (including History of the Peace) from 1800-1846. 5 vols. *N. S.*

MENZEL'S History of Germany, from the Earliest Period to the Crimean War. 3 Portraits. 3 vols.

MICHELET'S Autobiography of Luther. Trans. by W. Hazlitt. With Notes. *N. S.*

—— **The French Revolution** to the Flight of the King in 1791. *N. S.*

MIGNET'S The French Revolution, from 1789 to 1814. Portrait of Napoleon. *N. S.*

MILTON'S Prose Works. With Preface, Preliminary Remarks by J. A. St. John, and Index. 5 vols.

MITFORD'S (Miss) Our Village. Sketches of Rural Character and Scenery. 2 Engravings. 2 vols. *N. S.*

MOLIÈRE'S Dramatic Works. 1 English Prose, by C. H. Wall. With a Life and a Portrait. 3 vols. *N. S.*
'It is not too much to say that we have here probably as good a translation of Molière as can be given.'—*Academy.*

MONTAGU. Letters and Works of Lady Mary Wortley Montagu. Lord Wharncliffe's Third Edition. Edited by W. Moy Thomas. With steel plates. 2 vols. 5s. each. *N. S.*

MONTESQUIEU'S Spirit of Laws. Revised Edition, with D'Alembert's Analysis, Notes, and Memoir. 2 vols. *N. S.*

NEANDER (Dr. A.) History of the Christian Religion and Church. Trans. by J. Torrey. With Short Memoir. 10 vols.

—— **Life of Jesus Christ, in its Historical** Connexion and Development. *N. S.*

—— **The Planting and Training of** the Christian Church by the Apostles. With the Antignosticus, or Spirit of Tertullian. Trans. by J. E. Ryland. 2 vols.

—— **Lectures on the History of** Christian Dogmas. Trans. by J. E. Ryland. 2 vols.

—— **Memorials of Christian Life in** the Early and Middle Ages; including Light in Dark Places. Trans. by J. E. Ryland.

OCKLEY (S.) History of the Saracens and their Conquests in Syria, Persia, and Egypt. Comprising the Lives of Mohammed and his Successors to the Death of Abdalmelik, the Eleventh Caliph. By Simon Ockley, B.D., Prof. of Arabic in Univ. of Cambridge. Portrait of Mohammed.

PERCY'S Reliques of Ancient English Poetry, consisting of Ballads, Songs, and other Pieces of our earlier Poets, with some few of later date. With Essay on Ancient Minstrels, and Glossary. 2 vols. *N. S.*

PHILIP DE COMMINES. Memoirs of. Containing the Histories of Louis XI. and Charles VIII., and Charles the Bold, Duke of Burgundy. With the History of Louis XI., by J. de Troyes. With a Life and Notes by A. R. Scoble. Portraits. 2 vols.

PLUTARCH'S LIVES. Newly Translated, with Notes and Life, by A. Stewart, M.A., late Fellow of Trinity College, Cambridge, and G. Long, M.A. 4 vols. *N. S.*

POETRY OF AMERICA. Selections from One Hundred Poets, from 1776 to 1876. With Introductory Review, and Specimens of Negro Melody, by W. J. Linton. Portrait of W. Whitman. *N. S.*

RANKE (L.) History of the Popes, their Church and State, and their Conflicts with Protestantism in the 16th and 17th Centuries. Trans. by E. Foster. Portraits of Julius II. (after Raphael), Innocent X. (after Velasquez), and Clement VII. (after Titian). 3 vols. *N. S.*

—— **History of Servia.** Trans. by Mrs. Kerr. To which is added, The Slave Provinces of Turkey, by Cyprien Robert. *N. S.*

—— **History of the Latin and Teutonic** Nations. 1494-1514. Trans. by P. A. Ashworth, translator of Dr. Gneist's 'History of the English Constitution.' *N. S.*

REUMONT (Alfred de).—*See Carafas.*

REYNOLDS' (Sir J.) Literary Works. With Memoir and Remarks by H. W. Beechy. 2 vols. *N. S.*

RICHTER (Jean Paul). Levana, a Treatise on Education; together with the Autobiography, and a short Memoir. *N.S.*

—— **Flower, Fruit, and Thorn Pieces,** or the Wedded Life, Death, and Marriage of Siebenkaes. Translated by Alex. Ewing. *N. S.*
The only complete English translation.

ROSCOE'S (W.) Life of Leo X., with Notes, Historical Documents, and Dissertation on Lucretia Borgia. 3 Portraits. 2 vols.

—— **Lorenzo de' Medici,** called 'The Magnificent,' with Copyright Notes, Poems, Letters, &c. With Memoir and Portrait of Roscoe and Portrait of Lorenzo.

RUSSIA, History of, from the earliest Period to the Crimean War. By W. K. Kelly. 3 Portraits. 2 vols.

SCHILLER'S Works. 6 vols. *N. S.*
Vol. I.—Thirty Years' War—Revolt in the Netherlands. Rev A. J. W. Morrison, M.A. Portrait.
Vol. II.—Revolt in the Netherlands, *completed*—Wallenstein. By J. Churchill and S. T. Coleridge.—William Tell. Sir Theodore Martin. Engraving (after Vandyck).
Vol. III.—Don Carlos. R. D. Boylan—Mary Stuart. Mellish—Maid of Orleans. Anna Swanwick—Bride of Messina. A. Lodge, M.A. Together with the Use of the Chorus in Tragedy (a short Essay). Engravings.
These Dramas are all translated in metre.
Vol. IV.—Robbers—Fiesco—Love and Intrigue. Demetrius—Ghost Seer—Sport of Divinity.
The Dramas in this volume are in prose.
Vol. V.—Poems. E. A. Bowring, C.B.
Vol. VI.—Essays, Æsthetical and Philosophical, including the Dissertation on the Connexion between the Animal and Spiritual in Man.

SCHILLER and GOETHE. Correspondence between, from A.D. 1794-1805. With Short Notes by L. Dora Schmitz. 2 vols. *N. S.*

SCHLEGEL'S (F.) Lectures on the Philosophy of Life and the Philosophy of Language. By A. J. W. Morrison.

—— **The History of Literature,** Ancient and Modern.

—— **The Philosophy of History.** With Memoir and Portrait.

—— **Modern History,** with the Lectures entitled Cæsar and Alexander, and The Beginning of our History. By L. Purcell and R. H. Whitelock.

—— **Æsthetic and Miscellaneous** Works, containing Letters on Christian Art, Essay on Gothic Architecture, Remarks on the Romance Poetry of the Middle Ages, on Shakspeare, the Limits of the Beautiful, and on the Language and Wisdom of the Indians. By E. J. Millington.

SCHLEGEL (A. W.) Dramatic Art and Literature. By J. Black. With Memoir by A. J. W. Morrison. Portrait.

SCHUMANN (Robert), His Life and Works. By A. Reissmann. Trans. by A. L. Alger. *N. S.*

SHAKESPEARE'S Dramatic Art. The History and Character of Shakspeare's Plays. By Dr. H. Ulrici. Trans. by L. Dora Schmitz. 2 vols. *N. S.*

SHERIDAN'S Dramatic Works. With Memoir Portrait after Reynolds). *N. S.*

SKEAT Rev. W. W.)—*See Chaucer.*

SISMONDI'S History of the Literature of the South of Europe. With Notes and Memoir by T. Roscoe. Portraits of Sismondi and Dante. 2 vols.
The specimens of early French, Italian, Spanish, and Portugese Poetry, in English Verse, by Cary and others.

SMITH'S (Adam) The Wealth of Nations. An Inquiry into the Nature and Causes of. Reprinted from the Sixth Edition. With an Introduction by Ernest Belfort Bax. 2 vols. *N. S.*

SMITH'S (Adam) Theory of Moral Sentiments; with Essay on the First Formation of Languages, and Critical Memoir by Dugald Stewart.

SMYTH'S (Professor) Lectures on Modern History; from the Irruption of the Northern Nations to the close of the American Revolution. 2 vols.

—— **Lectures on the French Revolution.** With Index. 2 vols.

SOUTHEY.—*See Cowper, Wesley, and (Illustrated Library) Nelson.*

STURM'S Morning Communings with God, or Devotional Meditations for Every Day. Trans. by W. Johnstone, M.A.

SULLY. Memoirs of the Duke of, Prime Minister to Henry the Great. With Notes and Historical Introduction. 4 Portraits. 4 vols.

TAYLOR'S (Bishop Jeremy) Holy Living and Dying, with Prayers, containing the Whole Duty of a Christian and the parts of Devotion fitted to all Occasions. Portrait. *N. S.*

THIERRY'S Conquest of England by the Normans; its Causes, and its Consequences in England and the Continent. By W. Hazlitt. With short Memoir. 2 Portraits. 2 vols. *N. S.*

TROYE'S (Jean de).—*See Philip de Commines.*

ULRICI (Dr.)—*See Shakespeare.*

VASARI. Lives of the most Eminent Painters, Sculptors, and Architects. By Mrs. J. Foster, with selected Notes. Portrait. 6 vols., Vol. VI. being an additional Volume of Notes by J. P. Richter. *N. S.*

WERNER'S Templars in Cyprus. Trans. by E. A. M. Lewis. *N. S.*

WESLEY, the Life of, and the Rise and Progress of Methodism. By Robert Southey. Portrait. 5s. *N. S.*

WHEATLEY. A Rational Illustration of the Book of Common Prayer, being the Substance of everything Liturgical in all former Ritualist Commentators upon the subject. Frontispiece. *N. S.*

HISTORICAL LIBRARY.

22 *Volumes at* 5s. *each.* (5l. 10s. *per set.*)

EVELYN'S Diary and Correspondence, with the Private Correspondence of Charles I. and Sir Edward Nicholas, and between Sir Edward Hyde (Earl of Clarendon) and Sir Richard Browne. Edited from the Original MSS. by W. Bray, F.A.S. 4 vols. *N. S.* 45 Engravings (after Vandyke, Lely, Kneller, and Jamieson, &c.).

N.B.—This edition contains 130 letters from Evelyn and his wife, contained in no other edition.

PEPYS' Diary and Correspondence. With Life and Notes, by Lord Braybrooke. 4 vols. *N. S.* With Appendix containing additional Letters, an Index, and 31 Engravings (after Vandyke, Sir P. Lely, Holbein, Kneller, &c.).

JESSE'S Memoirs of the Court of England under the Stuarts, including the Protectorate. 3 vols. With Index and 42 Portraits (after Vandyke, Lely, &c.).

—— **Memoirs of the Pretenders and** their Adherents. 7 Portraits.

NUGENT'S (Lord) Memorials of Hampden, his Party and Times. With Memoir. 12 Portraits (after Vandyke and others). *N. S.*

STRICKLAND'S (Agnes) Lives of the Queens of England from the Norman Conquest. From authentic Documents, public and private. 6 Portraits. 6 vols. *N. S.*

—— **Life of Mary Queen of Scots.** 2 Portraits. 2 vols. *N. S.*

—— **Lives of the Tudor and Stuart** Princesses. With 2 Portraits. *N. S.*

PHILOSOPHICAL LIBRARY.

16 *Vols. at* 5s. *each, excepting those marked otherwise.* (3l. 14s. *per set.*)

BACON'S Novum Organum and Advancement of Learning. With Notes by J. Devey, M.A.

BAX. A Handbook of the History of Philosophy, for the use of Students. By E. Belfort Bax, Editor of Kant's 'Prolegomena.' 5s. *N. S.*

COMTE'S Philosophy of the Sciences. An Exposition of the Principles of the *Cours de Philosophie Positive.* By G. H. Lewes, Author of 'The Life of Goethe.'

DRAPER (Dr. J. W.) A History of the Intellectual Development of Europe. 2 vols. *N. S.*

HEGEL'S Philosophy of History. By J. Sibree, M.A.

KANT'S Critique of Pure Reason. By J. M. D. Meiklejohn. *N. S.*

—— **Prolegomena and Metaphysical** Foundations of Natural Science, with Biography and Memoir by E. Belfort Bax. Portrait. *N. S.*

LOGIC, or the Science of Inference. A Popular Manual. By J. Devey.

MILLER (Professor). History Philosophically Illustrated, from the Fall of the Roman Empire to the French Revolution. With Memoir. 4 vols. 3s. 6d. each.

SPINOZA'S Chief Works. Trans. with Introduction by R. H. M. Elwes. 2 vols. *N.S.*

Vol. I.—Tractatus Theologico-Politicus —Political Treatise.

Vol. II.— Improvement of the Understanding—Ethics—Letters.

TENNEMANN'S Manual of the History of Philosophy. Trans. by Rev. A. Johnson, M.A.

THEOLOGICAL LIBRARY.

15 *Vols. at 5s. each, excepting those marked otherwise.* (3*l*. 13*s*. 6*d*. *per set*.)

BLEEK. Introduction to the Old Testament. By Friedrich Bleek. Trans. under the supervision of Rev. E. Venables, Residentiary Canon of Lincoln. 2 vols. *N.S.*

CHILLINGWORTH'S Religion of Protestants. 3s. 6d.

EUSEBIUS. Ecclesiastical History of Eusebius Pamphilius, Bishop of Cæsarea. Trans. by Rev. C. F. Cruse, M.A. With Notes, Life, and Chronological Tables.

EVAGRIUS. History of the Church. —See *Theodoret*.

HARDWICK. History of the Articles of Religion; to which is added a Series of Documents from A.D. 1536 to A.D. 1615. Ed. by Rev. F. Procter. *N.S.*

HENRY'S (Matthew) Exposition of the Book of Psalms. Numerous Woodcuts.

PEARSON (John, D.D.) Exposition of the Creed. Edit. by E. Walford, M.A. With Notes, Analysis, and Indexes. *N.S.*

PHILO-JUDÆUS, Works of. The Contemporary of Josephus. Trans. by C. D. Yonge. 4 vols.

PHILOSTORGIUS. Ecclesiastical History of.—*See Sozomen*.

SOCRATES' Ecclesiastical History. Comprising a History of the Church from Constantine, A.D. 305, to the 38th year of Theodosius II. With Short Account of the Author, and selected Notes.

SOZOMEN'S Ecclesiastical History. A.D. 324-440. With Notes, Prefatory Remarks by Valesius, and Short Memoir. Together with the ECCLESIASTICAL HISTORY OF PHILOSTORGIUS, as epitomised by Photius. Trans. by Rev. E. Walford, M.A. With Notes and brief Life.

THEODORET and EVAGRIUS. Histories of the Church from A.D. 332 to the Death of Theodore of Mopsuestia, A.D. 427; and from A.D. 431 to A.D. 544. With Memoirs.

WIESELER'S (Karl) Chronological Synopsis of the Four Gospels. Trans. by Rev. Canon Venables. *N.S.*

ANTIQUARIAN LIBRARY.

35 *Vols. at 5s. each.* (8*l*. 15*s*. *per set*.)

ANGLO-SAXON CHRONICLE.—See *Bede*.

ASSER'S Life of Alfred. See *Six O. E. Chronicles*.

BEDE'S (Venerable) Ecclesiastical History of England. Together with the ANGLO-SAXON CHRONICLE. With Notes, Short Life, Analysis, and Map. Edit. by J. A. Giles, D.C.L.

BOETHIUS'S Consolation of Philosophy. King Alfred's Anglo-Saxon Version, with an English Translation on opposite pages, Notes, Introduction, and Glossary, by Rev. S. Fox, M.A. To which is added the Anglo-Saxon Version of the Metres of Boethius, with a free Translation by Martin F. Tupper, D.C.L.

BRAND'S Popular Antiquities of England, Scotland, and Ireland. Illustrating the Origin of our Vulgar and Provincial Customs, Ceremonies, and Superstitions. By Sir Henry Ellis, K.H., F.R.S. Frontispiece. 3 vols.

CHRONICLES of the CRUSADES. Contemporary Narratives of Richard Cœur de Lion, by Richard of Devizes and Geoffrey de Vinsauf; and of the Crusade at Saint Louis, by Lord John de Joinville. With Short Notes. Illuminated Frontispiece from an old MS.

DYER'S (T. F. T.) British Popular Customs, Present and Past. An Account of the various Games and Customs associated with different Days of the Year in the British Isles, arranged according to the Calendar. By the Rev. T. F. Thiselton Dyer, M.A.

EARLY TRAVELS IN PALESTINE. Comprising the Narratives of Arculf, Willibald, Bernard, Sæwulf, Sigurd, Benjamin of Tudela, Sir John Maundeville, De la Brocquière, and Maundrell; all unabridged. With Introduction and Notes by Thomas Wright. Map of Jerusalem.

ELLIS (G.) Specimens of Early English Metrical Romances, relating to Arthur, Merlin, Guy of Warwick, Richard Cœur de Lion, Charlemagne, Roland, &c. &c. With Historical Introduction by J. O. Halliwell, F.R.S. Illuminated Frontispiece from an old MS.

ETHELWERD. Chronicle of.—*See Six O. E. Chronicles.*

FLORENCE OF WORCESTER'S Chronicle, with the Two Continuations: comprising Annals of English History from the Departure of the Romans to the Reign of Edward I. Trans., with Notes, by Thomas Forester, M.A.

GEOFFREY OF MONMOUTH. Chronicle of.—*See Six O. E. Chronicles.*

GESTA ROMANORUM, or Entertaining Moral Stories invented by the Monks. Trans. with Notes by the Rev. Charles Swan. Edit. by W. Hooper, M.A.

GILDAS. Chronicle of.—*See Six O. E. Chronicles.*

GIRALDUS CAMBRENSIS' Historical Works. Containing Topography of Ireland, and History of the Conquest of Ireland, by Th. Forester, M.A. Itinerary through Wales, and Description of Wales, by Sir R. Colt Hoare.

HENRY OF HUNTINGDON'S History of the English, from the Roman Invasion to the Accession of Henry II.; with the Acts of King Stephen, and the Letter to Walter. By T. Forester, M.A. Frontispiece from an old MS.

INGULPH'S Chronicles of the Abbey of Croyland, with the CONTINUATION by Peter of Blois and others. Trans. with Notes by H. T. Riley, B.A.

KEIGHTLEY'S (Thomas) Fairy Mythology, illustrative of the Romance and Superstition of Various Countries. Frontispiece by Cruikshank. *N. S.*

LEPSIUS'S Letters from Egypt, Ethiopia, and the Peninsula of Sinai; to which are added, Extracts from his Chronology of the Egyptians, with reference to the Exodus of the Israelites. By L. and J. B. Horner. Maps and Coloured View of Mount Barkal.

MALLET'S Northern Antiquities, or an Historical Account of the Manners, Customs, Religions, and Literature of the Ancient Scandinavians. Trans. by Bishop Percy. With Translation of the PROSE EDDA, and Notes by J. A. Blackwell. Also an Abstract of the 'Eyrbyggia Saga' by Sir Walter Scott. With Glossary and Coloured Frontispiece.

MARCO POLO'S Travels; with Notes and Introduction. Edit. by T. Wright.

MATTHEW PARIS'S English History, from 1235 to 1273. By Rev. J. A. Giles, D.C.L. With Frontispiece. 3 vols.— *See also Roger of Wendover.*

MATTHEW OF WESTMINSTER'S Flowers of History, especially such as relate to the affairs of Britain, from the beginning of the World to A.D. 1307. By C. D. Yonge. 2 vols.

NENNIUS. Chronicle of.—*See Six O. E. Chronicles.*

ORDERICUS VITALIS' Ecclesiastical History of England and Normandy. With Notes, Introduction of Guizot, and the Critical Notice of M. Delille, by T. Forester, M.A. To which is added the CHRONICLE OF St. EVROULT. With General and Chronological Indexes. 4 vols.

PAULI'S (Dr. R.) Life of Alfred the Great. To which is appended Alfred's ANGLO-SAXON VERSION OF OROSIUS. With literal Translation interpaged, Notes, and an ANGLO-SAXON GRAMMAR and Glossary, by B. Thorpe, Esq. Frontispiece.

RICHARD OF CIRENCESTER. Chronicle of.—*See Six O. E. Chronicles.*

ROGER DE HOVEDEN'S Annals of English History, comprising the History of England and of other Countries of Europe from A.D. 732 to A.D. 1201. With Notes by H. T. Riley, B.A. 2 vols.

ROGER OF WENDOVER'S Flowers of History, comprising the History of England from the Descent of the Saxons to A.D. 1235, formerly ascribed to Matthew Paris. With Notes and Index by J. A. Giles, D.C.L. 2 vols.

SIX OLD ENGLISH CHRONICLES: viz., Asser's Life of Alfred and the Chronicles of Ethelwerd, Gildas, Nennius, Geoffrey of Monmouth, and Richard of Cirencester. Edit., with Notes, by J. A. Giles, D.C.L. Portrait of Alfred.

WILLIAM OF MALMESBURY'S Chronicle of the Kings of England, from the Earliest Period to King Stephen. By Rev. J. Sharpe. With Notes by J. A. Giles, D.C.L. Frontispiece.

YULE-TIDE STORIES. A Collection of Scandinavian and North-German Popular Tales and Traditions, from the Swedish, Danish, and German. Edit. by B. Thorpe.

ILLUSTRATED LIBRARY.

86 Vols. at 5s. each, excepting those marked otherwise.   (23l. 4s. per set.)

ALLEN'S (Joseph, R.N.) Battles of the British Navy. Revised edition, with Indexes of Names and Events, and 57 Portraits and Plans. 2 vols.

ANDERSEN'S Danish Fairy Tales. By Caroline Peachey. With Short Life and 120 Wood Engravings.

ARIOSTO'S Orlando Furioso. In English Verse by W. S. Rose. With Notes and Short Memoir. Portrait after Titian, and 24 Steel Engravings. 2 vols.

BECHSTEIN'S Cage and Chamber Birds: their Natural History, Habits, &c. Together with SWEET'S BRITISH WARBLERS. 43 Plates and Woodcuts. *N. S.*
— or with the Plates Coloured, 7s. 6d.

BONOMI'S Nineveh and its Palaces. The Discoveries of Botta and Layard applied to the Elucidation of Holy Writ. 7 Plates and 294 Woodcuts. *N. S.*

BUTLER'S Hudibras, with Variorum Notes and Biography. Portrait and 28 Illustrations.

CATTERMOLE'S Evenings at Haddon Hall. Romantic Tales of the Olden Times. With 24 Steel Engravings after Cattermole.

CHINA, Pictorial, Descriptive, and Historical, with some account of Ava and the Burmese, Siam, and Anam. Map, and nearly 100 Illustrations.

CRAIK'S (G. L.) Pursuit of Knowledge under Difficulties. Illustrated by Anecdotes and Memoirs. Numerous Woodcut Portraits. *N. S.*

CRUIKSHANK'S Three Courses and a Dessert; comprising three Sets of Tales, West Country, Irish, and Legal; and a Mélange. With 50 Illustrations by Cruikshank. *N. S.*
— **Punch and Judy.** The Dialogue of the Puppet Show; an Account of its Origin, &c. 24 Illustrations by Cruikshank. *N. S.*
— With Coloured Plates. 7s. 6d.

DIDRON'S Christian Iconography; a History of Christian Art in the Middle Ages. By the late A. N. Didron. Trans. by E. J. Millington, and completed, with Additions and Appendices, by Margaret Stokes. Vol. I. Numerous Illustrations.
Vol. II. The History of the Nimbus, the Aureole, and the Glory; Representations of the Persons of the Trinity.
Vol. II. The Trinity; Angels; Devils; The Soul; The Christian Scheme. Appendices.

DANTE, in English Verse, by I. C. Wright, M.A. With Introduction and Memoir. Portrait and 34 Steel Engravings after Flaxman. *N. S.*

DYER (Dr. T. H.) Pompeii: its Buildings and Antiquities. An Account of the City, with full Description of the Remains and Recent Excavations, and an Itinerary for Visitors. By T. H. Dyer, LL.D. Nearly 300 Wood Engravings, Map, and Plan. 7s. 6d. *N. S.*
— **Rome:** History of the City, with Introduction on recent Excavations. 8 Engravings, Frontispiece, and 2 Maps.

GIL BLAS. The Adventures of. From the French of Lesage by Smollett. 24 Engravings after Smirke, and 10 Etchings by Cruikshank. 612 pages. 6s.

GRIMM'S Gammer Grethel; or, German Fairy Tales and Popular Stories, containing 42 Fairy Tales. By Edgar Taylor. Numerous Woodcuts after Cruikshank and Ludwig Grimm. 3s. 6d.

HOLBEIN'S Dance of Death and Bible Cuts. Upwards of 150 Subjects, engraved in facsimile, with Introduction and Descriptions by the late Francis Douce and Dr. Dibdin. 7s. 6d.

HOWITT'S (Mary) Pictorial Calendar of the Seasons; embodying AIKIN'S CALENDAR OF NATURE. Upwards of 100 Woodcuts.

INDIA, Pictorial, Descriptive, and Historical, from the Earliest Times. 100 Engravings on Wood and Map.

JESSE'S Anecdotes of Dogs. With 40 Woodcuts after Harvey, Bewick, and others. *N. S.*
— With 34 additional Steel Engravings after Cooper, Landseer, &c. 7s. 6d. *N. S.*

KING'S (C. W.) Natural History of Gems or Decorative Stones. Illustrations. 6s.
— **Natural History of Precious** Stones and Metals. Illustrations. 6s.

KITTO'S Scripture Lands. Described in a series of Historical, Geographical, and Topographical Sketches. 42 Maps.
— With the Maps coloured, 7s. 6d.

KRUMMACHER'S Parables. 40 Illustrations.

LINDSAY'S (Lord) Letters on Egypt, Edom, and the Holy Land. 36 Wood Engravings and 2 Maps.

LODGE'S Portraits of Illustrious Personages of Great Britain, with Biographical and Historical Memoirs. 240 Portraits engraved on Steel, with the respective Biographies unabridged. Complete in 8 vols.

LONGFELLOW'S Poetical Works, including his Translations and Notes. 24 full-page Woodcuts by Birket Foster and others, and a Portrait. *N. S.*

—— Without the Illustrations, 3s. 6d. *N. S.*

—— **Prose Works.** With 16 full-page Woodcuts by Birket Foster and others.

LOUDON'S (Mrs.) Entertaining Naturalist. Popular Descriptions, Tales, and Anecdotes, of more than 500 Animals. Numerous Woodcuts. *N. S.*

MARRYAT'S (Capt., R.N.) Masterman Ready; or, the Wreck of the *Pacific*. (Written for Young People.) With 93 Woodcuts. 3s. 6d. *N. S.*

—— **Mission; or, Scenes in Africa.** (Written for Young People.) Illustrated by Gilbert and Dalziel. 3s. 6d. *N. S.*

—— **Pirate and Three Cutters.** (Written for Young People.) With a Memoir. 8 Steel Engravings after Clarkson Stanfield, R.A. 3s. 6d. *N. S.*

—— **Privateersman.** Adventures by Sea and Land One Hundred Years Ago. (Written for Young People.) 8 Steel Engravings. 3s. 6d. *N. S.*

—— **Settlers in Canada.** (Written for Young People.) 10 Engravings by Gilbert and Dalziel. 3s. 6d. *N. S.*

—— **Poor Jack.** (Written for Young People.) With 16 Illustrations after Clarkson Stanfield, R.A. 3s. 6d. *N. S.*

MAXWELL'S Victories of Wellington and the British Armies. Frontispiece and 4 Portraits.

MICHAEL ANGELO and RAPHAEL, Their Lives and Works. By Duppa and Quatremère de Quincy. Portraits and Engravings, including the Last Judgment, and Cartoons. *N. S.*

MILLER'S History of the Anglo-Saxons, from the Earliest Period to the Norman Conquest. Portrait of Alfred, Map of Saxon Britain, and 12 Steel Engravings.

MILTON'S Poetical Works, with a Memoir and Notes by J. Montgomery, an Index to Paradise Lost, Todd's Verbal Index to all the Poems, and Notes. 120 Wood Engravings. 2 vols. *N. S.*

MUDIE'S History of British Birds. Revised by W. C. L. Martin. 52 Figures of Birds and 7 Plates of Eggs. 2 vols. *N.S.*

—— With the Plates coloured, 7s. 6d. per vol.

NAVAL and MILITARY HEROES of Great Britain; a Record of British Valour on every Day in the year, from William the Conqueror to the Battle of Inkermann. By Major Johns, R.M., and Lieut. P. H. Nicolas, R.M. Indexes. 24 Portraits after Holbein, Reynolds, &c. 6s.

NICOLINI'S History of the Jesuits: their Origin, Progress, Doctrines, and Designs. 8 Portraits.

PETRARCH'S Sonnets, Triumphs, and other Poems, in English Verse. With Life by Thomas Campbell. Portrait and 15 Steel Engravings.

PICKERING'S History of the Races of Man, and their Geographical Distribution; with AN ANALYTICAL SYNOPSIS OF THE NATURAL HISTORY OF MAN. By Dr. Hall. Map of the World and 12 Plates.

—— With the Plates coloured, 7s. 6d.

PICTORIAL HANDBOOK OF Modern Geography on a Popular Plan. Compiled from the best Authorities, English and Foreign, by H. G. Bohn. 150 Woodcuts and 51 Maps. 6s.

—— With the Maps coloured, 7s. 6d.

—— Without the Maps, 3s. 6d.

POPE'S Poetical Works, including Translations. Edit., with Notes, by R. Carruthers. 2 vols.

—— **Homer's Iliad,** with Introduction and Notes by Rev. J. S. Watson, M.A. With Flaxman's Designs. *N. S.*

—— **Homer's Odyssey,** with the BATTLE OF FROGS AND MICE, Hymns, &c., by other translators, including Chapman. Introduction and Notes by J. S. Watson, M.A. With Flaxman's Designs. *N. S.*

—— **Life,** including many of his Letters. By R. Carruthers. Numerous Illustrations.

POTTERY AND PORCELAIN, and other objects of Vertu. Comprising an Illustrated Catalogue of the Bernal Collection, with the prices and names of the Possessors. Also an Introductory Lecture on Pottery and Porcelain, and an Engraved List of all Marks and Monograms. By H. G. Bohn. Numerous Woodcuts.

—— With coloured Illustrations, 10s. 6d.

PROUT'S (Father) Reliques. Edited by Rev. F. Mahony. Copyright edition, with the Author's last corrections and additions. 21 Etchings by D. Maclise, R.A. Nearly 600 pages. 5s. *N. S.*

RECREATIONS IN SHOOTING. With some Account of the Game found in the British Isles, and Directions for the Management of Dog and Gun. By 'Craven.' 62 Woodcuts and 9 Steel Engravings after A. Cooper, R.A.

REDDING'S History and Descriptions of Wines, Ancient and Modern. 20 Woodcuts.

RENNIE. Insect Architecture. Revised by Rev. J. G. Wood, M.A. 186 Woodcuts. *N. S.*

ROBINSON CRUSOE. With Memoir of Defoe, 12 Steel Engravings and 74 Woodcuts after Stothard and Harvey.

—— Without the Engravings, 3s. 6d.

ROME IN THE NINETEENTH CENTURY. An Account in 1817 of the Ruins of the Ancient City, and Monuments of Modern Times. By C. A. Laton. 34 Steel Engravings. 2 vols.

SHARPE (S.) The History of Egypt, from the Earliest Times till the Conquest by the Arabs, A.D. 640. 2 Maps and upwards of 400 Woodcuts. 2 vols. *N. S.*

SOUTHEY'S Life of Nelson. With Additional Notes, Facsimiles of Nelson's Writing, Portraits, Plans, and 50 Engravings, after Birket Foster, &c. *N. S.*

STARLING'S (Miss) Noble Deeds of Women; or, Examples of Female Courage, Fortitude, and Virtue. With 14 Steel Portraits. *N. S.*

STUART and REVETT'S Antiquities of Athens, and other Monuments of Greece; with Glossary of Terms used in Grecian Architecture. 71 Steel Plates and numerous Woodcuts.

SWEET'S British Warblers. 5s.—*See Bechstein.*

TALES OF THE GENII; or, the Delightful Lessons of Horam, the Son of Asmar. Trans. by Sir C. Morrell. Numerous Woodcuts.

TASSO'S Jerusalem Delivered. In English Spenserian Verse, with Life, by J. H. Wiffen. With 8 Engravings and 24 Woodcuts. *N. S.*

WALKER'S Manly Exercises; containing Skating, Riding, Driving, Hunting, Shooting, Sailing, Rowing, Swimming, &c. 44 Engravings and numerous Woodcuts.

WALTON'S Complete Angler, or the Contemplative Man's Recreation, by Izaak Walton and Charles Cotton. With Memoirs and Notes by E. Jesse. Also an Account of Fishing Stations, Tackle, &c., by H. G. Bohn. Portrait and 203 Woodcuts. *N. S.*

—— With 26 additional Engravings on Steel, 7s. 6d.

—— **Lives of Donne, Wotton, Hooker,** &c., with Notes. A New Edition, revised by A. H. Bullen, with a Memoir of Izaak Walton by William Dowling. 6 Portraits, 6 Autograph Signatures, &c. *N. S.*

WELLINGTON, Life of. From the Materials of Maxwell. 18 Steel Engravings.

—— **Victories of.**—*See Maxwell.*

WESTROPP (H. M.) A Handbook of Archæology, Egyptian, Greek, Etruscan, Roman. By H. M. Westropp. Numerous Illustrations. 7s. 6d. *N. S.*

WHITE'S Natural History of Selborne, with Observations on various Parts of Nature, and the Naturalists' Calendar. Sir W. Jardine, Edit., with Notes and Memoir, by E. Jesse. 40 Portraits. *N. S.*

—— With the Plates coloured, 7s. 6d. *N. S.*

YOUNG LADY'S BOOK, The. A Manual of Recreations, Arts, Sciences, and Accomplishments. 1200 Woodcut Illustrations. 7s. 6d.

—— cloth gilt, gilt edges, 9s.

CLASSICAL LIBRARY.

TRANSLATIONS FROM THE GREEK AND LATIN.

100 Vols. at 5s. each, excepting those marked otherwise. (24l. 10s. 6d. per set.)

ÆSCHYLUS, The Dramas of. In English Verse by Anna Swanwick. 4th edition. *N. S.*

—— **The Tragedies of.** In Prose, with Notes and Introduction, by T. A. Buckley, B.A. Portrait. 3s. 6d.

AMMIANUS MARCELLINUS. History of Rome during the Reigns of Constantius, Julian, Jovian, Valentinian, and Valens, by C. D. Yonge, B.A. Double volume. 7s. 6d.

ANTONINUS (M. Aurelius), The Thoughts of. Translated literally, with Notes, Biographical Sketch, and Essay on the Philosophy, by George Long, M.A. 3s. 6d. *N. S.*

APULEIUS, The Works of. Comprising the Golden Ass, God of Socrates, Florida, and Discourse of Magic. With a Metrical Version of Cupid and Psyche, and Mrs. Tighe's Psyche. Frontispiece.

CLASSICAL LIBRARY. 15

ARISTOPHANES' Comedies. Trans., with Notes and Extracts from Frere's and other Metrical Versions, by W. J. Hickie. Portrait. 2 vols.

ARISTOTLE'S Nicomachean Ethics. Trans., with Notes, Analytical Introduction, and Questions for Students, by Ven. Archdn. Browne.

—— **Politics and Economics.** Trans., with Notes, Analyses, and Index, by E. Walford, M.A., and an Essay and Life by Dr. Gillies.

—— **Metaphysics.** Trans., with Notes, Analysis, and Examination Questions, by Rev. John H. M'Mahon, M.A.

—— **History of Animals.** In Ten Books. Trans., with Notes and Index, by R. Cresswell, M.A.

—— **Organon;** or, Logical Treatises, and the Introduction of Porphyry. With Notes, Analysis, and Introduction, by Rev. O. F. Owen, M.A. 2 vols. 3s. 6d. each.

—— **Rhetoric and Poetics.** Trans., with Hobbes' Analysis, Exam. Questions, and Notes, by T. Buckley, B.A. Portrait.

ATHENÆUS. The Deipnosophists; or, the Banquet of the Learned. By C. D. Yonge, B.A. With an Appendix of Poetical Fragments. 3 vols.

ATLAS of Classical Geography. 22 large Coloured Maps. With a complete Index. Imp. 8vo. 7s. 6d.

BION.—*See Theocritus.*

CÆSAR. Commentaries on the Gallic and Civil Wars, with the Supplementary Books attributed to Hirtius, including the complete Alexandrian, African, and Spanish Wars. Trans. with Notes. Portrait.

CATULLUS, Tibullus, and the Vigil of Venus. Trans. with Notes and Biographical Introduction. To which are added, Metrical Versions by Lamb, Grainger, and others. Frontispiece.

CICERO'S Orations. Trans. by C. D. Yonge, B.A. 4 vols.

—— **On Oratory and Orators.** With Letters to Quintus and Brutus. Trans., with Notes, by Rev. J. S. Watson, M.A.

—— **On the Nature of the Gods,** Divination, Fate, Laws, a Republic, Consulship. Trans., with Notes, by C. D. Yonge, B.A.

—— **Academics, De Finibus, and Tusculan Questions.** By C. D. Yonge, B.A. With Sketch of the Greek Philosophers mentioned by Cicero.

CICERO'S Orations.—*Continued.*
—— **Offices;** or, Moral Duties. Cato Major, an Essay on Old Age; Lælius, an Essay on Friendship; Scipio's Dream; Paradoxes; Letter to Quintus on Magistrates. Trans., with Notes, by C. R. Edmonds. Portrait. 3s. 6d.

DEMOSTHENES' Orations. Trans., with Notes, Arguments, a Chronological Abstract, and Appendices, by C. Rann Kennedy. 5 vols.

DICTIONARY of LATIN and GREEK Quotations; including Proverbs, Maxims, Mottoes, Law Terms and Phrases. With the Quantities marked, and English Translations.

—— With Index Verborum (622 pages). 6s.

—— Index Verborum to the above, with the *Quantities* and Accents marked (56 pages), limp cloth. 1s.

DIOGENES LAERTIUS. Lives and Opinions of the Ancient Philosophers. Trans., with Notes, by C. D. Yonge, B.A.

EPICTETUS. The Discourses of. With the Encheiridion and Fragments. With Notes, Life, and View of his Philosophy, by George Long, M.A. *N. S.*

EURIPIDES. Trans., with Notes and Introduction, by T. A. Buckley, B.A. Portrait. 2 vols.

GREEK ANTHOLOGY. In English Prose by G. Burges, M.A. With Metrical Versions by Bland, Merivale, Lord Denman, &c.

GREEK ROMANCES of Heliodorus, Longus, and Achilles Tatius; viz., The Adventures of Theagenes and Chariclea; Amours of Daphnis and Chloe; and Loves of Clitopho and Leucippe. Trans., with Notes, by Rev R. Smith, M.A.

HERODOTUS. Literally trans. by Rev. Henry Cary, M.A. Portrait.

HESIOD, CALLIMACHUS, and Theognis. In Prose, with Notes and Biographical Notices by Rev. J. Banks, M.A. Together with the Metrical Versions of Hesiod, by Elton; Callimachus, by Tytler; and Theognis, by Frere.

HOMER'S Iliad. In English Prose, with Notes by T. A. Buckley, B.A. Portrait.

—— **Odyssey,** Hymns, Epigrams, and Battle of the Frogs and Mice. In English Prose, with Notes and Memoir by T. A. Buckley, B.A.

HORACE. In Prose by Smart, with Notes selected by T. A. Buckley, B.A. Portrait. 3s. 6d.

JULIAN THE EMPEROR. By the Rev. C. W. King, M.A.

JUSTIN, CORNELIUS NEPOS, and Eutropius. Trans., with Notes, by Rev. J. S. Watson, M.A.

JUVENAL, PERSIUS, SULPICIA, and Lucilius. In Prose, with Notes, Chronological Tables, Arguments, by L. Evans, M.A. To which is added the Metrical Version of Juvenal and Persius by Gifford. Frontispiece.

LIVY. The History of Rome. Trans. by Dr. Spillan and others. 4 vols. Portrait.

LUCAN'S Pharsalia. In Prose, with Notes by H. T. Riley.

LUCIAN'S Dialogues of the Gods, of the Sea Gods, and of the Dead. Trans. by Howard Williams, M.A.

LUCRETIUS. In Prose, with Notes and Biographical Introduction by Rev. J. S. Watson, M.A. To which is added the Metrical Version by J. M. Good.

MARTIAL'S Epigrams, complete. In Prose, with Verse Translations selected from English Poets, and other sources. 1 ble. vol. (670 pages). 7s. 6d.

MOSCHUS.—*See Theocritus.*

OVID'S Works, complete. In Prose, with Notes and Introduction. 3 vols.

PAUSANIAS' Description of Greece. Translated into English, with Notes and Index. By Arthur Richard Shilleto, M.A., sometime Scholar of Trinity College, Cambridge. 2 vols.

PHALARIS. Bentley's Dissertations upon the Epistles of Phalaris, Themistocles, Socrates, Euripides, and the Fables of Æsop. With Introduction and Notes by Prof. W. Wagner, Ph.D.

PINDAR. In Prose, with Introduction and Notes by Dawson W. Turner. Together with the Metrical Version by Abraham Moore. Portrait.

PLATO'S Works. Trans., with Introduction and Note. 6 vols.

—— **Dialogues.** A Summary and Analysis of. With Analytical Index to the Greek text of modern editions and to the above translations, by A. Day, LL.D.

PLAUTUS'S Comedies. In Prose, with Notes and Index by H. T. Riley, B.A. 2 vols.

PLINY'S Natural History. Trans., with Notes, by J. Bostock, M.D., F.R.S., and H. T. Riley, B.A. 6 vols.

PLINY. The Letters of Pliny the Younger. Melmoth's Translation, revised, with Notes and short Life, by Rev. F. C. T. Bosanquet, M.A.

PLUTARCH'S Morals. Theosophical Essays. Trans. by C. W. King, M.A. *N.S.*

—— **Lives.** *See page 7.*

PROPERTIUS, The Elegies of. With Notes, Literally translated by the Rev. P. J. F. Gantillon, M.A., with metrical versions of Select Elegies by Nott and Elton. 3s. 6d.

QUINTILIAN'S Institutes of Oratory. Trans., with Notes and Biographical Notice, by Rev. J. S. Watson, M.A. 2 vols.

SALLUST, FLORUS, and **VELLEIUS** Paterculus. Trans., with Notes and Biographical Notices, by J. S. Watson, M.A.

SENECA DE BENEFICIIS. Newly translated by Aubrey Stewart, M.A. 3s. 6d. *N.S.*

SENECA'S Minor Works. Translated by A. Stewart, M.A. [*In the press.*

SOPHOCLES. The Tragedies of. In Prose, with Notes, Arguments, and Introduction. Portrait.

STRABO'S Geography. Trans., with Notes, by W. Falconer, M.A., and H. C. Hamilton. Copious Index, giving Ancient and Modern Names. 3 vols.

SUETONIUS' Lives of the Twelve Cæsars and Lives of the Grammarians. The Translation of Thomson, revised, with Notes, by T. Forester.

TACITUS. The Works of. Trans., with Notes. 2 vols.

TERENCE and PHÆDRUS. In English Prose, with Notes and Arguments, by H. T. Riley, B.A. To which is added Smart's Metrical Version of Phædrus. With Frontispiece.

THEOCRITUS, BION, MOSCHUS, and Tyrtæus. In Prose, with Notes and Arguments, by Rev. J. Banks, M.A. To which are appended the METRICAL VERSIONS of Chapman. Portrait of Theocritus.

THUCYDIDES. The Peloponnesian War. Trans., with Notes, by Rev. H. Dale. Portrait. 2 vols. 3s. 6d. each.

TYRTÆUS.—*See Theocritus.*

VIRGIL. The Works of. In Prose, with Notes by Davidson. Revised, with additional Notes and Biographical Notice, by T. A. Buckley, B.A. Portrait. 3s. 6d.

XENOPHON'S Works. Trans., with Notes, by J. S. Watson, M.A., and others. Portrait. In 3 vols.

COLLEGIATE SERIES.
10 Vols. at 5s. each. (2l. 10s. per set.)

DANTE. The Inferno. Prose Trans., with the Text of the Original on the same page, and Explanatory Notes, by John A. Carlyle, M.D. Portrait. *N. S.*

—— **The Purgatorio.** Prose Trans., with the Original on the same page, and Explanatory Notes, by W. S. Dugdale. *N. S.*

NEW TESTAMENT (The) in Greek. Griesbach's Text, with the Readings of Mill and Scholz at the foot of the page, and Parallel References in the margin. Also a Critical Introduction and Chronological Tables. Two Fac-similes of Greek Manuscripts. 650 pages. 3s. 6d.

—— or bound up with a Greek and English Lexicon to the New Testament (250 pages additional, making in all 900). 5s. The Lexicon may be had separately, price 2s.

DOBREE'S Adversaria. (Notes on the Greek and Latin Classics.) Edited by the late Prof. Wagner. 2 vols.

DONALDSON (Dr.) The Theatre of the Greeks. With Supplementary Treatise on the Language, Metres, and Prosody of the Greek Dramatists. Numerous Illustrations and 3 Plans. By J. W. Donaldson, D.D. *N. S.*

KEIGHTLEY'S (Thomas) Mythology of Ancient Greece and Italy. Revised by Leonhard Schmitz, Ph.D., LL.D. 12 Plates. *N. S.*

HERODOTUS, Notes on. Original and Selected from the best Commentators. By D. W. Turner, M.A. Coloured Map.

—— **Analysis and Summary of,** with a Synchronistical Table of Events—Tables of Weights, Measures, Money, and Distances—an Outline of the History and Geography—and the Dates completed from Gaisford, Baehr, &c. By J. T. Wheeler.

THUCYDIDES. An Analysis and Summary of. With Chronological Table of Events, &c., by J. T. Wheeler.

SCIENTIFIC LIBRARY.
56 Vols. at 5s. each, excepting those marked otherwise. (14l. 10s. 6d. per set.)

AGASSIZ and GOULD. Outline of Comparative Physiology touching the Structure and Development of the Races of Animals living and extinct. For Schools and Colleges. Enlarged by Dr. Wright. With Index and 300 Illustrative Woodcuts.

BOLLEY'S Manual of Technical Analysis; a Guide for the Testing and Valuation of the various Natural and Artificial Substances employed in the Arts and Domestic Economy, founded on the work of Dr. Bolley. Edit. by Dr. Paul. 100 Woodcuts.

BRIDGEWATER TREATISES.

—— **Bell (Sir Charles) on the Hand;** its Mechanism and Vital Endowments, as evincing Design. Preceded by an Account of the Author's Discoveries in the Nervous System by A. Shaw. Numerous Woodcuts.

—— **Kirby on the History, Habits,** and Instincts of Animals. With Notes by T. Rymer Jones. 100 Woodcuts. 2 vols.

—— **Whewell's Astronomy and** General Physics, considered with reference to Natural Theology. Portrait of the Earl of Bridgewater. 3s. 6d.

BRIDGEWATER TREATISES.— *Continued.*

—— **Chalmers on the Adaptation of** External Nature to the Moral and Intellectual Constitution of Man. With Memoir by Rev. Dr. Cumming. Portrait.

—— **Prout's Treatise on Chemistry,** Meteorology, and the Function of Digestion, with reference to Natural Theology. Edit. by Dr. J. W. Griffith. 2 Maps.

—— **Buckland's Geology and Mineralogy.** With Additions by Prof. Owen, Prof. Phillips, and R. Brown. Memoir of Buckland. Portrait. 2 vols. 15s. Vol. I. Text. Vol. II. 90 large plates with letterpress.

—— **Roget's Animal and Vegetable** Physiology. 463 Woodcuts. 2 vols. 6s. each.

—— **Kidd on the Adaptation of External** Nature to the Physical Condition of Man. 3s. 6d.

CARPENTER'S (Dr. W. B.) Zoology. A Systematic View of the Structure, Habits, Instincts, and Uses of the principal Families of the Animal Kingdom, and of the chief Forms of Fossil Remains. Revised by W. S. Dallas, F.L.S. Numerous Woodcuts. 2 vols. 6s. each.

CARPENTER'S Works.—*Continued.*
— **Mechanical Philosophy, Astronomy,** and Horology. A Popular Exposition. 181 Woodcuts.
— **Vegetable Physiology and Systematic Botany.** A complete Introduction to the Knowledge of Plants. Revised by E. Lankester, M.D., &c. Numerous Woodcuts. 6s.
— **Animal Physiology.** Revised Edition. 300 Woodcuts. 6s.

CHEVREUL on Colour. Containing the Principles of Harmony and Contrast of Colours, and their Application to the Arts; including Painting, Decoration, Tapestries, Carpets, Mosaics, Glazing, Staining, Calico Printing, Letterpress Printing, Map Colouring, Dress, Landscape and Flower Gardening, &c. Trans. by C. Martel. Several Plates.
— With an additional series of 16 Plates in Colours, 7s. 6d.

ENNEMOSER'S History of Magic. Trans. by W. Howitt. With an Appendix of the most remarkable and best authenticated Stories of Apparitions, Dreams, Second Sight, Table-Turning, and Spirit-Rapping, &c. 2 vols.

HIND'S Introduction to Astronomy. With Vocabulary of the Terms in present use. Numerous Woodcuts. 3s. 6d. *N.S.*

HOGG'S (Jabez) Elements of Experimental and Natural Philosophy. Being an Easy Introduction to the Study of Mechanics, Pneumatics, Hydrostatics, Hydraulics, Acoustics, Optics, Caloric, Electricity, Voltaism, and Magnetism. 400 Woodcuts.

HUMBOLDT'S Cosmos; or, Sketch of a Physical Description of the Universe. Trans. by E. C. Otté, B. H. Paul, and W. S. Dallas, F.L.S. Portrait. 5 vols. 3s. 6d. each, excepting vol. v., 5s.
— **Personal Narrative of his Travels** in America during the years 1799–1804. Trans. with Notes, by T. Ross. 3 vols.
— **Views of Nature; or, Contemplations** of the Sublime Phenomena of Creation, with Scientific Illustrations. Trans. by E. C. Otté.

HUNT'S (Robert) Poetry of Science; or, Studies of the Physical Phenomena of Nature. By Robert Hunt, Professor at the School of Mines.

JOYCE'S Scientific Dialogues. A Familiar Introduction to the Arts and Sciences. For Schools and Young People. Numerous Woodcuts.
— **Introduction to the Arts and Sciences,** for Schools and Young People. Divided into Lessons with Examination Questions. Woodcuts. 3s. 6d.

JUKES-BROWNE'S Student's Handbook of Physical Geology. By A. J. Jukes-Browne, of the Geological Survey of England. With numerous Diagrams and Illustrations, 6s. *N.S.*
— **The Student's Handbook of** Historical Geology. By A. J. Jukes-Brown, B.A., F.G.S., of the Geological Survey of England and Wales. With numerous Diagrams and Illustrations. 6s. *N.S.*

KNIGHT'S (Charles) Knowledge is Power. A Popular Manual of Political Economy.

LECTURES ON PAINTING by the Royal Academicians, Barry, Opie, Fuseli. With Introductory Essay and Notes by R. Wornum. Portrait of Fuseli.

LILLY. Introduction to Astrology. With a Grammar of Astrology and Tables for calculating Nativities, by Zadkiel.

MANTELL'S (Dr.) Geological Excursions through the Isle of Wight and along the Dorset Coast. Numerous Woodcuts and Geological Map.
— **Petrifactions and their Teachings.** Handbook to the Organic Remains in the British Museum. Numerous Woodcuts. 6s.
— **Wonders of Geology; or, a** Familiar Exposition of Geological Phenomena. A coloured Geological Map of England, Plates, and 200 Woodcuts. 2 vols. 7s. 6d. each.

MORPHY'S Games of Chess, being the Matches and best Games played by the American Champion, with explanatory and analytical Notes by J. Lowenthal. With short Memoir and Portrait of Morphy.

SCHOUW'S Earth, Plants, and Man. Popular Pictures of Nature. And Kobell's Sketches from the Mineral Kingdom. Trans. by A. Henfrey, F.R.S. Coloured Map of the Geography of Plants.

SMITH'S (Pye) Geology and Scripture; or, the Relation between the Scriptures and Geological Science. With Memoir.

STANLEY'S Classified Synopsis of the Principal Painters of the Dutch and Flemish Schools, including an Account of some of the early German Masters. By George Stanley.

STAUNTON'S Chess-Player's Handbook. A Popular and Scientific Introduction to the Game, with numerous Diagrams and Coloured Frontispiece. *N.S.*

STAUNTON.—*Continued.*

—— **Chess Praxis.** A Supplement to the Chess-player's Handbook. Containing the most important modern Improvements in the Openings; Code of Chess Laws; and a Selection of Morphy's Games. Annotated. 636 pages. Diagrams. 6s.

—— **Chess-Player's Companion.** Comprising a Treatise on Odds, Collection of Match Games, including the French Match with M. St. Amant, and a Selection of Original Problems. Diagrams and Coloured Frontispiece.

—— **Chess Tournament of 1851.** A Collection of Games played at this celebrated assemblage. With Introduction and Notes. Numerous Diagrams.

STOCKHARDT'S Experimental Chemistry. A Handbook for the Study of the Science by simple Experiments. Edit. by C. W. Heaton, F.C.S. Numerous Woodcuts. *N. S.*

URE'S (Dr. A.) Cotton Manufacture of Great Britain, systematically investigated; with an Introductory View of its Comparative State in Foreign Countries. Revised by P. L. Simmonds. 150 Illustrations. 2 vols.

—— **Philosophy of Manufactures,** or an Exposition of the Scientific, Moral, and Commercial Economy of the Factory System of Great Britain. Revised by P. L. Simmonds. Numerous Figures. 800 pages. 7s. 6d.

ECONOMICS AND FINANCE.

GILBART'S History, Principles, and Practice of Banking. Revised to 1881 by A. S. Michie, of the Royal Bank of Scotland. Portrait of Gilbart. 2 vols. 10s. *N. S.*

REFERENCE LIBRARY.

28 *Volumes at Various Prices.* (8l. 10s. *per set.*)

BLAIR'S Chronological Tables. Comprehending the Chronology and History of the World, from the Earliest Times to the Russian Treaty of Peace, April 1856. By J. W. Rosse. 800 pages. 10s.

—— **Index of Dates.** Comprehending the principal Facts in the Chronology and History of the World, from the Earliest to the Present, alphabetically arranged; being a complete Index to the foregoing. By J. W. Rosse. 2 vols. 5s. each.

BOHN'S Dictionary of Quotations from the English Poets. 4th and cheaper Edition. 6s.

BUCHANAN'S Dictionary of Science and Technical Terms used in Philosophy, Literature, Professions, Commerce, Arts, and Trades. By W. H. Buchanan, with Supplement. Edited by Jas. A. Smith. 6s.

CHRONICLES OF THE TOMBS. A Select Collection of Epitaphs, with Essay on Epitaphs and Observations on Sepulchral Antiquities. By T. J. Pettigrew, F.R.S., F.S.A. 5s.

CLARK'S (Hugh) Introduction to Heraldry. Revised by J. R. Planché. 5s. 950 Illustrations.

—— *With the Illustrations coloured,* 15s. *N. S.*

COINS, Manual of.—*See Humphreys.*

DATES, Index of.—*See Blair.*

DICTIONARY of Obsolete and Provincial English. Containing Words from English Writers previous to the 19th Century. By Thomas Wright, M.A., F.S.A., &c. 2 vols. 5s. each.

EPIGRAMMATISTS (The). A Selection from the Epigrammatic Literature of Ancient, Mediæval, and Modern Times. With Introduction, Notes, Observations, Illustrations, an Appendix on Works connected with Epigrammatic Literature, by Rev. H. Dodd, M.A. 6s. *N. S.*

GAMES, Handbook of. Comprising Treatises on above 40 Games of Chance, Skill, and Manual Dexterity, including Whist, Billiards, &c. Edit. by Henry G. Bohn. Numerous Diagrams. 5s. *N. S.*

HENFREY'S Guide to English Coins. Revised Edition, by C. F. Keary, M.A., F.S.A. With an Historical Introduction. 6s. *N. S.*

HUMPHREYS' Coin Collectors' Manual. An Historical Account of the Progress of Coinage from the Earliest Time, by H. N. Humphreys. 140 Illustrations. 2 vols. 5s. each. *N. S.*

LOWNDES' Bibliographer's Manual of English Literature. Containing an Account of Rare and Curious Books published in or relating to Great Britain and Ireland, from the Invention of Printing, with Biographical Notices and Prices, by W. T. Lowndes. Parts I.-X. (A to Z), 3s. 6d. each. Part XI. (Appendix Vol.), 5s. Or the 11 parts in 4 vols., half morocco, 2l. 2s.

MEDICINE, Handbook of Domestic, Popularly Arranged. By Dr. H. Davies. 700 pages. 5s.

NOTED NAMES OF FICTION. Dictionary of. Including also Familiar Pseudonyms, Surnames bestowed on Eminent Men, &c. By W. A. Wheeler, M.A. 5s. *N. S*

POLITICAL CYCLOPÆDIA. A Dictionary of Political, Constitutional, Statistical, and Forensic Knowledge; forming a Work of Reference on subjects of Civil Administration, Political Economy, Finance, Commerce, Laws, and Social Relations. 4 vols. 3s. 6d. each.

PROVERBS, Handbook of. Containing an entire Republication of Ray's Collection, with Additions from Foreign Languages and Sayings, Sentences, Maxims, and Phrases. 5s.

— **A Polyglot of Foreign.** Comprising French, Italian, German, Dutch, Spanish, Portuguese, and Danish. With English Translations. 5s.

SYNONYMS and ANTONYMS; or, Kindred Words and their Opposites, Collected and Contrasted by Ven. C. J. Smith, M.A. 5s. *N. S.*

WRIGHT (Th.)—*See Dictionary.*

NOVELISTS' LIBRARY.

11 Volumes at 3s. 6d. each, excepting those marked otherwise. (2l. 1s. 6d. per set.)

BURNEY'S Evelina; or, a Young Lady's Entrance into the World. By F. Burney (Mme. D.Arblay). With Introduction and Notes by A. R. Ellis, Author of 'Sylvestra,' &c. *N. S.*

— **Cecilia.** With Introduction and Notes by A. R. Ellis. 2 vols. *N. S.*

EBERS' Egyptian Princess. Trans. by Emma Buchheim. *N. S.*

FIELDING'S Joseph Andrews and his Friend Mr. Abraham Adams. With Roscoe's Biography. *Cruikshank's Illustrations. N. S.*

— — **Amelia.** Roscoe's Edition, revised. *Cruikshank's Illustrations.* 5s. *N. S.*

FIELDING.—*Continued.*

— **History of Tom Jones, a Foundling.** Roscoe's Edition. *Cruikshank's Illustrations.* 2 vols. *N. S.*

GROSSI'S Marco Visconti. Trans. by A. F. D. *N. S.*

MANZONI. The Betrothed: being a Translation of 'I Promessi Sposi.' Numerous Woodcuts. 1 vol. (732 pages) 5s. *N. S.*

STOWE (Mrs. H. B.) Uncle Tom's Cabin; or, Life among the Lowly. 8 full-page Illustrations. *N. S.*

ARTISTS' LIBRARY.

7 Volumes at Various Prices. (1l. 18s. 6d. per set.)

BELL (Sir Charles). The Anatomy and Philosophy of Expression, as Connected with the Fine Arts. 5s. *N. S.*

DEMMIN. History of Arms and Armour from the Earliest Period. By Auguste Demmin. Trans. by C. C. Black, M.A., Assistant Keeper, S. K. Museum. 1900 Illustrations. 7s. 6d. *N. S.*

FAIRHOLT'S Costume in England. Third Edition. Enlarged and Revised by the Hon. H. A. Dillon, F.S.A. With more than 700 Engravings. 2 vols. 5s. each. *N. S.*
Vol. I. History. Vol. I. Glossary.

FLAXMAN. Lectures on Sculpture. With Three Addresses to the R.A. by Sir R. Westmacott, R.A., and Memoir of Flaxman. Portrait and 53 Plates. 6s. *N.S.*

HEATON'S Concise History of Painting. [*In the press.*

LEONARDO DA VINCI'S Treatise on Painting. Trans. by J. F. Rigaud, R.A. With a Life and an Account of his Works by J. W. Brown. Numerous Plates. 5s. *N. S.*

PLANCHÉ'S History of British Costume, from the Earliest Time to the 19th Century. By J. R. Planché. 400 Illustrations. 5s. *N. S.*

BOHN'S CHEAP SERIES.
PRICE ONE SHILLING EACH.

A Series of Complete Stories or Essays, mostly reprinted from Vols. in Bohn's Libraries, and neatly bound in stiff paper cover, with cut edges, suitable for Railway Reading.

ASCHAM (ROGER).—
SCHOLEMASTER. By Professor Mayor.

CARPENTER (DR. W. B.).—
PHYSIOLOGY OF TEMPERANCE AND TOTAL ABSTINENCE.

EMERSON.—
ENGLAND AND ENGLISH CHARACTERISTICS. Lectures on the Race, Ability, Manners, Truth, Character, Wealth, Religion, &c. &c.
NATURE: An Essay. To which are added Orations, Lectures and Addresses.
REPRESENTATIVE MEN: Seven Lectures on Plato, Swedenborg, Montaigne, Shakespeare, Napoleon, and Goethe.
TWENTY ESSAYS on Various Subjects.
THE CONDUCT OF LIFE.

FRANKLIN (BENJAMIN).—
AUTOBIOGRAPHY. Edited by J. Sparks.

HAWTHORNE (NATHANIEL).—
TWICE-TOLD TALES. Two Vols. in One.
SNOW IMAGE, and other Tales.
SCARLET LETTER.
HOUSE WITH THE SEVEN GABLES.
TRANSFORMATION; or the Marble Fawn. Two Parts.

HAZLITT (W.).—
TABLE-TALK: Essays on Men and Manners. Three Parts.
PLAIN SPEAKER: Opinions on Books, Men, and Things. Three Parts.
LECTURES ON THE ENGLISH COMIC WRITERS.
LECTURES ON THE ENGLISH POETS.

HAZLITT (W.).—Continued.
- LECTURES ON THE CHARACTERS OF SHAKE-SPEARE'S PLAYS.
- LECTURES ON THE LITERATURE OF THE AGE OF ELIZABETH, chiefly Dramatic.

IRVING (WASHINGTON).—
- LIFE OF MOHAMMED. With Portrait.
- LIVES OF SUCCESSORS OF MOHAMMED.
- LIFE OF GOLDSMITH.
- SKETCH-BOOK.
- TALES OF A TRAVELLER.
- TOUR ON THE PRAIRIES.
- CONQUESTS OF GRANADA AND SPAIN. Two Parts.
- LIFE AND VOYAGES OF COLUMBUS. Two Parts.
- COMPANIONS OF COLUMBUS: Their Voyages and Discoveries.
- ADVENTURES OF CAPTAIN BONNEVILLE in the Rocky Mountains and the Far West.
- KNICKERBOCKER'S HISTORY OF NEW YORK, from the Beginning of the World to the End of the Dutch Dynasty.
- TALES OF THE ALHAMBRA.
- CONQUEST OF FLORIDA UNDER HERNANDO DE SOTO.
- ABBOTSFORD AND NEWSTEAD ABBEY.
- SALMAGUNDI; or, The Whim-Whams and Opinions of LAUNCELOT LANGSTAFF, Esq.
- BRACEBRIDGE HALL; or, The Humourists.
- ASTORIA; or, Anecdotes of an Enterprise beyond the Rocky Mountains.
- WOLFERT'S ROOST, and Other Tales.

LAMB (CHARLES).—
- ESSAYS OF ELIA. With a Portrait.
- LAST ESSAYS OF ELIA.
- ELIANA. With Biographical Sketch.

MARRYAT (CAPTAIN).
- PIRATE AND THE THREE CUTTERS. With a Memoir of the Author.

The only authorised Edition; no others published in England contain the Derivations and Etymological Notes of Dr. Mahn, who devoted several years to this portion of the Work.

WEBSTER'S DICTIONARY
OF THE ENGLISH LANGUAGE.

Thoroughly revised and improved by CHAUNCEY A. GOODRICH, D.D., LL.D., and NOAH PORTER, D.D., of Yale College.

THE GUINEA DICTIONARY.

New Edition [1880], with a Supplement of upwards of 4600 New Words and Meanings.

1628 Pages. 3000 Illustrations.

The features of this volume, which render it perhaps the most useful Dictionary for general reference extant, as it is undoubtedly one of the cheapest books ever published, are as follows :—

1. COMPLETENESS.—It contains 114,000 words.
2. ACCURACY OF DEFINITION.
3. SCIENTIFIC AND TECHNICAL TERMS.
4. ETYMOLOGY.
5. THE ORTHOGRAPHY is based, as far as possible, on Fixed Principles.
6. PRONUNCIATION.
7. THE ILLUSTRATIVE CITATIONS.
8. THE SYNONYMS.
9. THE ILLUSTRATIONS, which exceed 3000.

Cloth, 21*s.* ; half-bound in calf, 30*s.* ; calf or half russia, 31*s.* 6*d.*; russia, 2*l.*

With New Biographical Appendix, containing over 9700 Names.

THE COMPLETE DICTIONARY

Contains, in addition to the above matter, several valuable Literary Appendices, and 70 extra pages of Illustrations, grouped and classified.

1 vol. 1919 pages, cloth, 31*s.* 6*d.*

'Certainly the best practical English Dictionary extant.'—*Quarterly Review*, 1873.

Prospectuses, with Specimen Pages, sent post free on application.

*** *To be obtained through all Booksellers.*

BOHN'S SELECT LIBRARY
OF
STANDARD WORKS.

THE texts in all cases will be printed without abridgment, and where Introductions, Biographical Notices and Notes, are likely to be of use to the Student, they will be given. The volumes, well printed and on good paper, will be issued at 1s. in paper covers, and 1s. 6d. in cloth.

NOW READY.

1. BACON'S ESSAYS. With Introduction and Notes.
2. LESSING'S LAOKOON. Beasley's Translation, revised, with Introduction, Notes, &c., by Edward Bell, M.A.
3. DANTE'S INFERNO. Translated, with Notes, by Rev. H. F. Cary.
4. GOETHE'S FAUST. Part I. Translated, with Introduction, by Anna Swanwick.
5. GOETHE'S BOYHOOD. Being Part I. of the Autobiography. Translated by J. Oxenford.
6. SCHILLER'S MARY STUART and THE MAID OF ORLEANS. Translated by J. Mellish and Anna Swanwick.
7. THE QUEEN'S ENGLISH. By the late Dean Alford.
8. LIFE AND LABOURS OF THE LATE THOMAS BRASSEY. By Sir A. Helps, K.C.B.
9. PLATO'S DIALOGUES: The Apology—Crito—Phaedo—Protagoras. With Introductions.
10. MOLIÈRE'S PLAYS: The Miser—Tartuffe—The Shopkeeper turned Gentleman. With brief Memoir.
11. GOETHE'S REINEKE FOX, in English Hexameters. By A. Rogers.
12. OLIVER GOLDSMITH'S PLAYS.
13. LESSING'S PLAYS: Nathan the Wise—Minna von Barnhelm.
14. PLAUTUS'S COMEDIES: Trinummus – Menaechmi — Aululeria — Captivi.

To be followed at intervals of a fortnight by

THE BATTLE DAYS of WATERLOO.

PAULI'S LIFE OF OLIVER CROMWELL.

STERNE'S SENTIMENTAL JOURNEY.

THE VICAR OF WAKEFIELD.

SHERIDAN'S PLAYS.

PAULI'S LIFE OF ALFRED THE GREAT.

HAUFF'S CARAVAN.

LONDON: GEORGE BELL AND SONS.

London: Printed by STRANGEWAY & SONS, Tower Street, Cambridge Circus, W.C.

www.ingramcontent.com/pod-product-compliance
Lightning Source LLC
Chambersburg PA
CBHW021354230426
43666CB00006B/524